GENDER AND CITIZENSHIP IN TRANSITION

Gender and Citizenship in Transition

Edited by

Barbara Hobson
Professor, Chair in Sociology and Gender Studies
Department of Sociology
and
Director
Advanced Research School in Comparative Gender Studies
Stockholm University

First published 2000 by
MACMILLAN PRESS LTD
Houndmills, Basingstoke, Hampshire RG21 6XS
and London
Companies and representatives
throughout the world

ISBN 0–333–75368–2 hardcover
ISBN 0–333–75369–0 paperback

A catalogue record for this book is available
from the British Library.

This book is printed on paper suitable for recycling and
made from fully managed and sustained forest sources.

10   9   8   7   6   5   4   3   2   1
09   08   07   06   05   04   03   02   01   00

Printed and bound in Great Britain by
Antony Rowe Ltd, Chippenham, Wiltshire

For my daughter Jenny

Contents

List of Tables

List of Figures

Preface

This volume represents a small proportion of exceptional and pathbreaking papers from a conference with 128 participants from 28 countries. In choosing papers for this volume we were faced with insoluble dilemmas as there were so many exceptional papers presented, provocative dialogues between East and West, rich and varied contextualized studies of gender and work, politics, human rights, and nationalism. There were two considerations that guided the selections: (1) that we include different national contexts; and (2) that we select those papers that most directly address the core question driving this conference: how were gendered boundaries of citizenship being redrawn and what were the arenas of conflict? Because of the growing implications of supranational policy contexts, Chapter 3, on Economic Citizenship, which focuses on the European Court of Justice, though not presented at the original conference, was added to volume.

The conference would not have taken place without the support of many sponsors. Most importantly, the Swedish Council for Planning and Coordination of Research (FRN) provided a large grant. We also received grants from the Swedish Institute, the Swedish Information Service in New York, and the German Marshall Fund. Their support enabled us to invite scholars from five continents. We wish to thank Christina Engfeldt, who was consul of New York at that time and currently is director of information and external relations in the UN HABITAT programme. She has over the years supported many forums for international exchange among feminist scholars and was a crucial resource for this conference. Finally, we are also grateful to Ann Marie Bergrenn, research secretary at the FRN, who was engaged in the organization of the conference and the compilation of papers for the FRN publication.

The opportunity to produce this volume and to continue comparative research on citizenship and welfare states has been made possible by the continued support of the Riksankens Jubileumsfond, and through the encouragement of its director, Dan Brandstöm, who is dedicated to developing an international dialogue among researchers in the social sciences.

Finally, we would like to thank Kathleen McCaughey for her important contribution to my project through her legal research skills. I am grateful to Lynn Chapman for her careful work on the index and her editorial support in the final stages of putting together this book.

Acknowledgements

The articles by Myra Marx Ferree, Hana Havelkova and Trudie Knijn were published in two special issues of *Social Politics: International Studies of Gender, State and Society*, Winter and Spring 1995. I would like to thank Richard Wentworth, the editor at the University of Illinois Press for his cooperation. A version of Ruth Lister's article was published in *Economy and Society* (Vol. 24, No. 1, February 1995) and a segment of Clare Ungerson's chapter appeared in *Journal of Social Policy*, 1995.

Notes on the Contributors

Lois Bryson, having recently formally retired from her academic post, is Emeritus Professor in Sociology. She is spending her post-retirement working life mainly teaching postgraduate students and doing research and social policy work. She was most recently Professor of Sociology at the University of Newcastle, Australia; her career has spanned the development of formal academic sociology in Australia. Her many publications have been particularly focused on gender and social issues. Her books include an international comparative study of welfare states – *Welfare and the State: Who Benefits?* The most recent (with Ian Winter) is *Social Change, Suburban Lives: an Australian Newtown 1960s to 1990s* (1999). This reports the effects of economic restructuring on the fate, in the 1990s, of an Australian suburb which she and Faith Thompson first studied in the 1960s.

Myra Marx Ferree is Professor of Sociology and Women's Studies at the University of Connecticut. She has published numerous books and articles on feminist movements and organizations and on German feminism, including most recently: 'Making Equality: the Women's Affairs Officers in the Federal Republic of Germany', in Dorothy Stetson and Amy Mazur, *Comparative State Feminism* (1995); 'After the Wall: Explaining the Status of Women in the Former GDR', in *Sociological Focus* (1995); '"The time of chaos was the best": Mobilization and Demobilization of the East German Women's Movement' in *Gender & Society* (1994). She is currently working on a large collaborative project analyzing abortion discourse in German and American newspapers from 1962 to 1994.

Nancy Fraser is Professor of Political Science at the graduate faculty of the New School for Social Research and co-editor of the journal, *Constellations*. Her books include: *Justice Interruptus: Critical Reflections on the 'Post Socialist' Condition* (1977), and *Unruly Practices: Power Discourse and Gender in Contemporary Social Theory* (1989). She is also co-editor of *Feminist Contentions: a Philosophical Exchange* (1994), and *Reevaluating French Feminism: Critical Essays on Difference, Agency, and Culture* (1992). Two new books will be published in 1999: a chapter in, *Adding Insult to Injury: Social Justice and the Politics of Recognition* (edited by Kevin Olson with an introduction by Richard Rorty) and *Redistribution and Recognition? a Political Philosophical Exchange*, co-authored with Axel Honneth.

Hana Havelkova is a sociologist and social philosopher, and currently Assistant Professor at the Charles University in Prague, Institute of Humanities. She has published numerous articles on gender and social transformation, especially on the political participation of women in the Czech Republic. She is the author of *Feminism and Modern Society* (1999). She is a member of the board of the IAWPh (International Association of Woman Philosophers), and of the board of the Gender Studies Centre in Prague.

Barbara Hobson is Professor of Sociology at Stockholm University and Director of the Advanced Research School in Comparative Gender Studies. She is a founder and a current editor of *Social Politics: International Studies of Gender, State, and Society*. She has published articles on the themes of gender and welfare states, gender and citizenship, women's power resources and welfare-state formation, and women's economic dependency and social citizenship. She is the author of 'Women's Collective Agency, Power Resources, and Citizenship Rights' in *Extending Citizenship: Reconfiguring States* (edited by Michael Hanagan and Charles Tilly, 1998) and 'The Parent-Worker Model: Lone Mothers in Sweden', in *Lone Mothers in European Welfare Regimes* (edited by Jane Lewis and Jessica Kingsley, 1997). Two forthcoming books based on international projects are: *Recognition Struggles: Political Identities and State Transition* and *Fathers and the State: Men, Masculinities and Gender Logics*.

Stina Johansson is Professor of Social Work at Umeå University. She is also research director at the Centre for Studies on Man, Technology and Organisation at Linköping University. Her own research is related to health professions and recent changes within the health care system. Recent publications include: 'Health Professions in the Transition of the Welfare State', in Elisabeth Sundin (ed.), *Om makt och kön – i spåren av offentliga organisationers ovandling*, Svenrka Offentliga Utredning 1997: 83, s 69–102; (1998): 'Vocabularies of

Citizenship and Gender: Sweden', *Critical Social Policy*, 1998: 18 (3), 397–415 (with Marie Jansson).

Trudie Knijn is Associate Professor at the Faculty of Social Sciences and senior researcher of the School for Social and Economical Policy Research. Her recent work focuses on social policies in the field of care, work and family and on gender and citizenship from a comparative perspective. Publications in English include 'Participation through Care? The Case of the Dutch Housewife', in J. Bussemaker and R. Voet (eds) *Gender, Participation and Citizenship in the Netherlands* 1997 (with Monique Kremer) and 'Gender and the Caring Dimension of Welfare States: Toward Inclusive Citizenship' in *Social Politics International Studies in Gender, State and Society* Vol. 4, no. 3 pp. 328–61. She edited with Clare Ungerson *Social Politics. International Studies in Gender, State and Society Special Issue: Gender and Care Work in Welfare States* Vol. 4, no. 3 Autumn 1997.

Wuokko Knocke, born in Finland, is a sociologist, and since 1979 has been a senior researcher at the National Institute for Working Life. Her research has principally focused on the working life and labour market situation of immigrants with concentration on issues related to gender, class and ethnicity. Her recent publications in English include: *Gender and Ethnicity at Work* (published in India in 1996); 'The Hidden Agenda of Post-war Immigration: Barriers to Women's Equal Rights', in *Transfer: European Journal of Labour and Research*, 1996, Vol. 2, no. 1:82–96; 'Problematizing Multiculturalism: Respect, Tolerance and the Limits to Tolerance' in *NORA*, Nordic Journal of Women's Studies (forthcoming). She has also acted as an expert member of the Joint Specialist Group on Migration, Cultural Diversity and the Equality between Women and Men at the Council of Europe, Strasbourg.

Ruth Lister is Professor of Social Policy at Loughborough University. She is a former Director of the Child Poverty Action Group and served on the Commission on Social Justice and the Opsahl Commission into the Future of Northern Ireland. She has published widely on poverty, income maintenance and women's citizenship. Her latest book is *Citizenship: Feminist Perspectives* (1997).

Clare Ungerson is Professor of Social Policy in the Department of Sociology and Social Policy at the University of Southampton. She has written for many years in the general area of women and social policy, and more particularly on the issue of informal care, especially from a gendered perspective. Her books on care include *Policy is Personal: Sex, Gender and Informal Care'* (1987) and *Gender and Caring: Work and Welfare in Britain and Scandinavia* (1990). She is currently working on the production and consumption of care, and developing empirical work on care workers who are situated at the boundary of paid and unpaid work.

Introduction

In the spring of 1994, 128 researchers from 28 countries met at Saltsjöbaden, a beautiful site by the sea near Stockholm, for an International conference, 'Crossing Borders: International Dialogues on Gender, Social Politics and Citizenship'.

'Crossing Borders' resonated on many levels. In a literal sense, we were moving across continents and traversing political contexts with participants from East, Central and Western Europe, from the US and Canada, from Australia, Asia, Africa, and the Middle East. Our meeting mirrored the historical moment and captured its sense of change and transformation, with scholars from a post-communist Europe, a new non-racial democratic South Africa and the first feminist researcher to travel to an academic conference from a self governing Palestine territory. 'Crossing Borders' reflected our sense of shifting political and economic terrains that called into question our scholarly paradigms and research agendas, the use of concepts, such as welfare state and citizenship, rooted in national policy frameworks with their own peculiar histories and discourses. On the one side, we were witnessing states breaking apart and a growing emphasis on decentralization and regional autonomy within national states, while on the other side we saw the growth and institutionalization of supranational political and economic arenas. We were confronting a world of less stable employment and more diverse families, and underlying all our discussions was the question: where would the new boundaries surrounding gender relations be redrawn in the family, market, and sexual and reproductive politics? Citizenship was a focal point for our discussions encircling questions of policy across borders – Eurocitizenship, or world citizenship, and even imagined communities among homosexuals, pacifists, environmentalists, feminists (De Swann 1998; Turner 1992; Jones 1994).

Citizenship as a concept has much currency in feminist theorizing and has fuelled many debates: is it possible to engender a concept that had such a long tradition of delegitimizing women's sphere of activity by designating it as a private domain (Landes 1999; Phillips 1993)? How are gendered dimensions

xviii

discernible in a construction of universal citizen, a disembodied individual who does not bear children and have the responsibility for their care? Is this citizen particularly male, and is his membership in the community gained through his paid work?

Citizenship is a keyword for unlocking the policy logics around gender in welfare states. These logics can make gender invisible through universalistic gender-neutral policies or they can render gender highly visible through policies that accentuate gender difference, through constructions of social, sexual, or biological difference. This is what Carole Patemen in her pioneer work on gender and citizenship analyzed as Wollstonecraft's dilemma, referring to the eighteenth-century feminist philosopher who first recognized the dilemma of difference.

In a framework where the ideal of citizenship is based upon a universalistic gender-neutral social world – which in our century is connected to paid work – women are lesser men. In a framework where women's special talents, needs, and capacities are acknowledged as different from the citizenship based on the rights and duties attached to paid work, then women are lesser citizens, since there is a lack respect for their contribution as mothers and carers.

The essays in this volume speak to this dilemma in new ways by confronting the meaning of gender difference in varied social contexts. They reveal the complex mechanisms of exclusion within and across national borders. To address gendered forms of exclusion within national borders is to recognize that citizenship is not just the relation of individuals to the state, but sets of social relationships between individuals (Lister 1997). When we begin looking at citizens as gendered subjects, these sets of relations are revealed in women's economic dependency in the family, weak position in the labour market, and lack of representation in local and national politics. Exclusion from without takes on new dimensions with the closing of many borders in Europe to non-Europeans and the treatment of immigrant women as spouses of migrant male workers. Taking these insights further, these articles reveal the multiple dilemmas in engendering citizenship through the mosaic of gender identities where race, ethnicity, class and sexual preference are brought into the picture.

Citizenship in the 1990s is a highly contested concept. In putting together this book, I have tried to map out some of that contested terrain. The book falls into three sections: 'The Dilemmas of Citizenship'; 'Transitions: Europolitics and Post-Communist Societies'; and 'Care, Commodification and Citizenship'. The authors, from different perspectives and in different contexts, reflect on where the boundaries of citizenship are being redrawn and what are the arenas of conflict.

THE DILEMMAS OF CITIZENSHIP

In this first section on the dilemmas of citizenship, both Ruth Lister and Nancy Fraser confront the current debates on the framing of public and private spheres as a gendered construction: both seek to go beyond the equality and difference dichotomy in feminist theorizing.

Ruth Lister reveals the dilemmas in engendering citizenship, through the many-sided prism of difference and diversity. The feminist challenge remains, not only to expose the false universalism lurking behind the abstract 'male' citizen, but also the false universalism in the unitary category of woman (through the recognition of multiple identities around race, ethnicity, class, sexual preference, and so on). In analyzing the strengths and weaknesses of liberal and radical feminists' views of the public and private divide, Lister asserts that it is an essentially contested and profoundly gendered debate. Nevertheless it is one that has to be confronted in any discussion of democratic citizenship, since it goes to the core of the project to engender citizenship rights and the contradictions that lie within the claims made around difference and equality.

Nancy Fraser,[1] in asking us to imagine a new gender order after the demise of the family wage, argues that any emancipatory vision must go beyond the dilemmas surrounding equality and difference. According to Fraser the feminist debates on equality and difference will always end in stalemate. Not equality or difference but the principle of equity is the way out of the impasse and the path toward a multi-layered conception of citizenship. Fraser evaluates two visions of gender equity in feminist theorizing, the Universal Breadwinner Model and the Caregiver Parity Model, the former embodying the equality position and the latter expressing feminist politics of difference. Her article not only challenges the equality – and difference-dichotomy but reinvigorates the search for new visions for old questions: what kind of welfare state could best support a new gender order?

GENDERED TRANSITIONS: POST COMMUNISM AND EUROPOLITICS

Part of the new interest in citizenship, and the meanings of exclusion and inclusion, can be traced to two crucial shifts in international politics: one being the emergence of supranational policymaking bodies – the European Union having direct influence on who will be included and excluded in the new Europe and indirect influence on social spending and social programmes in member states. The other is the collapse of the communist regime and the recasting of citizenship in former soviet societies. To understand these societies and the gendered dimensions of the transition, we have to go beyond the constitutional framing of citizenship and look at the construction of gendered political identities, the discursive framing of private and public and the emancipatory visions of feminists.

Barbara Hobson in theorizing gendered dimensions of economic citizenship recognizes the importance of supranational policymaking arenas as seen in the widening role of the European Court of Justice. Economic citizenship as dimension connects to the increased activity of women in the labour market and the instability of marriages, the growing number of solo mothers who are often the only or main breadwinners in their families. Hobson analyzes constraints within the framing of gender equality in the European Union, which are market derived rights, as compared to Sweden where policies to increase gender equality have been mainly in the sphere of care – both services and benefits – to increase women's activity in paid work. In developing a model of economic citizenship that would be empowering for women, Hobson reveals the need to construct policies that acknowledge the dynamic relationship between the institutional triangle (aimed at family, state and market) and the domestic triangle (man/woman and parents/children).

Wuokko Knocke provides another dimension to the discussion of policy across borders, by considering the implications of

European Union policy, which has created a dividing line between EU nationals (included) and other immigrants and migrants (excluded). These policies are highly gendered as they are centred around the market and the full-time worker. Knocke sees the challenge for feminist researchers as twofold: (1) to develop categories or concepts for analyzing women across societies, whether they are ethnic, immigrant, or migrant; and (2) to find new emancipatory strategies that will work against the trend toward a new ethnically defined female underclass.

In a dialogue between East and West, Myra Marx Ferree analyzes the two Germanies as expressions of public and private patriarchy. She reveals how different constructions of oppression have shaped feminist identities on the two sides of the Berlin Wall: whereas public patriarchy in the East supplanted the male head of household and women experienced state dependence, the private patriarchy in the west sustained the male breadwinner and women's economic dependence on husbands. Ferree argues for a pluralistic notion of feminisms; recognizing different interpretations of oppression as well as different emancipatory feminist visions, being the path toward building new coalitions and understanding different exclusionary processes.

Hana Havelkova continues this East–West dialogue and her work represents a growing body of literature among East European scholars, which translates and recontextualizes the meaning of feminism in order to articulate their versions of women's interests. Like Ferree she recognizes the misunderstandings and distortions of East European women's experiences and ideologies that have emerged from a theoretical overlay rooted in Western feminist traditions. Havelkova, in her analysis of women's situation in the Czech Republic, focuses on the pragmatic situations and varied arenas for contesting citizenship, particularly in the economic sphere where the sources of power and policymaking are perhaps more central for understanding the new gender order than the political spheres.

CARE, COMMODIFICATION AND CITIZENSHIP

Care is a dimension that has been linked to citizenship in feminist discussions of welfare states. By analyzing gendered work as carework, feminist scholarship has gone beyond the dichotomy of reproductive (women's work) versus productive (men's work) that has been embedded in Marxist feminist framing of gender inequalities. Care takes in a broader set of concerns than the concept of reproduction – the means by which the capitalist employer reproduced the working class – to the organization and provision of services, for the old, young and handicapped. Care as concept also problematizes the ways in which private and public are bound together: care could be paid work and unpaid work; it is emotional work in that caring for someone cannot be easily detached from caring about them, even for those who are paid to care (Ungerson 1993). Care often involves power relations, not only between client and caregiver, parent and child or adult children and elderly parents, but also between partners.

Care is a dimension that challenges basic assumptions in dominant theories of citizenship. Most fundamentally, care challenges the distinction between work (which in industrialized societies is defined as paid work) and domestic labour (which is unpaid and therefore not viewed as work). Carework, which can be paid and unpaid, or both, formal and informal, reveals the weakness of using dichotomies such as commodification and decommodification to develop theories of welfare state variation, to cluster welfare states into regime typologies, for example (Esping-Andersen 1990). That both family members and professionals are receiving pay as carers is apparent in new concepts such as quasi-wages, Clare Ungerson's term, and quasi-markets, employed by Stina Johansson in her analysis of the complex mix of private and public provisioning of care in many welfare states.

Clare Ungerson argues that the growing commodification of care requires us to reconceptualize care by following on the research of Kari Waerness (1984), she reveals the futility of separating formal from informal care. It is not only that conceptual boundaries are breaking down, but Ungerson illustrates that the empirical boundaries are no longer clearly marked. In the British case, it is hard to determine where to draw the line between unpaid and paid carework. In looking ahead to the general trends in the growing commodification of care, Ungerson concludes that commodification of carework involves gender, race and class issues. This type of women's work, extremely low paid and flexible work, will fall upon those with the fewest options, lowest educational and skills levels, and those who have limited rights of citizenship.

Analyzing the shifting forms of public and private care in Swedish municipalities, Stina Johansson underscores the explicit and implicit gendered formulas and calculations. In the case of elderly care, women care recipients are assumed to need less care, and cutbacks in care services will be filled by family members, particularly women. Rather than the needs of the client or the employee, the privatization process is structured to fit the work organization. Finally, the reorganization of care, that is the new forms of flexible, low-waged work, threaten the basic foundations of the gender contract in Sweden (Hirdman 1989) in which women were accorded rights to education, professional jobs and a living wage. At the heart of the contract within the social service state was the provision of care as a public responsibility.

Lois Bryson shows how the gender contract around care operates on the micro-level of time use and everyday life experiences among men and women in families. Through an analysis of the gendered organizations of care and employment among Finnish and Swedish families, she provides convincing evidence that men are advantaged in the public world of work through women's care work. Beginning from the perspective of the unequal division of labour, she reintroduces the concept of 'exploitation', but offers us new insights: not only are women the ones who do the most unpaid work, but they perform the routine tasks that have no definite time boundaries. Moreover she underscores a crucial aspect of exploitation is that it is most visible through a life-course perspective.

Trudie Knijn addresses the current debates on the crises of care in light of the pressures for women to enter the labour market present in all advanced industrialized societies. Societal solutions to the care deficit reflect both the unequal ratio of elderly to non-elderly and the inability of informal carers to pick up the slack brought about by cost-cutting measures and reduced state services (the so-called rationalization of care). The Netherlands, which has been one of the strongest and most entrenched male breadwinner societies, is a fascinating case from which to consider how the care deficit will be resolved. Much in the same way that Nancy Fraser calls on feminists to imagine a new gender order after the demise of the family wage of universal caregiving, Trudie Knijn urges us to view care, not as a gendered activity but as a human activity, a recognition that we will all need care and need to be responsible for caring.

* * * * *

The chapters in this book pose challenges to T.H. Marshall that he would have never imagined. Consider his classic formulation: 'Citizenship is a status bestowed on those who are full members of a community. All who possess the status are equal with respect to the rights and duties with which the status is endowed.' (1950, pp. 28–9).

In this era of transnational policy arenas, not only the gendering of citizenship, but the multidimensionality of gender raises poignant questions: what is equality? membership? What is community ? These questions take on particular significance in the 1990s, a period of global economic crisis, and of welfare state retrenchment and budget cuts. There is an implicitly gendered script in questions surrounding whose needs should be met, as seen in the growing care deficit and the tendency to shift the financial and actual caring responsibilities back to individuals and families.

In the Mastraacht and Amsterdam treaties of the European Union, there is a real shift in decisionmaking beyond the political borders of welfare states. These treaties are constructed within a framework of citizenship in which the market has been the arbiter of societal needs and rights. Taken together these consequences alter conditions for participatory democracy, which assume mobilization of constituencies to influence and shape policy, and of what its membership means in a democratic society.

Finally, in acknowledging the multidimensionality of gender, these essays suggest the need for new political coalitions and constituencies both within and across policy borders. Feminists in politics are now faced with the challenge of creating new coalitions and feminist communities among women of different classes, ages and ethnic groups.

NOTES

1   This article, originally presented at the 'Crossing Borders' conference was published as 'After the Family Wage: Gender Equity and Social Welfare', *Political Theory*, 22 November 1995.

REFERENCES

Ackers, Louise (1996) 'Citizenship, gender, and dependency, in the European Union: women and internal migration' in *Sex Equality and the Law in the European Union* (eds) Tarmara K. Hervey and David O'Keefe, Chichester, England: John Wiley & Sons.

De Swaan, Abram (1998) 'The Prospects for Transnational Social Policy – a Reappraisal' in *Recasting Citizenship* (eds) Michael Hannagan and Charles Tilly. Boulder, Colorado: Rowman and Littlefield.

Esping-Andersen, G. (1990) *The Three Worlds of Welfare Capitalism*. New Jersey: Princeton University Press.

Fraser, Nancy and Linda Gordon (1994) '"Dependency" Demystified: Inscriptions of Power in a Keyword of the Welfare State', *Social Politics: International Studies in Gender, State, and Society* 1:1: 4–32.

Hirdman, Yvonne. (1989). Att Lägga livet till rätta. studier I sventsk folkhems politik. Stockholm: Norstedts Förlag.

Hobson, Barbara (1990) 'No Exit, No Voice: Women's Economic Dependency and the Welfare State', *Acta Sociologica*, Vol. 33: 235–49.

Hobson, Barbara and Takahashi, Mieko (1996) 'Care Regimes, Solo Mothers, and the Recasting of Social Citizenship Rights' *Engendering Citizenship, Work, and Care,* Seminar 1 of the EC Programme, 'Gender and Citizenship'.

Jones, Kathleen B. (1994). 'Identity, Action, and Locale', *Social Politics: International Studies in Gender, State, and Society*, 1: 3: 256–71.

Landes, Joan (1988) *Women in the Public Sphere in the Age of the French Revolution.* Ithaca, NY: Cornell University Press.

Lister, Ruth (1998) *Citizenship: Feminist Perspectives.* London: Macmillian.

Marshall, T.H. (1950). *Citizenship and Social Class and Other Essays.* Cambridge, England: Cambridge University Press.

Pateman, Carole (1989) *The Disorder of Women: Democracy, Feminism and Political Theory*. Stanford, CA: Stanford University Press.

—— (1996) 'Democratization and Citizenship in the 1990's.' Gunnar Myrdal Memorial Lecture, Stockholm, Sweden: Stockholm University.

Philips, Ann (1993). *Democracy & Difference*. Cambridge: Polity Press.

Turner, Bryan (1992) 'Outline of a Theory of Citizenship' in *Dimensions of Radical Democracy: Pluralism, Citizenship, and Community* (ed.) Chantal Mouffe. London: Verso.

Ungerson, Clare (1993) *Gender and Caring: Work and Welfare in Britain and Scandinavia* Harvester/Wheatsheaf.

Waerness, K. (1984) 'The Rationality of Caring', *Economic and Industrial Democracy*. Vol. 5: 183–211.

1 After the Family Wage: a Postindustrial Thought Experiment

Nancy Fraser

The current crisis of the welfare state has many roots – global economic trends, massive movements of refugees and immigrants, popular hostility to taxes, the weakening of trade unions and labour parties, the rise of national and 'racial'–ethnic antagonisms, the decline of solidaristic ideologies, and the collapse of state socialism. One absolutely crucial factor, however, is the crumbling of the old gender order. Existing welfare states are premised on assumptions about gender that are increasingly out of phase with many people's lives and self-understandings. They therefore do not provide adequate social protection, especially for women and children.[1]

The gender order that is now disappearing descends from the industrial era of capitalism and reflects the social world of its origin. It was centred on the ideal of *the family wage*. In this world people were supposed to be organized into heterosexual, male-headed nuclear families, which lived principally from the man's labour market earnings. The male head of the household would be paid a family wage, sufficient to support children and a wife-and-mother, who performed domestic labour without pay. Of course countless lives did not fit this pattern. Still, it provided the normative picture of a proper family.

The family-wage ideal was inscribed in the structure of most industrial-era welfare states.[2] That structure had three tiers, with social-insurance programmes occupying the first rank. Designed to protect people from the vagaries of the labour market (and to protect the economy from shortages of demand), these programmes replaced the breadwinner's wage in case of sickness, disability, unemployment, or old age. Many countries also featured a second tier of programmes, providing direct support for full-time female homemaking and

1

mothering. A third tier served the 'residuum'. Largely leftover from traditional poor relief, public assistance programmes provided paltry, stigmatized, means-tested aid to needy people who had no claim to honourable support because they did not fit the family-wage scenario.[3]

Today, however, the family-wage assumption is no longer tenable – either empirically or normatively. We are currently experiencing the death throes of the old, industrial gender order with the transition to a new, *postindustrial* phase of capitalism. The crisis of the welfare state is bound up with these epochal changes. It is rooted in part in the collapse of the world of the family wage, and of its central assumptions about labour markets and families.

In the labour markets of postindustrial capitalism, few jobs pay wages sufficient to support a family single-handedly; many, in fact, are temporary or part-time and do not carry standard benefits.[4] Women's employment is increasingly common, moreover – although far less well-paid than men's.[5] Postindustrial families, meanwhile, are less conventional and more diverse.[6] Heterosexuals are marrying less and later, and divorcing more and sooner. And gays and lesbians are pioneering new kinds of domestic arrangements.[7] Gender norms and family forms are highly contested. Thanks in part to the feminist and gay and lesbian liberation movements, many people no longer prefer the male breadwinner/female homemaker model. One result of this trend is a steep increase in solo-mother families: growing numbers of women, both divorced and never married, are struggling to support themselves and their families without access to a male breadwinner's wage. Their families have high rates of poverty.

In short, a new world of economic production and social reproduction is emerging – a world of less stable employment and more diverse families. Though no one can be certain about its ultimate shape, this much seems clear: the emerging world, no less than the world of the family wage, will require a welfare state that effectively insures people against uncertainties. It is clear, too, that the old forms of welfare state, built on assumptions of male-headed families and relatively stable jobs, are no longer suited to providing this protection. We need something new; a postindustrial welfare state suited to radically new conditions of employment and reproduction.

What, then, should a postindustrial welfare state look like? Conservatives have lately had a lot to say about 'restructuring the welfare state', but their vision is counterhistorical and contradictory; they seek to reinstate the male breadwinner/female homemaker family for the middle class, while demanding that poor single mothers 'work'. Neoliberal proposals have recently emerged in the United States but they, too, are inadequate in the current context. Punitive, androcentric and obsessed with employment despite the absence of good jobs, they are unable to provide security in a postindustrial world.[8] Both these approaches ignore one crucial thing: a postindustrial welfare state, like its industrial predecessor, must support a gender order. But the only kind of gender order that can be acceptable today is one premised on gender equity.

Feminists, therefore, are in a good position to generate an emancipatory vision for the coming period. They, more than anyone, appreciate the importance of gender relations to the current crisis of the industrial welfare state and the centrality of gender equity to any satisfactory resolution. Feminists also appreciate the importance of carework for human well-being and the effects of its social organization on women's standing. They are attuned, finally, to potential conflicts of interest within families and to the inadequacy of androcentric definitions of work.

To date, however, feminists have tended to shy away from systematic reconstructive thinking about the welfare state. Nor have we yet developed a satisfactory account of gender equity that can inform an emancipatory vision. We need now to undertake such thinking. We should ask: what new, postindustrial gender order should replace the family wage? And what sort of welfare state can best support such a new gender order? What account of gender equity best captures our highest aspirations? And what vision of social welfare comes closest to embodying it?

Two different sorts of answers are presently conceivable, I think, both of which qualify as feminist. The first I call the Universal Breadwinner model. It is the vision implicit in the current political practice of most US feminists and liberals. It aims to foster gender equity by promoting women's employment; the centrepiece of this model is state provision of employment-enabling services such as child care. The second possible answer I call the Caregiver Parity model. It is the vision implicit in the current political practice of most Western European feminists and social democrats. It aims to promote gender equity chiefly by supporting informal carework; the centrepiece of this model is state provision of caregiver allowances.

Which of these two approaches should command our loyalties in the coming period? Which expresses the most attractive vision of a postindustrial gender order? Which best embodies the ideal of gender equity?

In this chapter, I outline a framework for thinking systematically about these questions. I analyze highly idealized versions of Universal Breadwinner and Caregiver Parity in the manner of a thought experiment. I postulate, contrary to fact, a world in which both these models are feasible in that their economic and political preconditions are in place. Assuming very favourable conditions, I then assess the respective strengths and weaknesses of each.

The result is not a standard policy analysis. For neither Universal Breadwinner nor Caregiver Parity will in fact be realized in the near future; and my discussion is not directed primarily at policymaking elites. My intent, rather, is theoretical and political in a broader sense. I aim, first, to clarify some dilemmas surrounding 'equality' and 'difference' by reconsidering what is meant by gender equity. In so doing, I also aim to spur increased reflection on feminist strategies and goals by spelling out some assumptions that are implicit in current practice and subjecting them to critical scrutiny.

My discussion proceeds in four parts. In the first section, I propose an analysis of gender equity that generates a set of evaluative standards. Then, in the second and third sections, I apply those standards to Universal Breadwinner and Caregiver Parity, respectively. I conclude, in the fourth section, that neither of those approaches, even in an idealized form, can deliver full gender equity. To achieve that, I contend, we must develop a new vision of a postindustrial welfare state, which effectively dismantles the gender division of labour.

GENDER EQUITY: A COMPLEX CONCEPTION

In order to evaluate alternative visions of a postindustrial welfare state, we need some normative criteria. Gender equity,

I have said, is one indispensable standard. But in what precisely does it consist?

Feminists have so far associated gender equity with either equality or difference, where 'equality' means treating women exactly like men, and where 'difference' means treating women differently insofar as they differ from men. Theorists have debated the relative merits of these two approaches as if they represented two antithetical poles of an absolute dichotomy. These arguments have generally ended in stalemate. Proponents of 'difference' have successfully shown that equality strategies typically presuppose 'the male as norm', thereby disadvantaging women and imposing a distorted standard on everyone. Egalitarians have argued just as cogently, however, that difference approaches typically rely on essentialist notions of femininity, thereby reinforcing existing stereotypes and confining women within existing gender divisions.[9] Neither equality nor difference, then, is a workable conception of gender equity.

Feminists have responded to this stalemate in several different ways. Some have tried to resolve the dilemma by reconceiving one or another of its horns; they have reinterpreted difference or equality in what they consider a more defensible form. Others have concluded 'a plague on both your houses' and sought some third, wholly other, normative principle. Still others have tried to embrace the dilemma as an enabling paradox, a resource to be treasured, not an impasse. Many feminists, finally, have retreated altogether from normative theorizing into cultural positivism, piecemeal reformism, or postmodern antinomianism.

None of these responses is satisfactory. Normative theorizing remains an indispensable intellectual enterprise for feminism, indeed for all emancipatory social movements. We need a vision or picture of where we are trying to go, and a set of standards for evaluating various proposals as to how we might get there. The equality/difference theoretical impasse is real, moreover; it cannot be simply sidestepped or embraced. Nor is there any 'wholly other' third term that can magically catapult us beyond it. What, then, should feminist theorists do?

I propose we reconceptualize gender equity as a complex, not a simple, idea. This means breaking with the assumption that gender equity can be identified with any single value or norm, whether it be equality, difference, or something else. Instead we should treat it as a complex notion comprising a plurality of distinct normative principles. The plurality will include some notions associated with the equality side of the debate, as well as some associated with the difference side. It will also encompass still other normative ideas that neither side has accorded due weight. Wherever they come from, however, the important point is this: each of several distinct norms must be respected simultaneously in order that gender equity be achieved. Failure to satisfy any one of them means failure to realize the full meaning of gender equity.

In what follows, I assume that gender equity is complex in this way. And I propose an account of it that is designed for the specific purpose of evaluating alternative pictures of a postindustrial welfare state. For issues other than welfare, a somewhat different package of norms might be called for. Nevertheless, I believe that the general idea of treating gender equity as a complex conception is widely applicable. The analysis here may serve as a paradigm case demonstrating the usefulness of this approach.

For this particular thought experiment, in any case, I unpack the idea of gender equity as a compound of seven distinct normative principles. Let me enumerate them one by one.

The Anti-Poverty Principle

The first and most obvious objective of social–welfare provision is to prevent poverty. Preventing poverty is crucial to achieving gender equity now, after the family wage, given the high rates of poverty in solo-mother families and the vastly increased likelihood that US women and children will live in such families.[10] If it accomplishes nothing else, a welfare state should at least relieve suffering by meeting otherwise unmet basic needs. Arrangements, such as those in the United States, that leave women, children, and men in poverty, are unacceptable according to this criterion. Any postindustrial welfare state that prevented such poverty would constitute a major advance. So far, however, this does not say enough. The anti-poverty principle might be satisfied in a variety of different ways, not all of which are acceptable. Some ways, such as the provision of targeted, isolating and stigmatized poor relief for solo-mother families, fail to respect several of the following normative principles, which are also essential to gender equity in social welfare.

The Anti-Exploitation Principle

Anti-poverty measures are important not only in themselves but also as a means to another basic objective: preventing exploitation of vulnerable people.[11] This principle, too, is central to achieving gender equity after the family wage. Needy women with no other way to feed themselves and their children, for example, are liable to exploitation – by abusive husbands, by sweatshops, and by pimps. In guaranteeing relief of poverty, then, welfare provision should also aim to mitigate exploitable dependency.[12] The availability of an alternative source of income enhances the bargaining position of subordinates in unequal relationships. The non-employed wife who knows she can support herself and her children outside of her marriage has more leverage within it; her 'voice' is enhanced as her possibilities of 'exit' increase.[13] The same holds for the low-paid nursing-home attendant in relation to her boss.[14] For welfare measures to have this effect, however, support must be provided as a matter of right. When receipt of aid is highly stigmatized or discretionary, the anti-exploitation principle is not satisfied.[15] At best the claimant would trade exploitable dependence on a husband or a boss for exploitable dependence on a caseworker's whim.[16] The goal should be to prevent at least three kinds of exploitable dependencies: exploitable dependence on an individual family member, such as a husband or an adult child; exploitable dependence on employers and supervisors; and exploitable dependence on the personal whims of state officials. Rather than shuttle people back and forth among these exploitable dependencies, an adequate approach must prevent all three simultaneously.[17] This principle rules out arrangements that channel a homemaker's benefits through her husband. It is likewise incompatible with arrangements that provide essential goods, such as health insurance, only in forms linked conditionally to scarce employment. Any postindustrial welfare state that satisfied the anti-exploitation principle would represent a major improvement over current US arrangements. But even it might not be satisfactory. Some ways of satisfying this principle would fail to respect several of the following normative principles, which are also essential to gender equity in social welfare.

The equality principles

A postindustrial welfare state could prevent women's poverty and exploitation and yet still tolerate severe gender inequality. Such a welfare state is not satisfactory. A further dimension of gender equity in social provision is redistribution, reducing inequality between women and men. Equality, as we saw, has been criticized by some feminists. They have argued that it entails treating women exactly like men according to male-defined standards, and that this necessarily disadvantages women. That argument expresses a legitimate worry, which I shall address below. But it does not undermine the ideal of equality *per se*. The worry pertains only to certain inadequate ways of conceiving equality, which I do not presuppose here. At least three distinct conceptions of equality escape the objection. These are essential to gender equity in social welfare.

Income Equality

One form of equality that is crucial to gender equity concerns the distribution of real per capita income. This sort of equality is highly pressing now, after the family wage, when US women's earnings are approximately 70 per cent of men's, when much of women's labour is not compensated at all, and when many women suffer from 'hidden poverty' due to unequal distribution within families.[18] As I interpret it, the principle of income equality does not require absolute levelling. But it does rule out arrangements that reduce women's incomes after divorce by nearly half, while men's incomes nearly double.[19] It likewise rules out unequal pay for equal work and the wholesale undervaluation of women's labour and skills. The income-equality principle requires a substantial reduction in the vast discrepancy between men's and women's incomes. In so doing, it tends, as well, to help equalize the life-chances of children, as a majority of US children are currently likely to live at some point in solo-mother families.[20]

Leisure-time Equality

Another kind of equality that is crucial to gender equity concerns the distribution of leisure time. This sort of equality is highly pressing now, after the family wage, when many women, but only a few men, do both paid work and unpaid primary carework and when women suffer disproportionately from 'time poverty'.[21] One recent British study found that 52 per cent of women surveyed, compared to 21 per cent of men, said they 'felt tired most of the time'.[22] The leisure-time-equality principle rules out welfare arrangements that would equalize incomes while requiring a double shift of work from women, but only a single shift from men. It likewise rules out arrangements that would require women, but not men, to do either the 'work of claiming' or the time-consuming 'patchwork' of piecing together income from several sources and of coordinating services from different agencies and associations.[23]

Equality of Respect

Equality of respect is also crucial to gender equity. This kind of equality is especially pressing now, after the family wage, when postindustrial culture routinely represents women as sexual objects for the pleasure of male subjects. The principle of equal respect rules out social arrangements that objectify and deprecate women – even if those arrangements prevent poverty and exploitation, and even if in addition they equalize income and leisure time. It is incompatible with welfare programmes that trivialize women's activities and ignore women's contributions – hence with 'welfare reforms' in the US that assume AFDC claimants do not 'work'. Equality of respect requires recognition of women's personhood and recognition of women's work.

A postindustrial welfare state should promote equality in all three of these dimensions. Such a state would constitute an enormous advance over present arrangements, but even it might not go far enough. Some ways of satisfying the equality principles would fail to respect the following principle, which is also essential to gender equity in social welfare.

The Anti-Marginalization Principle

A welfare state could satisfy all the preceding principles and still function to marginalize women. By limiting support to generous mothers' pensions, for example, it could render women independent, well-provided for, well-rested and respected, but enclaved in a separate domestic sphere, removed from the life of the larger society. Such a welfare state would be unacceptable. Social policy should promote women's full participation on a par with men in all areas of social life – in employment, in politics, in the associational life of civil society. The anti-marginalization principle requires provision of the necessary conditions for women's participation, including child care, elder care and provision for breast-feeding in public. It also requires the dismantling of masculinist work cultures and woman-hostile political environments. Any postindustrial welfare state that provided these things would represent a great improvement over current arrangements. Yet even it might leave - something to be desired. Some ways of satisfying the anti-marginalization principle would fail to respect the last principle, which is also essential to gender equity in social welfare.

The Anti-Androcentrism Principle

A welfare state that satisfied many of the foregoing principles could still entrench some obnoxious gender norms. It could assume the androcentric view that men's current life patterns represent the human norm and that women ought to assimilate to them. This is the real issue behind the previously noted worry about equality. Such a welfare state is unacceptable. Social policy should not require women to become like men, nor to fit into institutions designed for men, in order to enjoy comparable levels of well-being. Policy should aim instead to restructure androcentric institutions so as to welcome human beings who can give birth and who often care for relatives and friends, treating them not as exceptions, but as ideal–typical participants. The anti-androcentrism principle requires decentering masculinist norms – in part by revaluing practices and traits that are currently undervalued because they are associated with women. It entails changing men as well as changing women.

Here, then, is an account of gender equity in social welfare. On this account, gender equity is a complex idea comprising seven distinct normative principles, each of which is necessary and essential. No postindustrial welfare state can realize gender equity unless it satisfies them all.

How, then, do the principles interrelate? Here everything depends on context. Some institutional arrangements permit simultaneous satisfaction of several principles with a minimum of mutual interference; other arrangements, in contrast, set up zero-sum situations, in which attempts to satisfy one principle interfere with attempts to satisfy another. Promoting gender equity after the family wage, therefore, means attending to multiple aims that are potentially in conflict. The goal should be to find approaches that avoid trade-offs and maximize prospects for satisfying all – or at least most – of the seven principles.

In the next sections, I use this approach to assess two alternative models of a postindustrial welfare state. First, however, I want to flag four sets of relevant issues. One concerns the social organization of carework. Precisely how this work is organized is crucial to human well-being in general and to the social standing of women in particular. In the era of the family wage, carework was treated as the private responsibility of individual women. Today, however, it can no longer be treated in that way. Some other way of organizing it is required, but a number of different scenarios are conceivable. In evaluating postindustrial welfare state models, then, we must ask: how is responsibility for carework allocated between such institutions as the family, the market, civil society, and the state? And how is responsibility for this work assigned within such institutions: by gender? by class? by 'race'–ethnicity? by age?

A second set of issues concerns the basis of entitlement to provision. Every welfare state assigns its benefits according to a specific mix of distributive principles, which defines its basic moral quality. That mix, in each case, needs to be scrutinized. Usually it contains varying proportions of three basic principles of entitlement: need, desert and citizenship. Need-based provision is the most redistributive, but it risks isolating and stigmatizing the needy; it has been the basis of traditional poor relief and of modern public assistance, the least honourable forms of provision. The most honourable, in contrast, is entitlement based on desert, but it tends to be anti-egalitarian and exclusionary. Here one receives benefits according to one's 'contributions', usually tax payments, work, and service – where 'tax payments' means wage deductions paid into a special fund, 'work' means primary labour-force employment, and 'service' means the military, all interpretations of those terms that disadvantage women. Desert has usually been seen as the primary basis of earnings-linked social insurance in the industrial welfare state.[24] The third principle, citizenship, allocates provision on the basis of membership in society. It is honourable, egalitarian and universalist, but also expensive, hence hard to sustain at high levels of quality and generosity; some theorists worry, too, that it encourages free-riding, which they define, however, androcentrically.[25] Citizenship-based entitlements are most often found in social-democratic countries, where they may include single-payer universal health insurance systems and universal family or child allowances; they are virtually unknown in the United States – except for public education. In examining models of postindustrial welfare states, then, one must look closely at the construction of entitlement. It makes considerable difference to women's and children's well-being, for example, whether day care places are distributed as citizenship entitlements or as desert-based entitlements, that is, whether or not they are conditional on prior employment. It likewise matters, to take another example, whether carework is supported on the basis of need, in the form of a means-tested benefit for the poor, or whether it is supported on the basis of desert, as return for 'work' or 'service', now interpreted nonandrocentrically, or whether, finally, it is supported on the basis of citizenship under a universal Basic Income scheme.

A third set of issues concerns differences among women. Gender is the principal focus of this chapter, to be sure, but it cannot be treated en bloc. The lives of women and men are cross-cut by several other salient social divisions, including class, 'race'–ethnicity, sexuality, and age. Models of postindustrial welfare states, then, will not affect all women, nor all men, in the same way; they will generate different outcomes for differently situated people. For example, some policies will affect women who have children differently from those who do not; some, likewise, will affect women who have access to a second income differently from those who do not; and some, finally, will affect women employed full-time differently from those employed part-time, and differently yet again from those who are not employed. For each model, then, we must ask: which groups of women would be advantaged and which groups disadvantaged?

A fourth set of issues concerns desiderata for postindustrial welfare states other than gender equity. Gender equity, after all, is not the only goal of social welfare. Also important are non-equity goals, such as efficiency, community and individual liberty. In addition there remain other equity goals, such as 'racial'–ethnic equity, generational equity, class equity and equity among nations. All of these issues are necessarily backgrounded here. Some of them, however, such as 'racial'–ethnic equity, could be handled via parallel thought experiments: one might define 'racial'–ethnic equity as a complex idea, analogous to the way gender equity is treated here, and then use it, too, to assess competing visions of a postindustrial welfare state.

With these considerations in mind, let us now examine two strikingly different feminist visions of a postindustrial welfare state. And let us ask: Which comes closest to achieving gender equity in the sense I have elaborated here?

THE UNIVERSAL BREADWINNER MODEL

In one vision of postindustrial society, the age of the family wage would give way to the age of the Universal Breadwinner. This is the vision implicit in the current political practice of most US feminists and liberals. (It was also assumed in the former communist countries!) It aims to achieve gender equity principally by promoting women's employment. The point is to enable women to support themselves and their families through their own wage-earning. The breadwinner role is to be universalized, in sum, so that women, too, can be citizen-workers.

Universal Breadwinner is a very ambitious postindustrial scenario, requiring major new programmes and policies. One crucial element is a set of employment-enabling services, such as child care and elder care, aimed at freeing women from unpaid responsibilities so they could take full-time employment on terms comparable to men.[26] Another essential element is a set of workplace reforms aimed at removing equal-opportunity obstacles, such as sex discrimination and sexual harassment. Reforming the workplace requires reforming the culture, however, eliminating sexist stereotypes and breaking the cultural association of breadwinning with masculinity. Also required are policies to help change socialization, so as, first, to reorient women's aspirations toward employment and away from domesticity, and second, to reorient men's expectations toward acceptance of women's new role. None of this would work, however, without one additional ingredient: macroeconomic policies to create full-time, well paid, permanent jobs for women.[27] These would have to be true breadwinner jobs in the primary labour force, carrying full, first-class social-insurance entitlements. Social insurance, finally, is central to Universal Breadwinner. The aim here is to bring women up to parity with men in an institution that has traditionally disadvantaged them.

How would this model organize carework? The bulk of such work would be shifted from the family to the market and the state, where it would be performed by employees for pay.[28] Who, then, are these employees likely to be? In many countries today, including the US, paid institutional carework is poorly remunerated, feminized and largely racialized and/or performed by immigrants.[29] But such arrangements are precluded in this model. If the model is to succeed in enabling all women to be breadwinners, it must upgrade the status and pay attached to carework employment, making it, too, into primary labour force work. Universal Breadwinner, then, is necessarily committed to a policy of 'comparable worth'; it must redress the widespread undervaluation of skills and jobs currently coded as feminine and/or 'non-white,' and it must remunerate such jobs with breadwinner-level pay.

Universal Breadwinner would link many benefits to employment and distribute them through social insurance, with levels varying according to earnings. In this respect, the model resembles the industrial-era welfare state.[30] The difference is that many more women would be covered on the basis of their own employment records. And many more women's employment records would look considerably more like men's.

Not all adults can be employed, however. Some will be unable to work for medical reasons, including some not previously employed. Others will be unable to get jobs. Some, finally, will have carework responsibilities that they are unable or unwilling to shift elsewhere. Most of these last will be women. To provide for these people, Universal Breadwinner must include a residual tier of social welfare that provides need-based, means-tested wage replacements.[31]

Universal Breadwinner is far removed from present realities. It requires massive creation of primary labour-force jobs – jobs sufficient to support a family single-handedly. That, of course, is wildly askew of current postindustrial trends, which generate jobs not for breadwinners but for 'disposable workers'.[32] Let us assume for the sake of the thought experiment, however, that it's conditions of possibility could be met. And let us consider whether the resulting postindustrial welfare state could claim title to gender equity.

Anti-Poverty

We can acknowledge immediately that Universal Breadwinner would do a good job of preventing poverty. A policy that created secure breadwinner-quality jobs for all employable women and men, while providing the services that would enable women to take such jobs, would keep most families out of poverty. And generous levels of residual support would keep the rest out of poverty through transfers.[33]

Anti-Exploitation

The model should also succeed in preventing exploitable dependency for most women. Women with secure breadwinner jobs are able to exit unsatisfactory relations with men. And those who do not have such jobs but know they can get them will also be less vulnerable to exploitation. Failing that, the residual system of income support provides back-up protection against exploitable dependency, assuming that it is generous, nondiscretionary, and honourable.[34]

Income Equality

Universal Breadwinner is only fair, however, at achieving income equality; granted, secure breadwinner jobs for women – plus the services that would enable women to take them –

would narrow the gender wage gap.[35] Moreover, reduced inequality in earnings, translates into reduced inequality in
social-insurance benefits. And the availability of exit options
from marriage should encourage a more equitable distribution of resources within it. But the model is not otherwise
egalitarian. It contains a basic social faultline dividing breadwinners from others, to the considerable disadvantage of the
others – most of whom would be women. Apart from comparable worth, moreover, it does not reduce pay inequality among
breadwinner jobs. To be sure, the model reduces the weight of
gender in assigning individuals to unequally compensated
breadwinner jobs; but it thereby increases the weight of other
variables, presumably class, education, 'race'–ethnicity and
age. Women, and men, who are disadvantaged in relation to
those axes of social differentiation will earn less than those
who are not.

Leisure-time Equality

The model is quite poor, moreover, with respect to equality of
leisure time, as we know from the Communist experience. It
assumes that all of women's current domestic and carework responsibilities can be shifted to the market and/or the state. But
that assumption is patently unrealistic. Some things, such as
childbearing, attending to family emergencies, and much parenting work cannot be shifted – short of universal surrogacy
and other presumably undesirable arrangements. Other things,
such as cooking and (some) housekeeping, could – provided we
were prepared to accept collective living arrangements or high
levels of commodification. Even those tasks that are shifted, do
not disappear without a trace, but give rise to burdensome new
tasks of coordination. Women's chances for equal leisure, then,
depend on whether men can be induced to do their fair share of
this work. On this, the model does not inspire confidence. Not
only does it offer no disincentives to free-riding, but in valoriz-
ing paid work, it implicitly denigrates unpaid work, thereby fu-
elling the motivation to shirk.[36] Women without partners would
in any case be on their own. And those in lower-income households would be less able to purchase replacement services.
Employed women would have a second shift on this model,
then, albeit a less burdensome one than some have now and

there would be many more women employed full-time. Universal Breadwinner, in sum, is not likely to deliver equal leisure. Anyone who does not free-ride in this possible postindustrial world is likely to be harried and tired.

Equality of Respect

The model is only fair, moreover, at delivering equality of respect. Because it holds men and women to the single standard of the citizen–worker, its only chance of eliminating the gender respect gap is to admit women to that status on the same terms as men. This, however, is unlikely to occur. A more likely outcome is that women would retain more connection to reproduction and domesticity than men, thus appearing as breadwinners manqué. In addition, the model is likely to generate another kind of respect gap. By putting a high premium on breadwinner status, it invites disrespect for others. Participants in the means-tested residual system will be liable to stigmatization and most of these will be women. Any employment-centred model, even a feminist one, has a hard time constructing an honorable status for those it defines as 'non-workers'.

Anti-Marginalization

This model is also only fair at combating women's marginalization. Granted, it promotes women's participation in employment, but its definition of participation is narrow. Expecting full-time employment of all who are able, the model may actually impede participation in politics and civil society. Certainly, it does nothing to promote women's participation in those arenas. It fights women's marginalization, then, in a one-sided, 'workerist' way.

Anti-Androcentrism

Lastly, the model performs poorly in overcoming androcentrism. It valorizes men's traditional sphere – employment – and simply tries to help women fit in. Traditionally female carework, in contrast, is treated instrumentally; it is what must be sloughed off in order to become a breadwinner. It is not itself accorded social value. The ideal-typical citizen here is the

Table 1.1 Strengths and Weaknesses of the Universal Breadwinner Model

Anti-poverty	good
Anti-exploitation	good
Income equality	fair
Leisure-time equality	poor
Equality of respect	fair
Anti-marginalization	fair
Anti-androcentrism	poor

breadwinner, now nominally gender-neutral. But the content of the status is implicitly masculine; it is the male half of the old breadwinner/homemaker couple, now universalized and required of everyone. The female half of the couple has simply disappeared. None of her distinctive virtues and capacities has been preserved for women, let alone universalized to men. The model is androcentric.

We can summarize the merits of Universal Breadwinner in Table 1.1. Not surprisingly, Universal Breadwinner delivers the best outcomes to women whose lives most closely resemble the male half of the old family-wage ideal couple. It is especially good to childless women and to women without other major domestic responsibilities that cannot easily be shifted to social services. But for those women, as well as for others, it falls short of full gender equity.

THE CAREGIVER PARITY MODEL

In a second vision of postindustrial society, the era of the family wage would give way to the era of Caregiver Parity. This is the picture implicit in the political practice of most Western European feminists and social democrats. It aims to promote gender equity principally by supporting informal carework. The point is to enable women with significant domestic responsibilities to support themselves and their families either through carework alone or through carework plus part-time employment. (Women without significant domestic responsibilities would presumably support themselves through employment.) The aim is not to make women's lives the same as men's, but rather to 'make difference costless'.[37] Thus, childbearing, childrearing and informal domestic labour are to be elevated to parity with formal paid labour. The caregiver role is to be put on a par with the breadwinner role, so that women and men can enjoy equivalent levels of dignity and well-being.

Caregiver Parity is also extremely ambitious. On this model, many (though not all) women will follow the current US female practice of alternating spells of full-time employment, spells of full-time carework, and spells that combine part-time carework with part-time employment. The aim is to make such a life-pattern costless. To this end, several major new programmes are necessary. One is a programme of caregiver allowances to compensate childbearing, childraising, housework and other forms of socially-necessary domestic labour; the allowances must be sufficiently generous at the full-time rate to support a family – hence equivalent to a breadwinner wage.[38] Also required is a programme of workplace reforms. These must facilitate the possibility of combining supported carework with part-time employment and of making transitions between different life-states. The key here is flexibility. One obvious necessity is a generous programme of mandated pregnancy and family leave, so that caregivers can exit and enter employment without losing security or seniority. Another is a programme of retraining and job search for those not returning to old jobs. Also essential is mandated flex-time so that caregivers can shift their hours to accommodate their carework responsibilities, including shifts between full- and part-time employment. Finally, in the wake of all this flexibility, there must be programmes to ensure continuity of all the basic social-welfare benefits, including health, unemployment, disability and retirement insurance.

This model organizes carework very differently from Universal Breadwinner. Whereas that approach shifted carework to the market and the state, this one keeps the bulk of such work in the household and supports it with public funds. Caregiver Parity's social-insurance system also differs sharply. To assure continuous coverage for people alternating between carework and employment, benefits attached to both must be integrated in a single system. In this system, part-time jobs and supported carework must be covered on the same basis as full-time jobs. Thus, a woman finishing a spell of supported carework would be eligible for unemployment insurance benefits on the same basis as a recently laid off employee in the event she could not find a suitable job. And a supported care-worker who became disabled would receive disability payments on the same basis as a disabled employee. Years of supported carework would count on a par with years of employment toward eligibility for retirement pensions. Benefit levels would be fixed in ways that treat carework and employment equivalently. [39]

Caregiver Parity also requires another, residual tier of social welfare. Some adults will be unable to do either carework or waged work, including some without prior work records of either type. Most of these people will probably be men. To provide for them, the model must offer means-tested wage-and-allowance replacements.[40] Caregiver Parity's residual tier should be smaller than Universal Breadwinner's, however; nearly all adults should be covered in the integrated bread-winner–caregiver system of social insurance.

Caregiver Parity, too, is far removed from current US arrangements. It requires large outlays of public funds to pay caregiver allowances, hence major structural tax reform and a sea-change in political culture. Let us assume for the sake of the thought experiment, however, that its conditions of possibility could be met. And let us consider whether the re-sulting postindustrial welfare state could claim title to gender equity.

Anti-Poverty

Caregiver Parity would do a good job of preventing poverty – including those women and children who are currently most vulnerable. Sufficiently generous allowances would keep solo-mother families out of poverty during spells of full-time care-work. And a combination of allowances and wages would do the same during spells of part-time supported carework and part-time employment.[41] Since each of these options would carry the basic social-insurance package, moreover, women with 'feminine' work patterns would have considerable security.[42]

Anti-Exploitation

Caregiver Parity should also succeed in preventing exploitation for most women, including for those who are most vulnerable today. By providing income directly to non-employed wives, it reduces their economic dependence on husbands. It also provides economic security to single women with children, reducing their liability to exploitation by employers. Insofar as caregiver allowances are honourable and nondiscretionary, finally, recipients are not subject to caseworkers' whims.[43]

Income Equality

Caregiver Parity performs quite poorly, however, with respect to income equality, as we know from the Nordic experience. Although the system of allowances-plus-wages provides the equivalent of a basic minimum breadwinner wage, it also institutes a 'mommy track' in employment – a market in flexible, noncontinuous full – and/or part-time jobs. Most of these jobs will pay considerably less even at the full-time rate than comparable breadwinner-track jobs. Two-partner families will have an economic incentive to keep one partner on the breadwinner track rather than to share spells of carework between them; and given current labour markets, making the breadwinner the man will be most advantageous for heterosexual couples. Given current culture and socialization, moreover, men are generally unlikely to choose the mommy track in the same proportions as women. So the two employment tracks will carry traditional gender associations. Those associations are likely in turn to produce discrimination against women in the breadwinner track. Caregiver Parity may make difference cost less, then, but it will not make difference costless.

Leisure-time Equality

Caregiver Parity does somewhat better, however, with respect to equality of leisure time. It makes it possible for all women to avoid the double shift if they choose, by opting for full- or part-time supported carework at various stages in their lives. (Currently, this choice is available only to a small percentage of privileged US women.) We just saw, however, that this choice is not truly costless. Some women with families will not want to forego the benefits of breadwinner-track employment and will try to combine it with carework. Those not partnered with someone on the caregiver track will be significantly disadvantaged with respect to leisure time, and probably in their employment as well. Men, in contrast, will largely be insulated from this dilemma. On leisure time, then, the model is only fair.

Equality of Respect

Caregiver Parity is also only fair at promoting equality of respect. Unlike Universal Breadwinner, it offers two different routes to that end. Theoretically, citizen-workers and citizen-caregivers are statuses of equivalent dignity. But are they really on a par with one another? Caregiving is certainly treated more respectfully in this model than in current US society, but it remains associated with femininity. Breadwinning likewise remains associated with masculinity. Given those traditional gender associations, plus the economic differential between the two lifestyles, caregiving is unlikely to attain true parity with breadwinning. In general, it is hard to imagine how 'separate but equal' gender roles could provide genuine equality of respect today.

Anti-Marginalization

Caregiver Parity performs poorly, moreover, in preventing women's marginalization. By supporting women's informal carework, it reinforces the view of such work as women's work and consolidates the gender division of domestic labour. By consolidating dual labour markets for breadwinners and caregivers, moreover, the model marginalizes women within the employment sector. By reinforcing the association of caregiving with femininity, finally, it may also impede women's participation in other spheres of life, such as politics and civil society.

Anti-Androcentrism

Yet Caregiver Parity is better than Universal Breadwinner at combating androcentrism. It treats caregiving as intrinsically valuable, not as a mere obstacle to employment, thus challeng-

Table 1.2 Strengths and Weaknesses of the Caregiver Parity Model

Anti-poverty	good
Anti-exploitation	good
Income equality	poor
Leisure-time equality	fair
Equality of respect	fair
Anti-marginalization	poor
Anti-androcentrism	fair

ing the view that only men's traditional activities are fully human. It also accommodates 'feminine' life-patterns, thereby rejecting the demand that women assimilate to 'masculine' patterns. But the model still leaves something to be desired. Caregiver Parity stops short of affirming the universal value of activities and life-patterns associated with women. It does not value caregiving enough to demand that men do it, too; it does not ask men to change. Thus, Caregiver Parity represents only one-half of a full-scale challenge to androcentrism. Here, too, its performance is only fair.

Caregiver Parity's strengths and weaknesses are summarized in Table 1.2. In general, Caregiver Parity improves the lot of women with significant carework responsibilities. But for those women, as well as for others, it fails to deliver full gender equity.

TOWARD A UNIVERSAL CAREGIVER MODEL

Both Universal Breadwinner and Caregiver Parity are highly utopian visions of a postindustrial welfare state. Either one of them would represent a major improvement over current US arrangements. Yet neither is likely to be realized soon. Both models assume background preconditions that are strikingly absent today. Both presuppose major political-economic restructuring, including significant public control over corporations, the capacity to direct investment to create high-quality permanent jobs, and the ability to tax profits *and wealth* at rates sufficient to fund expanded high-quality social programmes.

Both models also assume broad popular support for a post-industrial welfare state that is committed to gender equity.

If both models are utopian in this sense, neither is utopian enough. Neither Universal Breadwinner nor Caregiver Parity can actually make good on its promise of gender equity – even under very favourable conditions. Although both are good at preventing women's poverty and exploitation, both are only fair at redressing inequality of respect: Universal Breadwinner holds women to the same standard as men, while constructing arrangements that prevent them from meeting it fully; Caregiver Parity, in contrast, sets up a double standard to accommodate gender difference, while institutionalizing policies that fail to assure equivalent respect for 'feminine' activities and life patterns. When we turn to the remaining principles, moreover, the two models' strengths and weaknesses diverge. The Universal Breadwinner model fails especially to promote equality of leisure time and to combat androcentrism, while Caregiver Parity fails especially to promote income equality and to prevent women's marginalization. Neither model, in addition, promotes women's full participation on a par with men in politics and civil society. And neither values female-associated practices enough to ask men to do them too; neither asks men to change. (The relative merits of Universal Breadwinner and Caregiver Parity are summarized in Table 1.3.) Neither model, in sum, provides everything feminists want. Even in a highly idealized form neither delivers full gender equity.

If these were the only possibilities, we would face a very difficult set of trade-offs. Suppose, however, we reject this Hobson's choice and try to develop a third alternative. The trick is to envision a postindustrial welfare state that combines the best of each model, while jettisoning the worst features of each. What third alternative is possible?

So far we have examined – and found wanting – two initially plausible approaches: one aiming to make women more like men are now; the other leaving men and women pretty much unchanged, while aiming to make women's difference costless. A third possibility is to *induce men to become more like most women are now* – viz. people who do primary carework.

Consider the effects of this one change on the models we have just examined. If men were to do their fair share of carework, Universal Breadwinner would come much closer to

Table 1.3   Relative Merits of the Universal Breadwinner and Caregiver
Parity Models

	Universal Breadwinner	*Caregiver Parity*
Anti-poverty	good	good
Anti-exploitation	good	good
Income equality	fair	poor
Leisure-time equality	poor	fair
Equality of respect	fair	fair
Anti-marginalization	fair	poor
Anti-androcentrism	poor	fair

equalizing leisure time and eliminating androcentrism, while
Caregiver Parity would do a much better job of equalizing
income and reducing women's marginalization. Both models, in
addition, would tend to promote equality of respect. If men
were to become more like women are now, in sum, both models
would begin to approach gender equity.

The key to achieving gender equity in a postindustrial
welfare state, then, is to make women's current life-patterns
the norm for everyone. Women today often combine breadwinning and caregiving, albeit with great difficulty and strain. A
postindustrial welfare state must ensure that men do the same,
while redesigning institutions so as to eliminate the difficulty
and strain.

We might call this vision *Universal Caregiver*.

What, then, might such a welfare state look like? Unlike
Caregiver Parity, its employment sector would not be divided
into two different tracks; all jobs would be designed for workers
who are caregivers, too; all would have a shorter work week
than full-time jobs have now; and all would have the support of
employment-enabling services. Unlike Universal Breadwinner,
however, employees would not be assumed to shift all carework
to social services. Some informal carework would be publicly
supported and integrated on a par with paid work in a single
social-insurance system. Some would be performed in households by relatives and friends, but such households would not
necessarily be heterosexual nuclear families. Other supported
carework would be located outside households altogether – in

civil society. In state-funded but locally organized institutions, childless adults, older people and others without kin-based responsibilities would join parents and others in democratic, self-managed carework activities.

A Universal Caregiver welfare state would promote gender equity by effectively dismantling the gendered opposition between breadwinning and caregiving. It would integrate activities that are currently separated from one another, eliminate their gender-coding and encourage men to perform them too. This, however, is tantamount to a wholesale restructuring of the institution of gender. The construction of breadwinning and caregiving as separate roles, coded masculine and feminine respectively, is a principal undergirding of the current gender order. To dismantle those roles and their cultural coding is in effect to overturn that order. It means subverting the existing gender division of labour and reducing the salience of gender as a structural principle of social organization.[44] At the limit, it suggests deconstructing gender.[45] By deconstructing the opposition between breadwinning and caregiving, moreover, Universal Caregiver would simultaneously deconstruct the associated opposition between bureaucratized public institutional settings and intimate private domestic settings. Treating civil society as an additional site for carework, it would overcome both the 'workerism' of Universal Breadwinner and the domestic privatism of Caregiver Parity. Thus, Universal Caregiver promises expansive new possibilities for enriching the substance of social life and for promoting equal participation.

Only by embracing the Universal Caregiver vision, moreover, can we mitigate potential conflicts among our seven component principles of gender equity and minimize the need for trade-offs. Rejecting this approach, in contrast, makes such conflicts and hence trade-offs, more likely. *Achieving gender equity in a postindustrial welfare state, then, requires deconstructing gender.*

Much more work needs to be done to develop this third – Universal Caregiver – vision of a postindustrial welfare state. A key is to develop policies that discourage free-riding. *Contra* conservatives, the real free-riders in the current system are not poor solo-mothers who shirk employment. Instead they are men of all classes who shirk carework and domestic labour, as well as corporations who free-ride on the labour of working people, both underpaid and unpaid.

A good statement of the Universal Caregiver vision comes from the Swedish Ministry of Labour: 'To make it possible for both men and women to combine parenthood and gainful employment, a new view of the male role and a radical change in the organization of working life are required'.[46] The trick is to imagine a social world in which citizens' lives integrate wage-earning, caregiving, community activism, political participation, and involvement in the associational life of civil society – while also leaving time for some fun. This world is not likely to come into being in the immediate future. But it is the only imaginable postindustrial world that promises true gender equity. And unless we are guided by this vision now, we will never get any closer to achieving it.

NOTES AND REFERENCES

1. Research for this essay was supported by the Center for Urban Affairs and Policy Research, Northwestern University. For helpful comments, I am indebted to Rebecca Blank, Joshua Cohen, Fay Cook, Barbara Hobson, Axel Honneth, Jenny Mansbridge, Linda Nicholson, Ann Shola Orloff, John Roemer, Ian Schapiro, Tracy Strong, Peter Taylor-Gooby, Judy Wittner, Eli Zaretsky, and the members of the Feminist Public Policy Work Group of the Center for Urban Affairs and Policy Research, Northwestern University.

2. Mimi Abramowitz, *Regulating the Lives of Women: Social Welfare Policy from Colonial Times to the Present* (Boston: South End Press, 1988); Nancy Fraser, 'Women, Welfare, and the Politics of Need Interpretation' in *Unruly Practices: Power, Discourse, and Gender in Contemporary Social Theory* (ed.) Fraser (Minneapolis: University of Minnesota Press, 1989); Linda Gordon, 'What Does Welfare Regulate?' Social Research 55, no. 4 (Winter 1988): 609–30; Hilary Land, 'Who Cares for the Family?' Journal of Social Policy 7, no. 3 (July 1978): 257–84. An exception to the built-in family-wage assumption is France, which from early on accepted high levels of female waged work. See Jane Jenson, 'Representations of Gender: Policies to "Protect" Women Workers and Infants in France and the United States before 1914', in *Women, the State, and Welfare* (ed.) Linda Gordon (Madison, WI: The University of Wisconsin Press, 1990).

3. This account of the tripartite structure of the welfare state represents a modification of the account I proposed in 'Women, Welfare, and the Politics of Need Interpretation', op. cit.. There I followed Barbara Nelson in positing a two-tier structure of ideal-typically 'masculine'

social insurance programmes and ideal-typically 'feminine' family support programmes. [See Nelson 'Women's Poverty and Women's Citizenship: Some Political Consequences of Economic Marginality,' *Signs: Journal of Women in Culture and Society* 10, no. 2 (Winter 1984): 209–31) and 'The Origins of the Two-Channel Welfare State: Workmen's Compensation and Mothers' Aid' in *Women, the State, and Welfare*, (ed.) Linda Gordon, op. cit..] Although that view was a relatively accurate picture of the US social–welfare system, I now consider it analytically misleading. The United States is unusual in that the second and third tiers are conflated. The main programme of means-tested poor relief – Aid to Families with Dependent Children (AFDC) – is also the main programme that supports women's childraising. Analytically, these are best understood as two distinct tiers of social welfare. When social insurance is added, we get a three tier welfare state.

4.   David Harvey, *The Condition of Postmodernity: An Inquiry into the Origins of Cultural Change* (Oxford: Blackwell, 1989); Scott Lash and John Urry, *The End of Organized Capitalism* (Cambridge: Polity Press, 1987); Robert Reich, *The Work of Nations: Preparing Ourselves for 21st Century Capitalism* (New York: Knopf, 1991).

5.   Joan Smith 'The Paradox of Women's Poverty: Wage-earning Women and Economic Transformation' *Signs: Journal of Women in Culture and Society* 9, no. 2 (Winter 1984): 291–310.

6.   Judith Stacey, 'Sexism By a Subtler Name? Postindustrial Conditions and Postfeminist Consciousness in the Silicon Valley' *Socialist Review* no. 96 (1987): 7–28.

7.   Kath Weston, *Families We Choose: Lesbians, Gays, Kinship.* (New York: Columbia University Press, 1991).

8.   Nancy Fraser 'Clintonism, Welfare, and the Antisocial Wage: The Emergence of a Neoliberal Political Imaginary' *Rethinking Marxism* 6, no. 1 (Spring 1993): 9–23.

9.   Some of the most sophisticated discussions are found in *Feminist Legal Theory: Readings in Law and Gender* (eds) Katharine T. Bartlett and Rosanne Kennedy (Boulder, Colorado: Westview Press, 1991).

10.   David T. Ellwood, *Poor Support: Poverty in the American Family* (New York: Basic Books, 1988).

11.   Robert Goodin, *Reasons for Welfare: The Political Theory of the Welfare State* (Princeton NJ: Princeton University Press, 1988).

12.   Not all dependencies are exploitable. In *Reasons for Welfare* (op. cit., pp. 175–6), Robert Goodin specifies the following four conditions that must be met if a dependency is to be exploitable: (1) the relationship must be asymmetrical; (2) the subordinate party must need the resource that the superordinate supplies; (3) the subordinate must depend on some particular superordinate for the supply of needed resources; (4) the superordinate must enjoy discretionary control over the resources that the subordinate needs from him/her.

13.   Albert O. Hirschman, *Exit, Voice, and Loyalty: Responses to Decline in Firms, Organizations, and States* (Cambridge, MA: Harvard University Press, 1970); Susan Moller Okin, *Justice. Gender, and the Family* (New York:

Basic Books, 1989); Barbara Hobson, 'No Exit, No Voice: Women's Economic Dependency and the Welfare State,' *Acta Sociologica* 33, no. 3 (Autumn 1990): 235–50.

14. Frances Fox Piven and Richard A. Cloward, *Regulating the Poor* (New York: Random House, 1971); Gosta Esping-Andersen, *The Three Worlds of Welfare Capitalism* (Princeton NJ: Princeton University Press, 1990).

15. Robert Goodin, *Reasons for Welfare*, op. cit.

16. Edward V. Sparer 'The Right to Welfare' in *The Rights of Americans: What They are – What They Should Be* (ed.) Norman Dorsen. (New York: Pantheon, 1970).

17. Ann Shola Orloff, 'Gender and the Social Rights of Citizenship: The Comparative Analysis of Gender Relations and Welfare States', *The American Sociological Review* 58, no. 3 (June 1993): 303–28. The anti-exploitation objective should not be confused with current US attacks on 'welfare dependency', which are highly ideological. These attacks define 'dependency' exclusively as receipt of public assistance. They ignore the ways in which such receipt can promote claimants' independence by preventing exploitable dependence on husbands and employers. For a critique of such views, see Nancy Fraser and Linda Gordon, 'A Genealogy of "Dependency": Tracing a Keyword of The US Welfare State', *Social Politics* Vol. 1, no. 1.

18. Ruth Lister, 'Women, Economic Dependency, and Citizenship', *Journal of Social Policy* 19, no. 4 (1990): 445–67; Amartya Sen, 'More Than 100 Million Women Are Missing', *The New York Review of Books* 37, no. 20 (20 December 1990): 61–6.

19. Lenore Weitzman, *The Divorce Revolution; The Unexpected Social Consequences for Women and Children in America* (New York: The Free Press, 1985).

20. David T. Ellwood, *Poor Support*, op. cit., p. 45.

21. Lois Bryson 'Citizenship, Caring and Commodification' paper presented at conference 'Crossing Borders: International Dialogues on Gender, Social Politics and Citizenship', Stockholm, Sweden, 27–9 May 1994) see Chapter 9; Arlie Hochschild, *The Second Shift: Working Parents and the Revolution at Home* (New York: Viking Press, 1989); Juliet Schor, *The Overworked American: The Unexpected Decline of Leisure* (New York: Basic Books, 1991).

22. Ruth Lister 'Women, Economic Dependency, and Citizenship', op. cit.

23. Laura Balbo, 'Crazy Quilts', in *Women and the State* (ed.) Ann Showstack Sassoon (London: Hutchinson, 1987).

24. Actually, there is a heavy ideological component in the usual view that public assistance is need-based, while social insurance is desert-based. Benefit levels in social insurance do not strictly reflect 'contributions'. Moreover, all government programmes are financed by 'contributions' in the form of taxation. Public assistance programmes are financed from general revenues, both federal and state. Welfare recipients, like others, 'contribute' to these funds, for example, through payment of sales taxes. See Nancy Fraser and Linda Gordon, 'Contract versus Charity: Why Is There No Social Citizenship in the United States?' *Socialist Review* 22, no. 3 (July–September 1992): 45–68.

25.   The free-rider worry is usually posed androcentrically as a worry about shirking paid employment. Little attention is paid, in contrast, to a far more widespread problem, namely, men's free-riding on women's unpaid domestic labour. A welcome exception is Peter Taylor-Gooby, 'Scrounging, Moral Hazard, and Unwaged Work: Citizenship and Human Need' (unpublished typescript, 1993).

26.   Employment-enabling services could be distributed according to need, desert or citizenship, but citizenship accords best with the spirit of the model. Means-tested child care targeted for the poor cannot help but signify a failure to achieve genuine breadwinner status; and desert-based child care sets up a Catch-22: one must already be employed in order to get what is needed for employment. Citizenship-based entitlement is best, then, but it must make services available to all. This rules out Swedish-type arrangements, which fail to guarantee sufficient day care places and are plagued by long queues. For the Swedish problem, see Barbara Hobson 'Economic Dependency and Women's Social Citizenship: Some Thoughts on Esping-Andersen's Welfare State Regimes' (unpublished typescript, 1993).

27.   That incidentally would be to break decisively with US policy, which has assumed since the New Deal that job creation is principally for men. Bill Clinton's 1992 campaign proposals for 'industrial' and 'infrastructural investment' policies were no exception in this regard. See Nancy Fraser, 'Clintonism, Welfare, and the Antisocial Wage', op. cit.

28.   Government could itself provide carework services in the form of public goods or it could fund marketized provision through a system of vouchers. Alternatively, employers could be mandated to provide employment – enabling services for their employees, either through vouchers or in-house arrangements. The state option means higher taxes, of course, but it may be preferable nevertheless. Mandating employer responsibility creates a disincentive to hire workers with dependents, to the likely disadvantage of women.

29.   Evelyn Nakano Glenn, 'From Servitude to Service Work: Historical Continuities in the Racial Division of Paid Reproductive Labour' *Signs: Journal of Women in Culture and Society* 18, no. 1 (Autumn 1992): 1–43.

30.   It, too, conditions entitlement on desert and defines 'contribution' in traditional androcentric terms as employment and wage deductions.

31.   Exactly what else must be provided inside the residual system will depend on the balance of entitlements outside it. If health insurance is provided universally as a citizen benefit, for example, then there need be no means-tested health system for the nonemployed. If, however, mainstream health insurance is linked to employment, then a residual health care system will be necessary. The same holds for unemployment, retirement and disability insurance. In general, the more that is provided on the basis of citizenship, instead of on the basis of desert, the less has to be provided on the basis of need. One could even say that desert-based entitlements create the necessity of need-based provision; thus, employment-linked social insurance creates the need for means-tested public assistance.

32. Peter Kilborn 'New Jobs Lack the Old Security in Time of "Disposable Workers"', *The New York Times* (15 March 1993) pp. A1, A6.

33. Failing that, however, several groups are especially vulnerable to poverty in this model: those who cannot work, those who cannot get secure, permanent, full-time, well paid jobs – disproportionately women and/or people of colour; and those with heavy, hard-to-shift, unpaid carework responsibilities – disproportionately women.

34. Failing that, however, the groups mentioned in the previous note remain especially vulnerable to exploitation – by abusive men, by unfair or predatory employers, by capricious state officials.

35. Exactly how much remains depends on the government's success in eliminating discrimination and in implementing comparable worth.

36. Universal Breadwinner presumably relies on persuasion to induce men to do their fair share of unpaid work. The chances of that working would be improved if the model succeeded in promoting cultural change and in enhancing women's voice within marriage. But it is doubtful that this alone would suffice, as the Communist experience suggests.

37. Christine A. Littleton 'Reconstructing Sexual Equality', in *Feminist Legal Theory* (eds) Katharine T. Bartlett and Rosanne Kennedy, op. cit.

38. Caregiver allowances could be distributed on the basis of need, as a means-tested benefit for the poor – as they have always been in the US. But that would contravene the spirit of Caregiver Parity. One cannot consistently claim that the caregiver life is equivalent in dignity to the breadwinner life, while supporting it only as a last-resort stop-gap against poverty. (This contradiction has always bedeviled mothers' pensions, and later Aid to Dependent Children, in the US. Although these programmes were intended by some advocates to exalt motherhood, they sent a contradictory message by virtue of being means-tested and morals-tested.) Means-tested allowances, moreover, would impede easy transitions between employment and carework. Since the aim is to make caregiving as deserving as breadwinning, caregiver allowances must be based on desert. Treated as compensation for socially necessary 'service' or 'work', they alter the standard androcentric meanings of those terms.

39. In *Justice. Gender, and the Family*, op. cit. Susan Okin has proposed an alternative way to fund carework. In her scheme the funds would come from what are now considered to be the earnings of the caregiver's partner. A man with a nonemployed wife, for example, would receive remuneration for one-half of 'his' salary; his employer would make the second half payable directly to the wife. Intriguing as this idea is, one may wonder whether it is really the best way to promote a wife's independence from her husband, as it ties her income so directly to his. In addition, Okin's proposal does not provide any carework support for women without employed partners. Caregiver Parity, in contrast, provides public support for all who perform informal carework. Who, then, are its beneficiaries likely to be? With the exception of pregnancy leave, all the model's benefits are open to everyone; men as well as women can opt for a 'feminine' life. Women, however, are considerably more likely

to do so. Although the model aims to make such a life costless, it includes no positive incentives for men to change. Some men, of course, may simply prefer such a life and will choose it when offered the chance; most will not, however, given current socialization and culture. We shall see, more over, that Caregiver Parity contains some hidden disincentives to male caregiving.

40.   In this respect it resembles the Universal Breadwinner model: what ever additional essential goods are normally offered on the basis of desert must be offered here too on the basis of need.

41.   Wages from full-time employment must also be sufficient to support a family with dignity.

42.   Adults with neither carework nor employment records would be most vulnerable to poverty in this model; most of these would be men. Children, in contrast, would be well protected.

43.   Once again, it is adults with neither carework nor employment records who are most vulnerable to exploitation in this model; and the majority of them would be men.

44.   Susan Okin, *Justice. Gender, and the Family*, op. cit.

45.   Joan Williams, 'Deconstructing Gender', in *Feminist Legal Theory*, (eds) Katharine T. Bartlett and Rosanne Kennedy, op. cit.

46.   Quoted in Ruth Lister, 'Women, Economic Dependency, and Citizenship' op. cit., p. 463.

2 Dilemmas in Engendering Citizenship
Ruth Lister

The ungendered nature of much of the mainstream literature on citizenship has been well established by now in feminist writings (see most recently, Walby, 1994). This chapter is an attempt, on the basis of a review of the literature on women's citizenship, to take stock of some of the dilemmas encountered in pursuit of a conception of citizenship which is genuinely inclusive of women as a differentiated category. As such, it poses more questions than it supplies answers and only touches the surface of some of the more difficult issues that it raises.

EXCLUSIONARY TENSIONS

Beyond the Nation-State

It is perhaps paradoxical that a concept, associated in modern times with the nation-state, is back on the political and academic agenda just at the time when the position of the nation-state is itself 'becoming ambiguous and uncertain'. (Bhavnani 1993) This reflects processes pulling in opposite directions (Turner 1990; Vogel and Moran 1991).

On the one hand, in many countries (the UK at present ex cluded) there is increased emphasis on regional autonomy; at the same time a number of nation-states have disintegrated into smaller, sometimes conflicting, units. On the other hand, the power of nation-states is being circumscribed by the development of supranational institutions such as the European Union (EU) which is, itself, promoting its own agenda of European citizenship (see for example Meehan, 1993). The growing power of international capital as part of a general process of 'economic and communicative globalization' (Yuval-

Davis 1992), together with ecological concerns (Heater 1990; Held 1991), has also served to underline the limits of nation-states. (See also, Roche 1992.)

The exclusionary force of nation-state-bound citizenship has been thrown into relief with the growth in the number of migrants and asylum-seekers in recent decades. This force is now being strengthened as members of the EU become European citizens behind the ramparts of Fortress Europe. As Bhavnani (1993) has argued, the borders between EU and non-EU countries have become sharper both symbolically and actually, reflecting new agreements on border controls and the admission of asylum-seekers as well as an official silence around racism. 'To organise a society around the categories of "citizenry" and "foreigners" – which is the basis of all nation-states – and to be simultaneously silent on racism can she argues, serve to legitimise and condone the lack of rights offered to immigrants' (p. 36). The same applies, writ large, at the level of the EU.

The lesson drawn by citizenship theorists from the weakening of the nation-state has not been to jettison the concept but to seek a more multi-layered conception, operating on several frontiers (Heater 1990; Parry 1991) and to argue for the development of an analysis of citizenship at a global level (Turner 1990; Roche 1992).

At the same time, given in part, the difficulties of such a project, there has been a tendency to sidestep the problem by identifying citizenship with the 'community' rather than the 'nation-state', following T.H. Marshall's definition of citizenship as 'full membership in the community'. However, as Yuval-Davis (1992) has warned, the assumptions implicit in notions of 'the community' – that is, those of an organic wholeness and of a given fixed collectivity – can be inimical to a politics of difference. Thus, for instance, the interests of women and men in mining 'communities' may not always coincide and minority ethnic women have protested when their interests have been rendered invisible by male leaders who purport to speak on behalf of their 'communities' (see for example Patel 1992). One question then is whether it is possible to link citizenship to a notion of community which explicitly distances itself from such assumptions.

Difference and Diversity

This leads us to another fundamental dilemma, described by Hall and Held (1989) as the 'irreconcilable tension' between the ideals of equality and universality embodied in the very idea of the citizen on the one hand and the 'post modern' emphasis on difference and diversity on the other. Central questions here are whether a concept originally predicated on the very exclusion of women can be reformulated so as satisfactorily to include (and not simply add) them (on); and whether, in doing so, it can give full recognition to the different and shifting identities that women simultaneously hold.

These two questions reflect how the feminist challenge to the false universalism of the language of abstract individualism, under the cloak of which lurked a definitely male citizen, has been followed by a similar challenge to the false universalism of the category 'woman'.

This second challenge has been spearheaded primarily by black feminists who have exposed the white prism through which the category 'woman' had been constructed. Other groups such as lesbians and disabled women have also contributed to its deconstruction. They have been aided by the growing influence of post-structuralism's rejection of any 'essentialist' categories which deny the multiple and fluid identities which, it is argued, make up each individual. In the words of the poetess June Jordan 'every single one of us is more than whatever race we represent or embody and more than whatever gender category we fall into. We have other kinds of allegiances, other kinds of dreams.' (quoted in Parmar, 1989, p. 61)

One does not need to be a signed-up postmodernist to accept that it is no longer good enough to adopt a one-dimensional gender analysis based on an understanding of women and men as unitary categories. Unfortunately, to quote Jean Leca, 'a conception of citizenship which would accommodate all social cleavages simultaneously has not yet been elaborated' (Leca 1992 p. 30).

The most thorough attempt at such an elaboration has been made by Iris Marion Young. In the name of 'a politics of difference', which rests on her critique of impartiality and a unified polity, Young (1990 p. 10) has argued that 'a conception of justice which challenges institutional domination and oppression should offer a vision of a heterogeneous public that acknowledges and affirms group differences'. She makes the case for a 'politics of group assertion' which 'takes as a basic principle that members of oppressed groups need separate organisations that exclude others, especially those from more privileged groups' (ibid. p. 167). To achieve this, 'a democratic public should', she argues, 'provide mechanisms for the effective recognition and representation of the distinct voices and perspectives of those of its constituent groups that are oppressed or disadvantaged' (ibid. p. 184). More specifically, these mechanisms should support the self-organization of groups; group generation of policy proposals in institutionalized contexts which require decisionmakers to have regard to them; and group veto power regarding specific policies which affect any group directly.

The critique of Young's proposals underscores some of the difficulties of elaborating a group-differentiated conception of citizenship. Although Young acknowledges that groups are differentiated within themselves, her prescription cannot really accommodate this. We face a Catch-22 summed-up by Razia Aziz (1992 pp. 299–300): that the very assertion of a difference tends to create 'fixed and oppositional categories which can result in another version of the suppression of difference'. Within each category, some people might face a multiplicity of oppressions; others might experience both disadvantage and privilege.

From a position sympathetic to Young, Phillips (1993) has argued that group representation is not the answer to the problems of democracy and difference for three main reasons: the difficulties of establishing which groups are most pertinent to political identity; the dangers of freezing identities and of 'group closure' so that change and the development of wider solidarities are blocked; and the near-impossibility of achieving accountability.

Phillips' own writing is infused with the dilemmas thrown up by her search for 'a politics that neither denies nor capitulates to the particularity of group identity' (1993 p. 5). It is also searching for a way of integrating both a politics of difference and 'a politics of greater generality and alliance' which is inspired by 'an aspiration or an impulse towards universality: a recognition of the partial, and potentially confining, nature of all our different and specific identities; a commitment to challenging and transforming the perspectives from which we have previously viewed the world' (ibid. p. 71).

Others have also warned of the dangers of abandoning all claims to universalism. Ursula Vogel (1988 p. 157), for instance, argues that the 'emancipatory *potential*' of the principle of equal rights 'cannot be disconnected from the claim to universality'. Similarly, Denise Riley (1992 p. 187), whilst recognizing the dangers in a claim to universal citizenship which masks real differences, points out that 'importantly, it also possesses the strength of it own idealism. Because of its claim to universality, such an ideal can form the basis for arguments for participation by everyone, as well as for entitlements and responsibilities for all.... Citizenship as a theory sets out a claim and an egalitarian promise, about real democratic participation; it envisages participation as a *potential*.'

Indeed, without this ideal, against which the denial of full and genuine citizenship to women and minority groups can be measured, the concept of citizenship loses all political force. It is precisely because of its universalist emancipatory potential that it has a resonance for many people. And it is for this reason that I believe the citizenship ideal is still worth pursuing from a feminist perspective, despite all the difficulties associated with it.

I would also argue that the deconstruction of the category 'woman' has not invalidated the project of engendering citizenship. The patterns of exclusion from citizenship are themselves sufficiently gendered to justify the exercize. (See also Walby 1994, who argues both for a gendered analysis of citizenship and for the centrality of citizenship to gender relations.) Whether the concept of citizenship can be reformulated so as successfully and genuinely to incorporate women is, however, still an open question.

The challenge is to pursue the project without slipping back into a false universalism within the gender categories and to maintain a truly differentiated analysis which does not degenerate into tokenism. Fiona Williams (1992, pp. 213–14) has suggested the image of a polyhedron 'reflecting different and changing experiences' to provide 'a more multi-faceted and interrelated model of the divisions through which people's lives are constituted'. This is helpful at a conceptual level in thinking about the ways in which women's position as citizens is mediated by other divisions such as those relating to 'race', ethnicity, class, disability, age and sexuality.

The Meaning(s) of Citizenship

Rights and participation
Returning to the dilemmas rehearsed by Phillips, caught between the politics of difference and those of a wider solidarity. For her the answer lies in earlier ideals of active citizen participation through which members of different groups would interact and debate and confront their differences. This brings us to the question of the meaning(s) of citizenship.

Like many such concepts, its meaning is contested. Leaving aside, for the moment, some of the specifically feminist debates, and over-simplifying for the sake of brevity, two broad contemporary approaches to citizenship can be identified.

One is that which focuses on individual rights, in the classical liberal tradition. Heavily influenced in the UK by Marshall's post-war conceptualization of civil, political and social citizenship rights, it has enjoyed something of a renaissance in recent years on the centre-left as the basis of a 'critique both of the undemocratic British state ... and of regressive social policies' (*New Statesman & Society* 1988). More dramatically, we have seen, in recent years, the culmination of struggles for political and civil rights in South Africa and former Communist regimes. The relationship between social citizenship rights and political and civil citizenship rights is an important issue, particularly for disadvantaged groups (Lister, 1990a).

At the same time the 'rights discourse' of the dominant post-war paradigm has come under challenge from a 'duties discourse' (Roche, 1992). The issue of citizen obligations versus citizen rights is not the focus of this paper but the gendered nature of those obligations, particularly in relation to the family and labour market, will be noted.

The other main approach, which indeed represents one strand of a 'duties discourse', stems from the civic republican tradition with its emphasis on the public community and political participation therein. This approach is particularly prominent today in the US. Writing from a feminist perspective,

Mary Dietz (1987 pp. 5–6) has dismissed as 'politically barren' the 'citizen as bearer of rights'. Instead, she argues that 'for a vision of citizenship, feminists should turn to the virtues, relations and practices that are expressly political and, more exactly, participatory and democratic ... . As long as feminists focus only on questions of social and economic concern ... they will not articulate a truly political vision, nor will they address the problem of citizenship. Only when they stress that the pursuit of those social and economic concerns must be undertaken through active engagement as citizens in the public world and when they declare the activity of citizenship itself a value, will feminists be able to claim a truly liberatory politics as their own.' (pp. 13–15)

In the UK, part of Phillips' case for politically participatory citizenship is that women's interests need to be articulated collectively and that such participation helps to address women's relative powerlessness.

One of the most prominent contemporary articulators of the republican position is Chantal Mouffe. She, like Dietz, emphasizes the limitations of a conception of the citizen as 'a bearer of rights' and instead claims that 'a radical, democratic citizen must be an active citizen, somebody who acts as a citizen, who conceives of herself as a participant in a collective undertaking' (1992 p. 4). However, Mouffe also recognizes the limitations of the republican tradition and claims that 'we need to go beyond the conceptions of citizenship of both the liberal and the civic republican traditions while building on their respective strengths.' (p. 225)

The case for such an approach, if citizenship is to provide a useful tool for feminist analysis of welfare and in the struggle for social rights, is exemplified by the work of Scandinavian feminist scholars such as Helga Hernes and Birte Siim. Hernes (1987), for example, writes: 'The welfare state literature, to the extent that it deals with individual citizens, deals with those aspects of citizenship that are related to social policy entitlements. Democratic theories and empirical studies of democratic politics emphasize the participatory aspects of citizenship. Any adequate account of contemporary citizenship in Scandinavia must include all these dimensions if the interplay between material rights, multi-level participation, and political identities is to be grasped.' (p. 138) She articulates what is a common refrain in the Scandinavian literature that 'what Scandinavian women are fighting for today is political power – the power to define, to circumscribe, to give content to policies – not material welfare.' (p. 163, see also for example Borchorst and Siim 1987).

The interplay between social and political citizenship has been a key in the development of women's position as citizens in the twentieth century (see for example Hernes, 1987; Gordon, 1990; Sarvasy, 1992). The nature of the social rights that have emerged has, in part, been a reflection of the extent to which women have been involved politically in their construction. Conversely, the extent of women's political involvement has, in part, been a reflection of the nature of the social and reproductive rights they have achieved and their mobilization has been, in part, a function of their relationship with the welfare state (see also below). And underlying the extension of women's social rights has, of course, been the possession of the vote, the significance of which it is all too easy to forget from the privilege of the late twentieth century. It's importance, however, has been brought home to us recently by the joy and seriousness with which the black peoples of South Africa seized their newly achieved right to vote after many years of struggle.

I would therefore argue that a rounded and fruitful theorization of citizenship, which can be of potential value to women, has to embrace both individual rights (and, in particular, social rights) and political participation and has also to analyze the relationship between the two (see for example Siim, 1993). However, this still begs the question as to what counts as political participation and, more specifically, what counts as citizen political participation; questions which this paper will just touch on briefly.

Active political citizenship
Feminist political scientists have done much to reconstruct 'our understanding of the body politic' (Pateman 1989 p. 52) so that it encompasses informal forms of political participation, in social movements or community groups, as well as more formal involvement in political parties and government itself. This has helped to highlight the contrast between women's continued underrepresentation (to different degrees in different countries) in the formal political system on the one hand (an under-

representation which is compounded for minority group women such as black and disabled women) and the vital role they play in keeping alive what Robert D. Putnam (1993 p. 41) has dubbed 'the capillaries of community life' on the other.

Within the context of the UK, this contrast is particularly stark in Northern Ireland where women are grossly underrepresented in the political system yet are at the centre of struggles for social rights within some of the most deprived working class communities. As a group of women from North Belfast explained to an independent commission into the future of Northern Ireland, 'We are involved with politics with a little "p" on the ground, but we get no recognition for it from politicians who are involved in politics with a big "p". There needs to be recognition for those engaged in politics with a little "p".' (Pollak, 1993, p. 12).

Women's engagement in politics with a little 'p' is important both for themselves and for their communities (be it a geographically defined community or one defined in terms of identity or interest). But as Anna Coote and Polly Pattullo (1990 p. 85) observed, in a study of women's political involvement in the UK, 'no matter how successful women were at organising at a grass-roots level, their power was limited while they remained outside the circles where key policy decisions were made and implemented'.

This dilemma is addressed elsewhere (Lister, 1993), where it is argued that it should be presented as facing not individual women (with the implication that the onus for change lies on them) but the very nature and conduct of formal politics and its interface with informal politics (see also below).

The issue remains whether, having recognized the political nature of women's involvement in social movements and community groups, it follows that this can be accorded the label of citizenship in the republican sense of the term.

According to Michael Waltzer, it cannot. He places those involved in the 'associational networks of civil society ... outside the republic of citizens as it is commonly conceived. They are only intermittently virtuous; they are too caught up in particularity.' (Waltzer 1992 p. 99) However, he writes as a sceptic when it comes to the heroic, ever-active citizen. For the true believers, the problem lies in the particularist nature of this kind of political involvement which does not accord with the republican ideal of the disinterested citizen, able to rise above his (and I mean his) particular interests, in working with other disinterested citizens, rising above their different interests, to work towards 'the common good'.

This brings us back to Iris Young (1989 p. 257) who has argued that to require the transcendence of 'particular affiliations and experiences to adopt a general view' in 'a society where some groups are privileged while others are oppressed ... serves only to reinforce that privilege'. To refuse to permit the label citizenship to be applied to the involvement of community activists, the struggles of poor women, of black or disabled women for justice, is to reactivate the very processes of exclusion which underpinned the classical republican practices of citizenship. It is to discount the empowering effect of political engagement of this kind on the individual women themselves, which can create a degree of self-confidence which is a prerequisite for effective citizenship, in contrast to more formal kinds of political activity which can be more alienating than personally empowering for some women. (The consequent enhancement of women's self-esteem, it has been argued, is important, too, for a 'kind of emotional independence' implicitly associated with citizenship in liberal political theory (James 1992 p. 60).)

The exclusion of such activities from definitions of citizenship is also to ignore the wider social and political impact they can have. Putnam (1993), for instance, has emphasized the importance of 'social capital', that is grassroots networks and organizations, as a prerequisite for effective public policy and as an expression of healthy citizenship.

To take an example from my own experience: in Bradford, a group of working class women got together to campaign against the imposition of water meters by the local water company post-privatization. This had led to soaring water bills and damaging water-rationing for many of them. Their actions helped to spearhead a national 'campaign for water justice' while also transforming the way in which these women now think about themselves. Susan Hyatt (1991), who has documented the campaign, has coined the term 'accidental activism' to describe 'such activism born of the immediate experience of social injustice', through which 'women who previously did not see themselves as in any way "political"' are becoming advocates and agents for social change'. As such, I would argue that they can also be described as active citizens, engaging in the political process on behalf of their own local community and others similarly placed, and thereby gaining greater control over their own lives.

This approach is consistent with that of political theorists such as John Keane who, in writing about civil society, have advocated 'a plurality of democratic public spheres' in which citizens can participate (Keane 1988 quoted in Phillips 1993 p. 144). This participation does not necessarily have to be directed at government but can simply involve the claiming of public space through, for example, Reclaim the Night marches (Jones 1990).

A less rigid definition of political citizenship of this kind, which includes the struggles of members of oppressed groups, invokes the spirit of a gendered political theory which 'redefines and enlarges the scope of politics, the practice of citizenship and authority, and the language of political action.' (Jones and Jonasdottir, 1988, p. 9) Nevertheless, it is not without its difficulties, as Phillips has highlighted with characteristic clarity. Where does sectional interest (bad) end and group identity (good) begin? 'What exactly' she asks is 'the dividing line between pressing one's own selfish and sectional interest and organising around your needs as disadvantaged or oppressed groups?' (1993 p. 82) And, one might add, who is to draw that line?

More fundamentally, Phillips suggests that, to embrace the notion of active political citizenship is to reassert the primacy of a public sphere separate from a private. To illustrate the point she suggests that we are acting as citizens if we campaign in public for men to do their fair share of housework; but not if we are simply sorting out the division of labour in our own home. Both are 'political' acts in the language of the 'personal is political' but, she contends 'citizenship acts on a different terrain' (ibid. 1993 p. 86). If this is so, some may ask: is there not a danger that the project of engendering citizenship might prove to be more of a liability than an asset for feminist theory and practice?

Back to the Public–Private Divide

To recognize a public terrain in which (a broadly defined) political citizenship is played out is not, I would argue, necessarily to fall back on the uncritical acceptance of a fixed public–private divide which has underpinned so much of traditional political theory. This 'patriarchal separation' (Pateman 1989 p. 183) between the domestic and the public has treated as irrelevant to citizenship whatever occurs in the 'private' sphere and has thereby helped to sustain the power of male citizens.

Some feminists have argued for the complete dissolution of the two categories. However, most would probably now agree with Mouffe (1992 p. 9) that 'what we need is a new way of understanding the nature of the private and the public, as well as a different mode of articulation between them.'

Young, for example, argues that there are good practical and theoretical reasons for maintaining the distinction, provided it is not construed as a hierarchical opposition. She suggests that, instead of defining the private as that which is excluded by the public, it should be understood as 'that aspect of his or her life and activity that any person has the right to exclude from others. The private in this sense is not what public institutions exclude, but what the individual chooses to withdraw from public view.' (Young 1990 pp. 119–20; see also Young 1987)

This is helpful but it does leave open the question as to which individuals have the power to make their choices stick. For example, some men would like to keep from public view the issue of domestic violence. In other words, it is not only public institutions which have tried to define as 'private' that which it has been in women's interests to define as matters of public concern.

The key point, therefore, is that the public–private divide has to be seen as an essentially contested concept. (It is also one which is profoundly gendered so that, for instance, Phillips' goal is the dissolution of the gendered quality of the distinction rather than the distinction itself.) The crucial question is: who has the power to decide where the line is drawn in any particular situation on any particular issue? It has been one of feminism's achievements that it has succeeded in shifting the boundaries between public and private on a number of important issues such as domestic violence and marital rape. But the legal boundaries ultimately have to be drawn through parliament or the courts, so that much depends on the openness of these institutions to women's demands which may not, themselves, be unified.

The contested nature of the distinction is one reason why it cannot be treated as a fixed given. Another reason is that, as Nira Yuval-Davis (1991, 1992) has argued, it is culturally-specific. As examples, she points to third world countries where the penetration of the modern state, especially in rural areas, is still quite limited on the one hand and the intrusiveness of the state in the former-communist societies of Eastern Europe on the other. With regard to the latter, Barbara Einhorn (1993 pp. 6–7) has contrasted the Western feminist interpretation of the public–private dichotomy with Eastern European women's idealization of the private sphere 'as both haven from and site of resistance to the long arm of the state ... in opposition to the over-politicized and didactic, exhortatory nature of the public sphere.' The boundaries between 'public' and 'private' have also shifted over time (Elshtain 1981).

Similarly, in any one society the line is drawn in different places for different groups according to the amount of power they can yield. Thus, for example, disabled people and those in poverty and/or without a home (especially if living on the streets) can find that their privacy is treated with rather less respect than that of more powerful groups. Jenny Morris (1991, p. 29), for instance, writes: 'Non-disabled people feel that our differentness gives them the right to invade our privacy and make judgements about our lives ... . Our physical difference makes our bodies public property.'

Black feminists have differed from white in their construction of the family as not just a source of sexual oppression but also a site of protection from and resistance to racist oppression (see for example Bhavnani and Coulson 1986). Patricia Hill Collins (1991 p. 47) has also suggested that the survival strategies of poor African-American families have created 'fluid public–private boundaries.'

What this adds up to is that far from being treated as a given, the public–private divide has to be seen as a shifting political construction, the understanding of which is central to the project of engendering citizenship. If treated in this way, there is no reason why the latter should weaken the feminist critique of the divide. Indeed, arguably the opposite is the case. As Phillips (1993 p. 107) has argued, 'under the rubric of citizenship, feminists are now exploring issues that used to be dealt with as economic or social policy, and the strategic significance of this is that it lifts the argument over sexual equality from the private to the public realm.'

This echoes Pateman's (1989) argument that the importance of the feminist critique lies in its illumination of the inter-relationship of the public and the private. Thus, for example, we cannot understand the gendered patterns of the exercize of political citizenship in the public sphere without understanding the sexual division of labour within the private.

A Gender-neutral or Gender-differentiated Citizenship?

This brings us to the next set of questions. Are we seeking a gender-neutral conception of citizenship which enables women to participate as equals with men in the public sphere or a gender-differentiated conception which recognizes and values women's responsibilities in the private sphere? Or does the answer lie in a gendered notion of citizenship which represents a synthesis of the two? This question can be formulated more specifically in relation to both republican and social rights for-mulations of citizenship, with implications for the nature of cit-izenship obligations. The article looks at both formulations but with the main emphasis on the latter.

Kathleen B. Jones (1988, p. 18) formulated the dilemma: 'how to recognise the political relevance of sexual differences and how to include these differences within definitions of politi-cal action and civic virtue without constructing sexually segre-gated norms of citizenship?'

Attempts to embody sexual difference in the definition of po-litical action have tended historically to focus on motherhood as the equivalent of a male civic republicanism grounded in active political participation and the ability to bear arms. Motherhood represented the epitome of difference, for only women, as mothers, could bear the next generation of citizens (Pateman 1992) The case made by Jean Elshtain (1981) for a 'social feminism', which draws on Sara Ruddick's notion of 'ma-ternal thinking' (1980) to create an 'ethical polity', imbued with the values and practices which women, supposedly, bring from the social practice of mothering, can be seen as a modern variant.

However, such approaches run the real risk of constructing the sexually segregated norms of citizenship which Jones warned against. (They are also in danger of privileging hetero-sexist assumptions about the family (Carabine 1992).) Pateman (1992 p. 20) argues that to insist 'that women's distinctive at-tributes, capacities and activities be revalued and treated as a contribution to citizenship is to demand the impossible; such "difference" is precisely what patriarchal citizenship excludes.'

Certainly, to argue today that motherhood (and presumably other forms of care) *per se* constitute the equivalent of active po-litical forms of citizenship seems a dangerous strategy. As Pateman (1992) observes, women were, in effect, incorporated into the political order on this basis and were thereby subordi-nated to men. Lip-service might be paid to the importance of care work but political power would remain in the hands of the true political citizens and the impetus for increasing women's political representation would be undermined, while the tradi-tional sexual division of labour would be legitimated.

Ultimately, women have to participate politically as citizens if they are to transform the conditions under which caring work is performed. As Stacey and Price (1981 p. 189) concluded their study of women and power over a decade ago: 'if women wish to make changes in the societies they live in, they must seek and achieve power positions. It is essential that women should enter the political arena ... for men certainly cannot be relied upon to initiate or carry through the necessary changes.' Nor, of course, can women, if it comes to that, but the more women there are in positions of power or close to positions of power, and the more women there are engaging with the political system even if within the sphere of informal politics (see for example Dahlerup 1986), the more likely it is that women's different in-terests will be articulated and acted upon.

Of course not all women (nor men for that matter) are going to want to be active politically at any level and there are dangers in idealizing collective political activity in such a way that not to engage in it becomes another source of guilt for already overburdened women.

That said, I do believe there is some mileage in a more prag-matic approach which on the one hand validates the different informal forms of political activity discussed earlier and on the other both addresses the processes which still exclude so many women from effective participation in formal politics (see for example Lovenduski 1986; Randall 1987) and the way those politics are conducted. At the same time the relationship between the two needs to be reconstructed so that the former are more accountable to the latter (Fraser 1990). This two-fold challenge to politics opens up the potential for a more permeable form of politics, open both to individual women and to the influence of the more informal forms of politics in which many women will probably still prefer to participate. In this way the legitimacy of the latter as a form of political activity and as a means of political citizenship is recognized and enhanced (although one has to guard against the tendency for men then to come in and take over). Yet men's grip on the tillers of power in the formal political arenas and on the gateways to them is not left undisturbed.

Without subscribing to the 'maternal thinking' thesis or essentialist notions of women's moral superiority, it is possible to argue that politics could be enriched by the concerns and ways of working that women can (which does not mean they always do) bring to it. Welfare issues are still all too often treated as belonging to the second division of politics (except when they become the scapegoat for public spending crises); politics is still all too often conducted in an unnecessarily adversarial way (which research, such as that by Coote and Pattullo (1990) suggests puts some women off) and on the assumption that participants are unencumbered by family responsibilities. Bacchi (1990 p. 253) argues, in similar vein, that 'it is possible to insist upon the necessity of "different" political values without suggesting that women embody them'.

At the same time we need to continue to press for better collective support for the care of children and older and disabled people and the kind of reforms which might help to shift the sexual division of labour and time within the home, as well as to press men to change their practices so as to free women to participate as political citizens more easily (see also below). Siim (1993) has argued from the Scandinavian experience that family factors no longer hinder women's political participation. Nevertheless, she contrasts this with the position in the UK where, perhaps more typically, there is still a strong case for focusing on this constraint on women's entry into politics, especially more formal forms of politics.

The accessibility of political institutions and activities is also affected by a range of other policies such as those to do with

public transport, public safety, the accessibility of public build-
ings to disabled people, sexual and racial harassment (Lister
1990b). Questions of accessibility, in its broadest sense, are especially significant for poorer women; minority groups such as
black women and disabled women face particular constraints
which need to be addressed.

This kind of pragmatic approach will not satisfy those who
argue for a more radical sexual differentiation of the construction of political citizenship. Nevertheless, it does attempt to
steer a path between a narrow equal rights stance and one
which recognizes the differences which frame men's and
women's relationship to politics so that it is not simply seeking
to 'transform women to accommodate the practice of citizenship as it traditionally has been defined.' (Jones 1990 p. 811)

Social Citizenship Rights

Who is a citizen in the welfare state?
The argument that motherhood (and, from a contemporary
stance, other forms of care) should be treated as the equivalent
of more public duties as a criterion of citizenship made more
sense in the context of the struggle for the basic political right
of the female suffrage than it does now in relation to the conceptualization of active political citizenship.

There was, though, a parallel debate which is still as relevant
today relating to the question as to which activities should
attract social citizenship rights, reflecting the gendered nature
of conceptions of citizenship obligations. Pateman (1989) has
noted how employment has replaced military service as the key
to welfare citizenship; should unpaid caring work in the private
sphere be treated as its equivalent so that earning is no longer
privileged over caring in the allocation of social rights of citizenship? Or should the aim be to improve women's access to
the labour market so that they can compete on equal terms
with men, thereby gaining the same employment-linked social
citizenship rights? Or once again, does the answer lie in a synthesis of the two approaches?

The meaning of citizenship has been a focal point – explicitly
or implicitly – of twentieth-century debates about women's relationship to the emerging welfare state. The model handed down
from the classic theorists of the British welfare state was, Susan

Pederson (1990 p. 983) observes, one in which the citizen 'not only participates in the political life of the community and holds political rights but also contributes to its social and economic well-being, drawing from it social and economic entitlements ... . By imagining a polity in which social rights stem from social functions, they begged the question of which forms of activity would properly be considered citizenship functions. If soldiering and working are to bring with them citizenship entitlements, will housekeeping or mothering do so as well?'

There was a strong strand in British feminism during and after the First World War that argued they should. The campaign for the endowment of motherhood appealed to a 'rhetoric of motherhood as national service' (Pederson 1990 p. 1006), the ethical equivalent of military service, as a basis for social citizenship and economic independence. Similarly, there was a strand in North American post-suffrage feminism which, according to Sarvasy (1992), argued the comparability of men's and women's separate services to the state as soldiers and mothers in the debate there about the endowment of motherhood.

Others, such as Ada Nield Chew in Britain, argued that participation in waged work was the key to women's economic independence. Eleanor Rathbone attempted to synthesize the two positions by arguing that the endowment of motherhood would encourage equal pay through the undermining of the case for the family wage (Land 1979; Lewis 1980; Pederson 1989).

Nevertheless, this long-standing tension between these different approaches to women's social citizenship has not been dissolved. Pateman (1989 p. 197) has conceptualized it as 'Wollstonecraft's dilemma'. On the one hand, she writes, women 'have demanded that the ideal of citizenship be extended to them, and the liberal-feminist agenda for a "gender-neutral" social world is the logical conclusion of one form of this demand.' On the other hand, women have also insisted, often simultaneously, as did Mary Wollstonecraft, that as women, 'they have specific capacities, talents, needs and concerns', so that the expression of their citizenship will be differentiated from that of men. Their unpaid work providing welfare could be seen, as Wollstonecraft saw 'women's tasks as mothers, as women's work as citizens, just as their husbands' paid work is central to men's citizenship.'

Beyond Equality versus Difference

This dilemma epitomises what is commonly known as the 'equality and difference' dichotomy, a dichotomy which a growing number of feminist writers are challenging.

The dichotomous pairing of equality and difference is, it is being argued, a logical, conceptual and political misconstruction. Equality and difference are not incompatible; indeed, the very notion of political equality implies differences to be discounted so that, despite them, people are treated as equals for a specific purpose (Scott 1988; see also O'Connor 1993, who distinguishes between the meanings of equality for purposes of civil and social rights).

The opposite of equality is inequality (Meehan and Sevenhuijsen 1991). To posit it as difference disguises the relations of subordination (Pateman 1992), hierarchy (Scott 1988) and consequent disadvantage (Bacchi 1991; Rhode, 1992) that underlie the dichotomy and distorts the political choices open to us (Scott 1988).

It also acts to suppress the differences within the categories of man and woman (Scott 1988) while implicitly taking 'man' as the standard against which 'woman' is measured. 'When men and women are treated the same, it means women being treated as if they were men; when men and women are treated differently, the man remains the norm, against which the woman is peculiar, lacking, different.' (Phillips 1993 p. 45) This norm is predicated on an implicit conception of 'men as abstract individuals without family commitments' (Bacchi 1990 p. 83) so that, conveniently, the experiences and qualities associated with such commitments are, of the essence, 'different'.

The problem does not lie in either 'equality' or 'difference', neither of which feminists can afford to discard, but in their misrepresentation as opposites. 'How then', Scott (1988 p. 44) asks, 'do we recognise and use notions of sexual difference and yet make arguments for equality?' The answer, she suggests, lies in 'the unmasking of the power relationship constructed by posing equality as the antithesis of difference and the refusal of its consequent construction of political choices.'

If equality and difference are to be reconstructed so that they open up rather than close off political choices, one inference which Scott draws is the need to recognize the contingent and specific nature of any political claims. Thus, there are certain political situations and historical moments when it makes sense to emphasize women's citizenship claims with reference to arguments associated with 'difference' (although avoiding the pitfalls of essentialism) and others when arguments associated with 'equality' are likely to have more purchase. (See also Rhode 1992.) Similarly, Bacchi (1990) suggests that historically disagreements between feminists over the two approaches can only be understood in the context of the political conditions under which they had to operate.

Also drawing on historical example, Sarvasy (1992) argues for a synthesis of equality and difference, possibly through 'the redefinition of equality as comparable treatment' (p. 356).[1] She takes inspiration from a group of North American post-suffrage feminists who 'groped for a theoretical and practical synthesis of equality and difference as the basis for women's citizenship and as the defining characteristic of public policies in a feminist welfare state.' (p. 330) They developed a conception of 'the feminist citizen–mother who performed a role both gender differentiated and equal'(p. 358). This 'citizen–mother' would be validated in her role but would not be confined to it; she would be a citizen in her own right, both politically and economically independent. (See also Rathbone's arguments for family endowment, noted above.)

Sarvasy describes three steps in what she terms 'a feminist method of synthesis': 'the uncovering of the negative aspects of gender difference as substantive gender inequality, the proposing of public policy remedies that embodied a new relationship between equality and difference, and the drawing out of the emancipatory potential of gender difference within a new context of greater substantive and formal gender equality.'

This process, she suggests, can help to resolve the tension between equality and difference and to distinguish policies which, in the name of difference, reinforce traditional gender relations from those based on the feminist potential of gender difference. It 'provides both a framework for reconceiving women's citizenship and an ideological motor for developing a feminist welfare state' (p. 359).

Sarvasy's idea of synthesis suggests a way forward in working through the dilemmas raised in this paper. Also helpful is Bacchi's thesis that a false choice between equal and different treatment diverts attention from the more fundamental issues of 'social responsibility for basic human needs such as child-bearing and child nurture' (1990 pp. 83–4). Instead of the abstract male model implicit in the equality versus different choice, she calls for a 'social model which includes women in the human standard' (ibid. p. 266).

What Price Citizen – the Carer?

Arnlaug Leira (1989, 1992) has adopted a similar stance in her work on welfare citizenship and working mothers. She analyzes the ways in which even the more progressive Scandinavian welfare states privilege citizen the wage-earner over citizen the carer, reflecting 'the hierarchy of work forms, which accords primacy to wage-work, however useless, over other forms of work, however useful' (1992 p. 171). She concludes that 'what is lacking is a concept of citizenship which recognises the importance of care to society' (1989 p. 208).

The problem is how to provide this recognition without locking women further into a caring role which serves to exclude them from the power and influence which can derive from participation in the public sphere of the economy and the polis.

One, minimalist, path is to provide adequate protection of social-insurance records during periods when people are out of the labour market providing care for either children or older or disabled people. This, one could argue, represents the bottom line of recognition of caring work in the allocation of social security rights. The provision of non-contributory (and non-means-tested) pensions, as is the case in the Nordic countries and the Netherlands, ensures that all women get a pension in their own right regardless of breaks in their employment record. Tove Stang Dahl (1984 p. 41) argues that, through such pensions 'old age liberates women financially', even though their level tends to be pretty low (Brocas *et al.* 1990) and women rely disproportionately on the basic pension alone (although less so in Finland where women have a longer history of labour market participation (Osterberg and Hedman 1988)).

Of course Dahl's claim is partly a reflection of the extent to which social security provisions do not liberate women under pension age financially. Generally unemployment insurance schemes exclude, to a greater or lesser extent, the increasingly typical 'atypical' worker who is combining paid work and family responsibilities. In some countries, greater flexibility is shown in accommodating part-time workers in sickness and maternity benefit schemes and, in a few, some provision is made in such schemes for women not in paid employment (Maier 1991). There is considerable scope for the reform of social insurance benefits so as to provide adequate protection for part-time workers and, in the UK at least, this is now seen by some (outside government) as a priority.[2]

So far, so relatively easy (in principle, if not necessarily in practice). Where the dilemma arises is with the question of the nature of the recognition, if any, that should be given through direct cash payments to those at home providing care. Two contrasting viewpoints are to be found in the first edition of *Social Politics*. According to Trudie Knijn (1994 p. 103) 'caring for children is a social activity as important as many other social activities and . . . women should be allowed to claim the right to an income from that activity.' Bettina Cass (1994 pp. 110–11), whilst agreeing that 'care-giving work should be legitimated and supported', warns that 'to do only this, however, would enshrine care-giving as women's work. If the social welfare system legitimated and (inadequately) financially supported women as care-givers, why should activists concerned with women's rights insist on more equitable participation of women in paid employment and, thus, more equitable participation of men in care-giving work?'

In this contemporary variant of Wollstonecraft's dilemma we are torn between wanting to validate and support, through some form of income maintenance provision, the caring work for which women still take the main responsibility in the 'private' sphere and to liberate them from this responsibility so that they can achieve economic and political autonomy in the 'public' sphere. One aspect of the dilemma is neatly encapsulated in Clare Ungerson's conclusion in *Gender and Caring* (1990 p. 189): it is 'essential that policies which are woman-centred develop, rather than policies that are paid worker centred, but this hangs crucially on the ability of mothers and carers to insert their needs and rights into the political and economic process.'

In the UK, the debate as to what are the appropriate woman-centred policies tends to differentiate between mothers and other carers, reflecting the particular meaning of 'care' in British social policy compared with, for example, Scandinavia (Ungerson 1990). Pateman's exposition of Wollstonecraft's dilemma, and her suggested way through it, provides a possible framework for the discussion of the policy options with regard to both types of care.

Pateman (1989 p. 203) poses the question: 'what form must democratic citizenship take if a primary task of all citizens is to ensure that the welfare of each living generation of citizens is secured?' Part of her answer is that 'if women's knowledge of and expertise in welfare are to become part of their contribution as citizens, as women have demanded during the twentieth century, the opposition between men's independence and women's independence has to be broken down, and a new understanding and practice of citizenship developed.' (p. 204)

Such an approach usefully encourages a shift in the focus of attention from women to men as well as to wider societal responsibilities for children and others in need of care. It raises questions about the gendered nature of the link between citizenship obligations and citizenship rights.

Shifting the Sexual Division of Labour

Susan Moller Okin (1989) has argued the centrality of a more equal sexual division of labour, if women are to enjoy genuine equal opportunities with men within the family 'or in any of the other spheres of distribution – from politics to free time, from recognition to security to money' (p. 116). Justice to women (and children), she argues, requires that family and work institutions 'encourage the avoidance of socially created vulnerabilities by facilitating and reinforcing the equal sharing of paid and unpaid work between men and women, and consequently the equalizing of their opportunities and obligations in general.' (p. 169)

A similar philosophy informs the EU's 3rd Action Programme on Equal Opportunities for Women and Men 1991–1995 (Commission of European Communities, 1991). An earlier declaration on equality between women and men in political and public life, from a 1986 European Ministerial conference made the link with citizenship, endorsing 'the view that de facto equality between women and men in the world of work, in the family and other areas of life, will not come about without the full sharing between women and men of the duties and responsibilities that democratic citizenship implies.'

Taylor-Gooby (1991) and Cass (1994) have developed the point, the former using the concept of 'moral hazard' in relation to men's evasion of caring work, which is encouraged by government policies. Cass turns the argument on its head with the claim that men should not be 'accorded full citizenship if they do not fulfil their responsibilities for care-giving work.' (p. 115)

While it is difficult to see how the state could enforce such a notion of citizenship, there are certainly a number of ways in which it could encourage it. Indeed, it has been a central tenet of European Community Action Programmes on women that member states should. Perhaps the most wholehearted attempt has been made with regard to child care in the Scandinavian countries by means of parental leave provisions and campaigns to encourage men to take the leave and more generally to undertake their fair share of domestic responsibilities. These have had some limited impact but not as much as had been hoped and women continue to carry the main responsibility for care and housework (Siim 1993). In some instances, this has raised questions as to whether part of the parental leave period should be restricted to fathers in two-parent families (Leira 1993; Lewis 1994).[3] However, so long as men can command, on average, higher rewards from the labour market than women, it will make economic sense for women to make greater use of parental leave provisions than men.

Another constraint on male participation in the home is the long hours that some men work, particularly in the UK (Hewitt 1993). A study for the Equal Opportunities Commission observes that 'there seems no way in which a style of work which involved such a long commitment to paid employment could be emulated by anyone who had a major responsibility for children.' (Marsh 1991, p. 80) It suggests that the single most effective way of promoting equality might be to regulate the hours of work that men work and notes the right of Swedish parents to reduce their hours of work to within school hours while their children are young.[4] Of course, any reduction in the hours men devote to paid work will not automatically translate into an increase in the hours they devote to unpaid care work, but it could help, especially if backed up by education campaigns directed at men.

A more equal division of paid and unpaid work between women and men does, I believe, form one important element of any strategy for the realization of women's full potential as citizens.[5] The importance of both sides of the equation does, though, need to be stressed. An increase in women's paid work contribution without an equivalent increase in men's unpaid contribution would have implications for women's time, and also possibly their health; witness the experience of many Eastern European women under the former communist regimes (see for example Einhorn 1993). This might limit rather than enhance the opportunities for them to participate as active political citizens.

There are also other provisos. First, is the difficult one. We cannot assume that men's participation in the family is always a blessing. Men may not have a total monopoly on violence and sexual, abuse within the family, but there can be no doubt that they are it's main perpetrators. The evidence about the extent of violence and abuse suggests that a degree of caution is in order when claiming greater male involvement in parenting as 'the' solution.

The other proviso is less problematic, in that it is simply that a fairer division of responsibility for the provision of care between men and women is only one part of the equation, particularly in the case of lone parent families; the other concerns the division of responsibility between individual families and the wider community, as expressed through state provision. This state provision can be aimed at enabling parents and other carers to take paid work or at providing financial support for them to provide care themselves at home.

Children

With regard to the care of children, the availability of affordable, good quality child care is a key to the achievement of the first aim. Cass (1994 p. 120), for instance, maintains that 'resolving Wollestonecraft's dilemma requires that a priority be placed on substantially increased support of child care.'

The European Commission Childcare Network has identified both considerable variation in the level of publicly financed pro-

vision between member states and significant levels of unmet
need overall (Commission of the European Communities,
1990). According to the Network's analysis, Denmark, followed
by France and Belgium, top the league; the UK, together with
Ireland and the Netherlands are at the bottom, although the
Netherlands has since embarked on a policy of expansion.

The UK's position exemplifies the extent to which child care
is seen as the responsibility of the individual parent and not the
state, to the particular detriment of lone parent families. It
has been a central tenet of British social policy under the
Conservatives to attempt to shift the boundaries of responsibility more firmly on to individual families and away from the
state. 'Accepting responsibility for yourself and your family and
not shuffling it off to the state' is part of the 'Back to Basics'
credo preached by Prime Minister John Major.

This residualist philosophy stands in contrast to that of
Scandinavian governments where, it has been suggested (Siim
1988) a new partnership has been forged between families, and
to some extent, women and the state (although the partnership
is now under strain in some cases as these welfare states face
cutbacks).

This partnership is most advanced in Denmark and Sweden.
Jane Lewis (1992) has described how the latter has adopted a
model which treats women as citizen-workers and then grafts
on their claims as mothers through parental leave schemes
(which have extended steadily in length). In an earlier work
(1990), she suggested that this model might offer an example
of a synthesis of claims based on equality and difference
strengthening women's rights as citizens. However, she has
since warned that it has served to reinforce the highly sexually
segregrated Swedish labour market and suggests that therefore, the Swedish model has 'considerably less to offer than
France, which provides almost as much for the working mother
. . . and has also taken equal opportunities legislation further'
(1992 p. 169).[6]

The lesson would therefore appear to be not to abandon the
idea of parental leave (which is a means of placing value on the
care of young children) but to make it harder for men to evade
taking at least a share of the leave on the one hand and to back
it up with much tougher equal opportunities and sex discrimination measures, plus decent child care provisions on the other.

However, there remains the danger that so long as it is women who are more likely to take advantage of parental leave, long breaks from the labour market will disadvantage their long-term position within it (Joshi 1991). This danger would be even greater if an allowance were paid to those who stay at home to care for children after the end of any parental leave period.

Such an allowance has been introduced in Finland in the shape of the home care allowance, payable after nine months until the child is aged three. Even though there is a complementary right to a place in a communal day centre and a partial home care allowance where a parent chooses to work shorter hours, its introduction has been interpreted by some as a shift in ideology to encourage mothers to stay at home for longer. Fears have also been expressed that it will increase divisions between working- and middle-class women, as it is the former who are more likely to take up the allowance (Simonen 1991).

An alternative approach would be to pay a benefit to all those raising children, after the end of any parental leave period. This would reduce the disincentive to mothers to take paid employment (although not remove it altogether) and would recognize that raising children incurs costs, including 'time-costs', regardless of the parents' employment status. Payable per family rather than per child it would have a different function from family allowances. Esam and Berthoud (1991) have modelled such a benefit in the UK context on the basis of lower payments where the youngest child is of school age. They suggest that one advantage of such a benefit might be to 'enable mothers and fathers to develop more flexible and more equal arrangements for sharing the responsibilities for caring and earning' (p. 48). However, such a benefit would be expensive and in the current context of welfare state retrenchment it seems something of a pipedream.

The same could be said for the even more radical option of a basic or citizen's income scheme under which every individual would receive a tax-free payment regardless of employment status and without any conditions or citizenship obligations attached. (This also raises the question, relevant to citizenship, of whether and under what conditions an obligation to seek paid work should be attached to social security entitlements, an issue of increasing salience for lone parents (see Lister 1990a; 1994a).) However, citizen's income would also provide the same basic benefit irrespective of care responsibilities. Thus, although it has been argued that a citizen's income would provide recognition of women's unpaid work in the home (Parker 1993), it would do so on a totally indiscriminatory basis, providing the same recognition for basic housework as care work. Moreover, if not combined with measures aimed at tackling the sexual division of labour, it could inadvertently serve to reinforce it as well as men's economic advantage over women, if men could simply add their higher wages to their citizens' income payment.

Adults

The failure of citizens' income to recognize the specific work of caring has also been noted by Clare Ungerson (1993) in a review of the options for underwriting the citizenship rights of carers (meaning, in the British literature, those providing care for older and/or disabled people). The growing literature on payment for carers underlines some of the difficulties in developing an approach which enhances the citizenship not only of those providing care but also of those receiving it, the majority of whom are also women.

McLaughlin and Glendinning (1994) have identified two main models of paying for care. The first is the social security model under which financial support is based on clear, if restricted, rights. The main examples given are Italy, France, Germany, the Republic of Ireland and the UK, although only in the latter two cases does the right to payment lie with the carers themselves.

The British invalid care allowance provides an interesting example of the strengths and limitations of the social security approach to paying for care in a system which privileges wage-earning in the allocation of rights. The invalid care allowance is an income replacement benefit for those providing at least 35 hours a week of care and not earning more than £50 a week, neither subject to contribution nor means test. As such, it can be said to represent a citizenship approach (Ungerson 1992; Pascall 1993), which recognizes the impact of caring on the ability to undertake paid work without policing the actual care work undertaken.

However, it's status as an independent citizenship benefit is compromised by eligibility criteria which link it to the receipt or non-receipt of other benefits by the care-recipient. More fundamentally, it's payment at only 60 per cent of the equivalent adult contributory benefit rate, so as to preserve the social insurance principle, together with the original exclusion of married/cohabiting women on the grounds that 'they might be at home in any event' (eventually abandoned in the face of a European court case) underlines the essentially second-class citizenship status it embodies.

More generally, McLaughlin and Glendinning (1994) criticize the social security approach on the grounds that, whilst recognizing the role of carers, it does not attempt to reward the actual work they perform (although many of those interviewed in a study by McLaughlin (1991) saw the invalid care allowance as a payment for care). As a consequence entitlement cannot begin after retirement age.

Whether the alternative model – that of payment for care undertaken – provides a firmer underpinning of carers' citizenship is, however, debatable. The disadvantages of the commodification of care in this way, highlighted in the literature (Ungerson 1992; McLaughlin and Glendinning 1993, 1994), include the low rates of pay and lack of employment rights typical of such schemes with possible implications for those employed in the formal care sector; the increase in control over carers; the dangers of increased professionalization of care work. Mclaughlin and Glendinning's (1993) assessment of the Finnish home care allowance scheme reaches the pessimistic conclusion that, like the UK's social security approach, it has 'so far failed to mount an effective challenge to either the "invisibility" of care-giving work or to the lack of value which is conventionally assigned to it. Even in the context of a highly developed Scandinavian welfare state, there has been clear resistance to the transformation of unpaid, private care-giving work into paid employment' (p. 250).

A danger common to both models is that mentioned earlier with regard to payment for child care: that it could serve to institutionalize further the sexual division of caring labour. This is a point that has been made by Finch (1990), amongst others, but she herself qualifies her objection with the observation 'that it would be wrong not to continue to press for more support for women who currently do take on unpaid caring with little or no financial or practical support for the sake of potential longer-term gains' (p. 52). Thus, more limited short-term demands need, she argues, to be complemented by longer-term strategies which address the sexual division of labour in both the private and public spheres.

At the same time, short-term demands need to be mindful of their possible negative effects and seek to minimize them. Thus, for example, any scheme for providing financial support for carers should be sufficiently flexible to enable carers of working age to combine their caring work with paid work, if they so wish.

Such an approach also underlines the importance of adequate service provision. McLaughlin and Glendinning (1994) are critical of a strategy which aims solely at enabling carers to participate in the labour market, partly on the grounds that, once again, it denies the value for citizenship of unpaid care work. It also ignores the needs of carers over pension age (Ungerson 1993) and, if not combined with other measures, could increase women's overall (combined paid and unpaid) work load.

Ungerson (1992) argues that it is fruitless trying to decide *in general* whether one approach or another is in or against women's interests. Instead, she suggests that what is needed is a set of agreed criteria for judging whether any *particular* scheme is in the interests of all involved in the caring relationship, in particular those of women carers. While such a set of criteria would be useful, one should not underestimate the difficulty in reaching agreement, particularly as Ungerson side-steps the issue of the potential conflict of interests between the different parties.

This is a point taken up by McLaughlin and Glendinning whose other main criticism of a carers' employment service-based strategy is that it ignores the needs and rights of care-recipients for whom 'the very language of day care and respite care services may be experienced as insulting', portraying 'disabled people as a burden from which their carer needs or "deserves" to be rescued' (1994 p. 56). This raises the critical issue, all too often overlooked in the care literature, of the perspective of the recipients of care and their rights as citizens.

Indeed some disabled people are challenging the very language of care as carrying with it 'the notion of "dependent people"' (Morris 1993 p. 150) and are arguing that the ideology of caring is incompatible with a commitment to disabled people's right to be equal citizens. In policy terms, there is a potential conflict of interests between demands for the payment of carers and the growing demand among some disabled people for direct payments to disabled people so that they can pay for and thereby control the way in which their care needs are met.

Both sets of demands can be justified with reference to the autonomy and citizenship of the members of each group. As McLaughlin and Glendinning (1994) observe, the interests of members of neither group are best served by policies which create financial dependence on the other so that 'there is a delicate path to be trod in negotiating dependence and independence between carers and disabled people with care needs' (p. 60).

They suggest, drawing on the work of Tronto, that this path might fruitfully be approached at a theoretical level using the concept of the 'ethics of care' thereby focusing 'on the terms and conditions under which we engage in caring relationships' (p. 61). Sevenhuijsen (1992) suggests that an ethics of care involves recognition of care as a relational activity rather than just as labour, as well as the balancing of needs of carer and care-recipient, often in situations of dependence and inequalities of power and resources. A commitment to see issues from different perspectives, one of the characteristics of an ethics of care, is, she suggests, a precondition for 'discussions about which needs should be met and how, in individual as well as in collective contexts' (p. 18).

A tendency in some of the literature to counterpose a (female) ethic of care or responsibility as antithetical to the dominant (male) ethic of justice or rights is being overtaken by arguments for a synthesis of the two (Siim 1990; Phillips 1993). Indeed, Bacchi (1990) quotes an article by Carol Gilligan and others which, drawing on Gilligan's 'inclusion model' argues that it is 'no longer either simply about justice or simply about caring; rather it is about bringing them together to transform the domain' (Du Bois *et al.* 1985 p. 45).

Such a synthesis is necessary if our understanding of citizenship is to be enriched by an ethic of care on the one hand and if the practice of care is to be underwritten by the social rights associated with citizenship on the other. This approach helps meet Clare Ungerson's doubts about applying the 'public construct of citizenship' to the 'essentially private constructs of love and kinship' involved in care relations (1993 p. 144). In fact, Ungerson's piece concludes by partially overcoming her own scepticism when it suggests that, in the context of high quality, reliable support services, which enable those who wish to remain in their own homes, 'the private aspects of care – the parts that contain the love and watchfulness – can flourish within a public framework, underwritten by the collectively guaranteed provision of caring services by the state.' (p. 150)

SOCIAL CITIZENSHIP AND (IN)DEPENDENCE

(In)dependence and Interdependence

Attempts to synthesise the ethics of care and justice are also relevant to the vexed issue of women's economic (in)dependence. A synthesis of the two could provide a framework in which due recognition can be given to the interdependence which is quintessential to human relationships – and in particular those involving care-giving – while not losing the cutting edge of the feminist critique of women's economic dependency upon men and the negation of rights and autonomy which it entails. In similar vein, Karen Offen (1992 p. 85) has made the case for 'reintegrating individualistic claims for women's self-realization and choices, with its emphasis on rights, into the more socially conscious relational framework, with its emphasis on mutual responsibility' as a model for contemporary feminist politics.

The case for women's economic independence, through their ability 'to earn their own subsistence, independent of men' as 'enlightened citizens', was made 200 years ago by Mary Wollstonecraft (1792/1985 p. 283). Two centuries later many women still do not enjoy genuine economic independence, despite a significant presence in the labour market (Lister 1992). The relevance of economic (in)dependence to women's citizenship has therefore continued to be emphasized in feminist analysis (Pascall 1986; Lister 1990b; Cass 1994).[7]

Dependence, has not, however, been an unproblematic concept; its opposition to independence is ideologically charged and constructed (Fraser and Gordon 1994).

It is a racialized concept, not only in the context of US debates about welfare (Fraser and Gordon 1994) but also in that of feminist analysis of women's position in the family. Black feminists have been critical of white feminists' preoccupation with women's economic dependence, pointing out that it is much less common among African-Caribbean households (Carby 1982; Hooks 1982). Nevertheless, it is only the more privileged women who are completely immune to the impact of the ideology of women's economic dependency which still governs the general position of women in the labour market. Thus black women, and other women heads of household such as lesbian women, can still be affected adversely by it.

The other main issue, as noted above, concerns the potential contradiction between demands for women's economic independence on the one hand and a rejection of the false dichotomy between dependence and independence in favour of notions of interdependence on the other (Wilson 1983; Land 1989; Gordon 1990). Diana Pearce (1990 p. 275) argues that 'the campaign against women's poverty should not be premised, implicitly or explicitly, on a false distinction between those who are economically "independent" and those who are "dependent"' that is between those who work in the home and those who work in the marketplace. The latter's independence is, she argues, made possible by their hidden dependence on the former. (See also Graham 1983; Pateman 1989.)

In a recent essay, which sketches the beginnings of 'an alternative semantics premised on the inescapable fact of human interdependence', Fraser and Gordon (1994 p. 23) quote Pearce and suggest that a feminist response needs to revalue the devalued side of the dichotomy 'ie to rehabilitate dependency as a normal, even valuable, human quality.' However, they recognize that this needs to be done cautiously, given that 'dependence' on welfare (would reliance be a less charged word to use in this context?) can reduce self-esteem and autonomy.

I would argue for similar caution in the rehabilitation of dependency in the context of the family for similar reasons. Moreover, in this context, there is a danger of losing sight of what Fraser and Gordon themselves earlier refer to as 'dependency as a social relation of subordination' (ibid. p. 21). The unequal power relationship that underpins women's economic dependency upon men means that the interdependence of which it is a part is skewed in men's favour.[8] It is not surprising, therefore, that men's dependence on women for care and servicing, which, as noted above, facilitates their own independence as workers and citizens, is thereby conveniently obscured.

Part of the feminist project has to be to distinguish between the different kinds of dependence involved in this relationship of interdependence. Fraser and Gordon (p. 24) go on to argue for a differentiation between what they term 'socially necessary' and 'surplus' dependence. The former represents the need for care which is 'an inescapable feature of the human condition'; the latter, in contrast, 'is rooted in unjust and potentially remediable social institutions.' The goal would be to eliminate the surplus dependency which currently adheres to the care-giving involved in the socially necessary dependency. 'The utopian end would be abolition of the current link between caring for dependants and thereby being rendered dependent oneself.' (p. 24) Similarly, Julia O'Connor (1993 p. 512) points out that 'the absence of involuntary economic dependence does not imply the absence of interdependence. Whereas interdependence implies choice, equality and reciprocity, involuntary economic dependence implies an unequal power relationship and the absence of choice.'

Another element of the feminist project is the illumination of the asymmetrical nature of relations of interdependence which involve involuntary economic dependence and its implications for both men's and women's citizenship.

One aspect of this is to problematize men's independence. This is the approach taken by Cass (1994 p. 114) who maintains that the problem for public policy lies not in women's dependence but in 'men's independence, with the negation of welfare that it implies and which is its consequence.' While agreeing with Cass on the need to problematize men's independence, I would nevertheless argue that women's economic dependence does not thereby cease to be a problem for public policy and for their position as citizens.

The continued problem of women's economic dependence
The nature of this problem can be analyzed from the perspectives of philosophy, poverty and power. In his defence of state welfare, Taylor-Gooby (1991) argues that basic human needs constitute rights against the state, as components of citizen-

ship. He identifies human freedom or autonomy as 'a basic principle' in 'the field of needs as goals for social welfare policy' and as 'an essential component in any account of human welfare' (p. 172). According to Hall and Held (1989 p. 19) citizenship rights can be 'thought of as a measure of the autonomy an individual citizen enjoys as a result of his or her status as "free and equal" members of a society.'

Sapiro also draws on the concept of autonomy, citing Weale's claim that the principle of autonomy 'asserts that all persons are entitled to respect as deliberative and purposive agents capable of formulating their own projects, and that as part of this respect there is a governmental obligation to bring into being or preserve the conditions in which this autonomy can be realised' (Weale 1983 quoted in Sapiro 1990 p. 51). Sapiro points out that this is precisely what has been missing in a social policy which is content to prescribe dependency for women.

The relationship between autonomy or human freedom and economic independence is explored in Tove Stang Dahl's treatise on feminist jurisprudence (1987). Within a framework of the central values underlying 'women's law' – those of justice, freedom and dignity – she argues that 'a minimum amount of money for oneself is a necessary prerequisite for personal freedom, self-determination and self-realisation' (p. 91). Conversely, economic dependency is portrayed as the negation of freedom. From a human rights perspective, women's economic dependency on men is, she contends, 'a moral problem, both on an individual and a societal level' (p. 97). Dahl thus argues that 'access to one's own money should be considered a minimum welfare requirement in a monetary economy ... . An independent income of one's own is a prerequisite for participation in and enjoyment of life, privately as well as publicly. Lack of money, on the other hand, gives a person little freedom of movement and a feeling of powerlessness' (p. 111).

Dahl quotes research showing that women experience economic dependency as a threat to their dignity. (See too Cragg and Dawson 1984; McLaughlin 1991; Callender 1992 for examples of British research which highlights the importance to many women of an independent source of income.) Dahl's account points us also to the relationship between economic dependency and a gendered understanding of poverty.

As the economist, A.B. Atkinson (1991 pp. 9, 10) observes, if poverty is conceptualized in relation to a 'right to a minimum level of resources', 'we may question whether the dependency of one partner, typically the woman, on the other is acceptable.' Stephen Jenkins (1991 p. 464) develops this to suggest that a feminist conception of poverty 'concerns the individual right to a minimum degree of potential economic independence'.

Both the actuality and the ideology of women's economic dependency serve to make them more vulnerable than men to poverty (Glendinning and Millar 1992; Lister 1992). The long-standing failure to recognize the family as 'an important sphere of distribution' (Okin 1989 p. 31), reflected in the typical measurement of poverty at the level of the family or household, means that the poverty of some women, fully or partially economically dependent on men, remains invisible.

The distribution of resources (including work and time as well as money) within the family is partly a function of power relationships which, in turn, reflect to some extent the relative economic resources that each partner commands independently (Fuchs 1988; Okin 1989; Pahl 1989). The unequal power relationship, already noted as typical of full or partial economic dependency, is experienced by many women as a lack of control over resources; a lack of rights and a sense of obligation and deference (Pahl 1989). Such relations are corrosive of women's citizenship.

Economic (In)dependence and Welfare State Regimes

If it is accepted that the question of economic (in)dependence is critical to women's welfare and citizenship, it needs to be incorporated into cross-national analysis of welfare states and regimes (Hobson 1991). Langan and Ostner (1991 p. 130) point out that, as it stands, 'the question of gender is not systematically built into' the influential framework developed by Esping-Anderson (1990). In particular, they argue that his use of the concept 'decommodification' – 'the degree to which individuals, or families, can uphold a socially acceptable standard of living independently of market participation' (Esping-Anderson 1990 p. 37) (note the elision of individuals and families here) – takes no account of gender differences. Lewis (1992) has taken the argument further, analyzing welfare regimes according to the strength of the male breadwinner family model.

In a paper written a couple of years ago (published as Lister, 1994a), I suggested that decommodification needs also to be complemented by what we might call 'defamilialization', if it is to provide a rounded measure of economic independence. Welfare regimes might then also be characterized according to the degree to which individual adults can uphold a socially acceptable standard of living, independently of family relationships, either through paid work or through social security provisions.

A very similar line of thought is being pursued by a number of feminist scholars (O'Connor 1993; Orloff 1993; McLaughlin and Glendinning 1994). McLaughlin and Glendinning use exactly the same term 'defamilialization'[9] and virtually the same definition of it. They argue that, as with decommodification, it is not a question of all or nothing. Instead, at issue is 'the extent to which packages of legal and social provisions have altered the balance of power between men and women, between dependents and non-dependents, and hence the terms and conditions under which people engage in familial or caring arrangements.' (p. 66) In this way, they suggest that the concept might provide a more structured way of approaching the questions raised by an analysis of women's economic position and their relationship to the state as well as a set of criteria for assessing different strategies around paying for care from the perspectives of both those receiving and providing care.

Orloff and O'Connor develop the notion of autonomy as a means of complementing the concept of decommodification. O'Connor's (1993 p. 514) formulation of 'personal autonomy or insulation from dependence' differs slightly from that of defamilialization in that it includes, in dependence, 'public dependence on the state agencies' as well as 'personal dependence on family members'. However, by public dependence on state agencies, O'Connor appears to be referring specifically to benefits and services subject to a 'dependency-enhancing means test' in contrast to those available as a citizenship right. While I would agree with the importance of the distinction and that means-tested benefits and services provide, at best, second-class citizenship (see Lister 1990a), under my formulation they could, in certain circumstances, contribute to the defamilialization process. I am thinking, in particular, of the way in which means-tested social assistance schemes, with all their restrictions and inadequacies, have at least enabled mothers to live separately from the fathers of their children. (However, in the UK the independence this has permitted is now being compromised under the new Child Support Act which, in effect, makes fathers liable for the support of the mother as well as the children, (Lister 1994b.))

'Women's capacity to form and maintain an autonomous household' is one of two dimensions (the other being that of access to paid work) which Orloff (1993 p. 319) adds to that of decommodification. But this formulation does not include the capacity to achieve financial autonomy within marriage (or its equivalent) other than through paid work, or indirectly through the increased leverage the possibility of this autonomy might give. Orloff then suggests that all three dimensions could be subsumed under the generic one of measuring independence or autonomy, that is 'individuals' freedom from compulsion to enter into potentially oppressive relationships in a number of spheres' (p. 320).

Both she and O'Connor make the link here with sexual autonomy, another important piece in the jigsaw of women's fractured citizenship. 'In sum', writes Orloff, 'relations of domination based on control of women's bodies in the family, the workplace, and public spaces undermine women's abilities to participate as "independent individuals" – citizens – in the polity, which in turn affect their capacities to demand and utilise social rights.' (p. 309) O'Connor stresses the necessity of guaranteed sexual as well as social rights to personal autonomy. (See also Jones (1990) and note 7 below.)

Leaving aside differences of detail, what the formulations described above share is an attempt to theorize social citizenship rights in terms of the degree to which they promote the personal autonomy and economic independence of women with caring responsibilities. As a complement to the concept of decommodification, they provide a framework for cross-national analysis of welfare state regimes which pays due regard to the different relationship of men and women to welfare states.

Women's Citizenship in Welfare States

They also constitute an approach which can distinguish between the ways in which welfare states can, at the same time, both deny many women genuine social citizenship through, for example, the operation of two-tier benefits systems (Nelson 1984, 1990; Acker 1988; Fraser 1987) yet, despite their patriarchal nature, also help to 'provide a basis for women's autonomous citizenship' (Pateman 1989, p. 195), particularly by providing support for lone parent families.

Such a perspective on women's relationship to welfare states – critical, yet recognizing the gains that have been made, often as a result of women's own struggles – is exemplified by much of the Scandinavian literature (see for example Hernes 1987) and by North American works such as Linda Gordon's edited collection, *Women, the State and Welfare* (1990, see also Acker 1988).

This literature points to how some women have been able to gain a degree of economic independence from men, both as recipients and as paid providers of welfare. It also suggests that welfare institutions have offered political resources to women and served to mobilize them as political citizens in a number of ways (Hernes 1987; Fox-Piven 1990; Orloff 1993; O'Connor 1993), bringing us back to the relationship between the social and political dimensions of citizenship.

The provision of public welfare services has both provided jobs for women and enabled them to 'go beyond the home and private relations, to enter the world of work and new areas of civil society' (Sassoon 1987 p. 172). The process of negotiation with welfare state institutions, the main responsibility for which tends to fall to women, has been described as a form of political citizenship (Nelson 1984; Jones 1990) and it can lead to more collective forms of action to extend and defend social rights, action which may unite the interests of different groups of women both as recipients and providers (Fox-Piven 1990).

Growing demands for user-involvement in the provision of welfare services creates a link between rights and participatory based forms of citizenship. Siim's research into women's local political involvement as parents in child care institutions and schools has led her to conclude, in the Danish context, that 'the new politics of reproduction can be interpreted as a new form of social citizenship that has empowered women by giving them new welfare and participatory rights as citizens *vis-à-vis* the state.' (1993 p. 34)

Siim (1988) has analyzed the contradictory nature of the Scandinavian welfare states; both patriarchal and in some ways empowering of women. Although on balance her assessment is a relatively optimistic one, she does not subscribe uncritically to Hernes' thesis that the Scandinavian or Nordic welfare states 'embody a state form that makes it possible to transform them into woman-friendly societies.' (Hernes 1987 p. 15)

One source of reservation, shared by Leira (1993), is that the notion of the 'woman-friendly state' glosses over the 'the growing economic and political polarization among women, which on a political level makes it more difficult to treat women as a group with common experiences and common interests.' (Siim 1993 p. 30) Siim is referring mainly to a growing class polarization which could become increasingly significant in societies such as the UK and the US where inequalities are widening generally and where the gap between the life-chances of poorer and more successful women is becoming more acute.

The point also has a wider purchase in the context of the more differentiated understanding of citizenship discussed at the beginning of this article. The earlier reference to the potential conflict of interests between women as carers and recipients of care is one example. A recent critique of the heterosexist assumptions underpinning welfare policies provides another (Carabine 1992).

The characterization of welfare states as racially structured as well as patriarchal is of particular importance here (Williams 1989). Gordon (1990 p. 25), for instance, reviewing Afro-Americans' contribution to the development of public welfare in the US, notes that 'this history suggests how racially specific have been what whites regard as mainstream welfare proposals; how deeply our welfare debates have taken place within a uniquely white set of political, economic, and familial assumptions.' In the British context, Mama (1992 p. 86), among others (see for example Bryan *et al.*), has identified black women's particular relations to the British state, arguing that it has, 'through various ideological mechanisms and administrative practices' behaved 'punitively and coercively' towards marginalized groups such as black women rather than treating them as citizens. This, she continues 'is evidenced most clearly in the differential service delivery to black people', underlining the importance for citizenship of the way in which welfare benefits and services are delivered. The everyday relations involved in negotiating with welfare institutions in two-track benefits systems are thus not only gendered but also racialized.[10]

Pringle and Watson (1992) point out that a perspective of women's heterogeneous interests means that no one policy will necessarily represent a gain for all women. They go on to suggest that this absence of a single feminist position 'mirrors the lack of coherence, interest or clarity within the state arenas' (p. 69) themselves. This is part of their wider argument that it is no longer helpful to view the state as 'a coherent, if contradictory, unity'; instead it can be better understood as an 'erratic and disconnected ... series of arenas' (pp. 63, 70) within which different interests and power relations are played out.

This abandonment of a monolithic conception of the state for a more nuanced approach is helpful to the kind of analysis adopted here. The relationship between welfare states and women's position as citizens is not a straightforward one. It is complicated, Pringle and Watson remind us, both by the complex nature of modern states on the one hand and by the differentiation between the interests of the various groups that make up the category 'woman' on the other.

CONCLUSION

The difficult task of elaborating a conception of citizenship which is sensitive to differences, of and within gendered categories, while not losing the emancipatory potential of citizenship's universalist aspirations which gives it much of its force, has been one example of a recurrent theme running through this chapter: that the most fruitful approach to resolving the dilemmas created by the attempt to engender citizenship in a way which genuinely incorporates women on women's terms lies in a process of synthesis.

In similar vein, it has been argued that a rounded conception of citizenship needs to embrace notions of both individual rights (taking account also of the gendered nature of citizenship obligations) and of 'republican' political involvement, defined in the broadest terms, and the relationship between the two. This involves an acceptance of a 'public' sphere but on the basis of an understanding of its interdependence with the 'private' domestic sphere and of the contested and shifting nature of the boundaries between the two. The critical issue for citizenship is who has the power to decide where the line is drawn on any particular issue.

The article has begun to sketch out the outlines of a possible gendered conceptualization of citizenship. The aim is a 'woman-friendly' conception of citizenship: one which combines the gender-neutrality of an approach which seeks to enable women to participate with men as equals in the public sphere (suitably transformed) with a gender-differentiated recognition and valuing of women's responsibilities in the private sphere.

From the perspective of political citizenship, it has tried to steer a path between a narrow equal rights stance and one which recognizes the differences which frame women's and men's relationship to politics so that the onus of change is placed on politics rather than on women.

The dilemmas faced in modelling a gendered notion of social citizenship epitomise the longstanding tension between equality and difference. This formulation is, though, in danger of leading us into a political cul de sac. Instead, our understanding of equality and difference needs to be refashioned so as to open up rather than close off political choices.

Part of the answer, it has been suggested, lies in problematizing men's failure to fulfil the obligations of citizen – the carer. A fairer share of the division of caring responsibilities between women and men (although not totally unproblematic), as well as between individual families and the wider community, through better publicly financed provision, would help to diffuse a key dilemma with regard to women's social citizenship: how to value the caring work that still falls mainly to women without trapping women into a privatized caring role that is in danger of reinforcing their exclusion from citizenship's public face.

The chapter has explored some of the possibilities of such an approach with regard to policies for the care of children and of older people. At a more philosophical level, it has supported the case for a synthesis of an ethic of care and of justice or rights. Our understanding of citizenship could be enriched by an ethic of care while the practice of care could be underwritten by an ethic of rights.

Such a synthesis might also provide a framework in which it is possible to acknowledge human interdependence without losing the cutting edge of feminism's traditional critique of women's economic independence on men. This critique, it is argued, is still essential for reasons of philosophy, women's poverty and men's power, and not least because of the continued force of the ideology of women's economic dependence which can still disadvantage women who are not actually economically dependent upon a man, for instance, black or lesbian women.

The chapter ends by suggesting a formulation for the incorporation of the dimension of women's economic independence and autonomy into cross-national analysis of welfare state regimes. It is an approach consistent with a recognition that welfare states can at the same time open the door of citizenship to many women while still relegating them to the status of second-class citizens. It is also consistent with theorizations of women's relationship to the state which treats neither as a monolithic block.

The chapter does not offer firm conclusions. Rather, it has been an attempt to articulate an approach to a number of dilemmas that arise in engendering citizenship. One aspect of this approach is a recognition of the need to balance women's short term interests with the more transformative longer term changes needed if women in all their diversity are to become full citizens. As Fiona Williams has argued, 'it is vitally important to attempt to weave a relationship between' short term 'practical' and longer term 'strategic' gender interests. (Williams 1989 p. 67, citing Molyneux 1984).

More fundamentally, the approach proposed is one which tries to avoid the polarized oppositions with which we are so often presented, in favour of a process of synthesis. This is an approach advocated by a number of contemporary feminist writers (for example Bacchi 1990; Phillips 1993; Sarvasy 1992; Scott 1988). It is one which arguably bears a closer relationship to the untidy realities of human existence and which has now been graced with the label 'fuzzy logic' (Kosko 1993) which accepts that things are not necessarily 'either/or' but can often be 'both'.[11]

But there are dangers. Fuzzy logic is not to be confused with woolly thinking. Synthesis requires critical analysis; it is no easy escape hatch into the apparent safety of the middle ground. For we cannot afford to lose the sharpness which has characterized much feminist analysis. In particular, an appreciation of the differences within and of the interdependence between binary categories must not be at the expense of a gendered analysis of the power relations which still underpin these categories and which thereby serve to perpetuate women's exile as a group from full citizenship.

This revised version of the original paper given at the 'Crossing Borders' conference has been published in *Economy and Society*, Vol. 21, no. 1, February 1995, pp. 1–40.

NOTES

1. Cynthia Cockburn (1992) has similarly promoted the notion of parity rather than equality, following usage of the term by the Council of Europe as a means of recognizing difference through positive action. She goes on to argue 'a stringently strategic political case' for women being able to claim both similarity to and difference from men, so long as this is necessary, on the basis that 'difference is relevant when, and only when, WE say it is'.
2. See, for example, the final report of the Commission on Social Justice (1994).
3. Such a restriction has recently been agreed in Sweden.
4. A working-time directive was agreed by the European Commission in 1993 but the final version is very limited, reflecting the opposition of the British Government. The Government also negotiated a ten year period of grace before the UK is required to implement the directive's 48 hour maximum working week which can, in any case, be breached where longer hours are voluntary, subject to safeguards against abuse.
5. A very similar conclusion was reached by Nancy Fraser (1994) in a paper given at the same conference as the original version of this paper.
6. There are, though, other ways in which Lewis (1993) argues that the Scandinavian model is nevertheless superior to the French, most notably in its promotion of relatively high levels of female political participation.
7. Susan James (1992) has also analyzed how fear of violence and sexual harassment can mean that women lack the physical independence enjoyed by men, thereby inhibiting their ability to participate as political citizens.
8. Sapiro (1990 p. 49) makes a similar point, arguing that true interdependence implies greater symmetry of power.

9.   They take care to distinguish their use of the term 'familialisation' from the more familiar meaning given to it by Barrett and Macintosh (1982).
10. There is a slowly growing British literature on the treatment of minority ethnic groups under the social security system. See for example Amin with Oppenheim 1992; NACAB 1991; *Benefits* No. 9 1994.
11. *The Independent* (1994) 'according to your viewpoint, fuzzy logic is a theoretical concept with profound implications, or merely a marketing gimmick for Japanese electronic goods!'

REFERENCES

Acker, J. (1988) 'Class, gender and the relations of distribution', *Signs*, Vol. 13, no. 3.

Amin, K. with C. Oppenheim (1992) *Poverty in Black and White,* London: Child Poverty Action Group/Runneymede Trust.

Andermahr, S. (1992) 'Subjects or citizens? Lesbians in the New Europe', in A. Ward, J. Gregory and N. Yuval-Davis (eds) *Women and Citizenship in Europe.* Stoke: Trentham Books and EFSF.

Atkinson, A.B. (1991) *Poverty, statistics and progress in Europe,* London: STICERD/LSE.

Aziz, R. (1992) 'Feminism and the challenge of racism: deviance or difference?' in H. Crowley and S. Himmelweit (eds) *Knowing Women,* Cambridge: Polity Press/Open University.

Bacchi, C. (1990) *Same Difference,* Sydney, Allen & Unwin.

Barrett, M. and M. Macintosh (1982) *The Anti-Social Family,* London: Verso.

Benefits (1994) 'Race' *Benefits* no. 9.

Bhavnani, K. (1993) 'Towards a multicultural Europe?: 'Race', Nation and Identity in 1992 and beyond', *Feminist Review*, no. 45 pp. 30–45.

Bhavnani, K. and M. Coulson (1986) 'Transforming socialist-feminism: the challenge of racism', *Feminist Review*, no. 23, pp. 81–92.

Bock, G. and S. James (eds) (1992) *Beyond Equality and Difference,* London: Routledge.

Borchorst, A. and B. Siim (1987) 'Women and the advanced welfare state: a new kind of patriarchal power?' in Showstack A. Sassoon (ed.) *Women and the State,* London: Hutchinson.

Brocas, A., A. Cailloux and V. Oget (1990) *Women and Social Security Progress Towards Equality of Treatment,* Geneva: International Labour Office.

Bryan, B., S. Dadzie and S. Scafe (1985) *The Heart of the Race,* London: Virago.

Callender, C. (1992) 'Redundancy, unemployment and poverty' in C. Glendenning and J. Millar, (eds) *Women and Poverty in Britain: The 1990s,* Hemel Hempstead: Harvester Wheatsheaf.

Carabine, J. (1992) 'Constructing women: women's sexuality and social policy' *Critical Social Policy*, no. 34, pp. 23–37.

Carby, H. (1984) 'White women listen: black feminism and the boundaries of sisterhood' in Centre for Contemporary Cultural Studies, *The Empire Strikes Back*, London: Hutchinson.

Cass, B. (1994) 'Citizenship, work and welfare: the dilemma for Australian women', *Social Politics*, Vol. 1, no. 1.

Cockburn, C. (1992) *Arguing for parity*, London: Charter 88 Women and Democracy Conference.

Collins, P.H. (1991) *Black Feminist Thought*, London: Routledge.

Commission of the European Communities (1990), 'Children in the European Communities, 1985–1990', Brussels.

Commission of the European Communities (1991) 'Equal Opportunities for Women and Men' *Social Europe*, Luxembourg.

Coote, A. and P. Pattullo (1990) *Power and Prejudice*, London: Weidenfield & Nicholson.

Cragg, A. and T. Dawson (1982) *Unemployed Women: A Case Study of Attitudes and Experiences*, London: Department of Employment.

Dahl, T.S. (1987) *Women's Law: An Introduction to Feminist Jurisprudence*, Oslo: Norwegian University Press.

Dahlerup, D. (1986) *The New Womens Movement*, London: Sage.

Dietz, M. (1987) 'Context is all: feminism and theories of citizenship' *Daedalus* Vol. 116, no. 4, pp. 1–24.

Du Bois, E., M. Dunlop, C., Gilligan, C. MacKinnon, Menkel-Meadow, C. (1985) 'Feminist discourse, moral values and the law – a conversation', *Buffalo Law Review* Vol. 54, no. 2, pp. 20–28, 37–49, 73–5.

Einhorn, B. (1993) *Cinderella goes to Market*, London: Verso.

Elshtain, J.B. (1981) *Public Man, Private Woman*, Oxford: Martin Robertson.

Esam, P. and R. Berthoud, (1991) *Independent Benefits for Men and Women*, London: Policy Studies Institute.

Esping-Anderson, G. (1990) *The Three Worlds of Welfare Capitalism*, Cambridge: Polity Press.

Finch, J. (1990) 'The politics of community care in Britain' in C. Ungerson, (ed.) *Gender and Caring*, Hemel Hempstead: Harvester Wheatsheaf.

Fox-Piven, F. (1990) 'Ideology and the state: women, power and the welfare state in L. Gordon, (ed.) *Women, the State and Welfare*, Madison University and Wiscon Press.

Fraser, N. (1987) 'Women, welfare and the politics of need interpretation' *Hypatia*, Vol. 2, no. 1.

Fraser, N. (1990) R*ethinking the public sphere: a contribution to the critique of actually existing democracy*, Madrid: World Sociological Conference.

Fraser, N. (1994) *After the Family Wage: Gender Equity and the Welfare State*, Stockholm, Sweden: Crossing Borders Conference.

Fraser, N. and L. Gordon (1994) '"Dependency" demystified: Inscriptions of power in a keyword of the welfare state', *Social Politics*, Vol. 1, no. 1.

Fuchs, V.C. (1988) *Women's Quest for Economic Equality*, Cambridge MA: Harvard University Press.

Glendenning, C. and E. McLaughlin (1993) (Paying for Informal Care: Lessons from Finland), *Journal of European Social Policy*, Vol. 3, no. 4. pp. 239–53.

Glendenning, C. and J. Millar (1992) *Women and Poverty in Britain: The 1990s*, Hemel Hempstead, Harvester Wheatsheaf.

Gordon, L. (ed.) (1990) *Women, the State and Welfare*, Madison University and Wisconsin Press.

Graham, H. (1983) 'Caring: a labour of love' in J. Finch, and D. Groves, (eds) *A Labour of Love: Women, Work and Caring*, London: Routledge and Kegan Paul.

Hall, S. and D. Held, (1989) 'Left and rights' *Marxism Today*, June pp. 16–23.

Heater, D. (1990) *Citizenship*, London: Longman.

Held, D. (1991) 'Between state and civil society: citizenship' in G. Andrews (ed.) *Citizenship*, London: Lawrence and Wishart.

Hernes, H. (1987) *Welfare State and Women Power*, Oslo, Norway: Norwegian University Press.

Hewitt, P. (1993) *About Time: The Revolution in Work and Family Life*, London: Institute for Public Policy Research.

Hobson, B. (1991) 'No exit, no voice: a comparative analysis of women's economic dependency and the welfare state', Aalborg, Denmark European Feminist Research Conference.

Hooks, B. (1982) *Ain't I a Woman?*, London: Pluto Press.

Hyatt, S. (1991) *Accidental activists: women and politics on a council estate*, Chicago: American Anthropological Association Annual Meeting.

Independent,The (1994) M. Kuhn, 'The logic that washes whiter' 5 May.

James, S. (1992) 'The good-enough citizen: citizenship and independence' in G. Bock, and S. James, (eds) *Beyond Equality and Difference*, London: Routledge.

Jenkins, S. (1991) 'Poverty measurement and the within-household distribution: agenda for action' *Journal of Social Policy*, Vol. 20, no. 4, pp. 457–83.

Jones, K. B. (1988) 'Towards the revision of politics' in K.B. Jones and A.G. Jonasdottir, (eds) *The Political Interests of Gender*, London: Sage.

Jones, K.B. (1990) 'Citizenship in a woman-friendly polity', *Signs*, Vol. 15, no. 4, pp. 781–812.

Jones, K.B. and A.G. Jonasdottir (1988) *The Political Interests of Gender*, London: Sage.

Joshi, H. (1991) 'Sex and motherhood as handicaps in the labour market' in M. Maclean and D. Groves, (eds) in *Women's Issues in Social Policy*, London: Routledge.

Keane, J. (1988) *Democracy and Civil Society*, London: Verso.

Knijn, T. (1994) 'Fish without bikes: revision of the Dutch welfare state and its consequences for the (in)dependence of single mothers' *Social Politics*, Vol. 1, no. 1.

Kosko, B. (1993) *Fuzzy Thinking: The New Science of Fuzzy Logic*, London: Harper Collins.

Land, H. (1979) 'The Introduction of Family Allowances: An Act of Historic Justice?' in P. Hall, H. Land, R. Parker and A. Webb, *Change, Choice and Conflict in Social Policy*, London: Heinemann.

Land, H. (1989) 'The construction of dependency' in M. Bulmer, J. Lewis and D. Piachaud (eds) *The Goals of Social Policy*, London: Unwin Hyman.

Langan, M. and I. Ostner (1991) 'Gender and welfare' in G. Room (ed.) *Towards a European Welfare State?*, Bristol: School for Advanced Urban Studies.

Leca, J. (1992) 'Questions on Citizenship' in C. Mouffe (ed.) *Dimensions of Radical Democracy*, London: Verso.

Leira, A. (1989) *Models of Motherhood*, Oslo, Norway: Institutt for Samfunns Forskning.

Leira, A. (1992) *Welfare States and Working Mothers*, Cambridge: Cambridge University Press.

Leira, A. (1993) 'The "woman-friendly" welfare state?: The case of Norway and Sweden' in J. Lewis (ed.) Women and Social Policies in Europe, Aldershot: Edward Elgar.

Lewis, J. (1980) *The Politics of Motherhood*, London: Croom Helm.

Lewis, J. (1990) *Equality, difference and state welfare: the case of labour market and family policies in Sweden*, insert.

Lewis, J. (1992) 'Gender and the Development of Welfare Regimes', *Journal of European Social Policy*, 2 (3): 159–73.

Lewis, J. (1993) *Women and Social Policies in Europe*, Aldershot: Edward Elgar.

Lister, R. (1990a) *The Exclusive Society: Citizenship and the Poor*, London: Child Poverty Action Group.

Lister, R. (1990b) 'Women, economic dependency and citizenship', *Journal of Social Policy*, Vol. 19, no. 4, pp. 445–67.

Lister, R. (1992) *Women: Economic Dependency and Social Security*, Manchester: Equal Opportunities Commission.

Lister, R. (1993) 'Tracing the contours of women's citizenship' *Policy and Politics* Vol. 21, no. 1, pp. 3–16.

Lister, R. (1994a) '"She has other duties" – Women, citizenship and social security' in S. Baldwin and J. Falkingham (eds) *Social Security and Social Change: New Challenges to the Beveridge Model*, Hemel Hempstead: Harvester Wheatsheaf.

Lister, R. (1994b) 'The Child Support Act: Shifting Family Financial Obligations in the United Kingdom', *Social Politics*, Vol. 1, no. 2.

Lovenduski, J. (1986) *Women and European Politics, Contemporary Feminism and Public Policy*, Brighton: Harvester Press.

Maier, F. (1991) 'Part-time work, social security protection and labour law: an international comparison', Policy and Politics, Vol. 19, no. 1, pp. 1–11.

Mama, A. (1992) in P. Braham *et al.* (eds) *Racism and Anti-racism*, London: Sage.

Marsh, C. (1991) *Hours of Work of Women and Men in Britain*, London: Equal Opportunities Commission/HMSO.

McLaughlin, E. (1991) *Social Security and Community Care: The Case of the Invalid Care Allowance*, London: Department of Social Security//HMSO.

McLaughlin, E. and Glendenning, C. (1994) 'Paying for Care in Europe: is there a feminist approach?' in L. Hantrais and S. Mangen, (eds) *Family Policy and the Welfare of Women*, Loughborough: Cross-National Research Group.

Meehan, E. and S. Sevenhuijsen (1991) *Equality, Politics and Gender* London: Sage.

Molyneux, M. (1984) 'Mobilisation without emancipation?', *Critical Social Policy*, no. 10.

Morris, J. (1991) *Pride against Prejudice*, London: Women's Press.

Morris, J. (1993) *Independent Lives*, Basingstoke: Macmillan.

Mouffe, C. (1992) *Dimensions of Radical Democracy*, London: Verso.

NACAB (1991) *Barriers to Benefit*, London: National Association of Citizens Advice Bureaux.

Nelson, B.J. (1984) 'Women's poverty and women's citizenship: some political consequences of economic marginality' *Signs* Vol. 10, no. 2, pp. 209–31.

Nelson, B.J. (1990) 'The origins of the two-channel welfare state: workmen's compensation and mothers' aid' in L. Gordon (ed.) *Women, the state and welfare*, Madison University and Wisconsin Press.

New Statesman and Society (1988) Editorial, 10 June.

O'Connor, J. (1993) 'Gender, Class and Citizenship in the comparative analysis of welfare state regimes: theoretical and methodological issues', *British Journal of Sociology*, Vol. 44, no. 3.

Offen, K. (1992), 'Defining feminism: a comparative historical approach' in G. Bock and S. James (eds) *Beyond Equality and Difference*, London: Routledge.

Okin, S.M. (1989) *Justice, Gender and the Family*, New York: Basic Books.

Orloff, A. (1993) 'Gender and the social rights of citizenship', the comparative analysis of gender relations and the welfare states', *American Sociological Review*, Vol. 58, June, pp. 303–28.

Osterberg, C. and B. Hedman (1988) *Women and Men in the Nordic Countries*, Copenhagen: Nordic Council of Ministers.

Pahl, J. (1989) *Money and Marriage*, London: Macmillan.

Parker, H. (1993) *Citizen's Income and Women*, London: Citizen's Income.

Parmar, P. (1989) 'Other Kinds of Dreams', *Feminist Review* no. 31, pp. 55–65.

Parry, G. (1991) 'Conclusion: paths to citizenship' in U. Vogel and M. Moran (eds) *The frontiers of Citizenship*, Basingstoke: Macmillan.

Pascall, G. (1986) *Social Policy: A Feminist Analysis*, London: Tavistock.

Pascall, G. (1993) 'Citizenship – a feminist analysis' in G. Drover and P. Kerans (eds) *New Approaches to Welfare Theory*, Aldershot: Edward Elgar.

Patel, P. (1992) 'Citizenship: whose rights' in A. Ward, J. Gregory and N. Yuval-Davis (eds) *Women and Citizenship in Europe Stoke*, Stoke: Trentham Books and European forum of Socialist Feminists.

Pateman, C. (1989) *The Disorder of Women*, Cambridge: Polity Press.

Pateman, C. (1992) 'Equality, difference, subordination: the politics of motherhood and women's citizenship in G. Bock and S. James (eds) *Beyond Equality and Difference*, London: Routledge.

Pearce, D. (1990) 'Welfare is not for women: why the war on poverty cannot conquer the feminization of poverty', in L. Gordon (ed.) *Women, the State and Welfare*, Madison University and Wisconsin Press.

Pederson, S. (1989) 'The failure of feminism in the making of the British welfare state', *Radical History Review*, No. 43, pp. 86–110.

Pederson, S. (1990) 'Gender, welfare and citizenship in Britain during the Great War', *The American Historical Review*, Vol. 95, no. 4, pp. 983–1006.

Phillips, A. (1993) *Democracy & Difference*, Cambridge: Polity Press.

Pollak, A. (ed.) (1993) A Citizens' Enquiry: *The Opsahl Report on Northern Ireland*, Dublin: Lilliput Press/Initiative '92.

Pringle, R. and S. Watson (1992) '"Women's interests" and the post-structuralist state' in M. Barret and A. Phillips, (eds) *Destabilising Theory* London: Polity.

Putnam, R.D. (1993) 'The prosperous community: social capital and public life' *The American Prospect*, no. 13, pp. 35–42.

Randall, V. (1987) *Women & Politics*, Basingstoke: Macmillan.

Rhode, D.L. (1992) 'The politics of paradigms: gender difference and gender disadvantage' in G. Bock and S. James (eds) *Beyond Equality and Difference*, London: Routledge.

Riley, D. (1992) 'Citizenship and the welfare state' in J. Allen and P. Lewis (eds) *Political and Economic Forms of Modernisation*, Cambridge: Polity Press.

Roche, M. (1992) *Rethinking Citizenship*, Cambridge: Polity Press.

Ruddick, S. (1980) 'Maternal thinking', *Feminist Studies*, Vol. 6, no. 2, pp. 342–67.

Sapiro, V. (1990) 'The gender basis of American social policy' in L. Gordon (ed.) *Women, the State and Welfare*, Madison University and Wisconsin Press.

Sarvasy, W. (1992) 'Beyond the difference versus equality policy debate: post-suffrage feminism, citizenship and the quest for a feminist welfare state' *Signs* Vol. 17, no. 2, pp. 329–62.

Sassoon, A.S. (1987) 'Women's new social role: contradictions of the welfare state' in A.S. Sassoon (ed.) *Women and the State*, London: Hutchinson.

Scott, J.W. (1988) 'Deconstructing equality versus difference: or, the uses of poststructuralist theory for feminism', *Feminist Studies* Vol. 14, no. 1, pp. 33–50.

Sevenhuijsen, S. (1992) *Paradoxes of Gender: Ethical and epistemological perspectives on care in feminist political theory*, London: BSA/PSA Conference 'The politics of care'.

Siim, B. (1988) 'Towards a feminist rethinking of the welfare state' in Jones, K.B. and Jonasdottir A.G. (eds) *The Political Interests of Gender*, London: Sage.

Siim, B. (1990) *Models of Citizenship – Gender Relations, Citizenship and Democracy in the Scandinavian Welfare States*, April, Bochum: ECPR Joint Sessions.

Siim, B (1993) 'The gendered Scandinavian welfare states: The interplay between women's roles as mothers, workers and citizens in Denmark' in J. Lewis (1993) *Women and Social Policies in Europe*, Aldershot: Edward Elgar.

Simonen, L. (1991) *The Finnish caring state in transition – Reversing the emancipatory mothering?* Aalborg, Denmark: European Feminist Research Conference.

Stacey, M. and M. Price (1981) *Women, power and politics*, London: Tavistock.

Taylor-Gooby, P. (1991) *Social Change, Social Welfare and Social Science*, Hemel Hempstead: Harvester Wheatsheaf.

Turner, B. (1990) 'Outline of a theory of Citizenship' *Sociology*, Vol. 24, no. 2, pp. 189–217.

Ungerson, C. (ed.) (1990) *Gender and Caring*, Hemel Hempstead: Harvester Wheatsheaf.

Ungerson, C. (1992) *Payment for Caring – Mapping a Territory*, Nottingham: Social Policy Association Annual Conference.

Ungerson, C. (1993), 'Caring and citizenship: a complex relationship', in J. Bornat, C. Pereira, D. Pilgrim and F. Williams (eds) *Community Care: A Reader*, Basingstoke: Macmillan/Open University.

Vogel, U. and M. Moran (1991) *The Frontiers of Citizenship*, Basingstoke: Macmillan.

Walby, S. (1994) 'Is Citizenship Gendered?' *Sociology*, Vol. 28, no. 2.

Waltzer, M. (1992) 'The civil society argument' in C. Mouffe (ed.) *Dimensions of Radical Democracy*, London: Verso.

Weale, A. (1983) *Political Theory and Social Policy*, London: Macmillan.

Williams, F. (1989) *Social Policy: A Critical Introduction*, Cambridge: Polity Press.

Williams, F. (1992) 'Somewhere over the rainbow: universality and diversity in social policy' in N. Manning and R. Page (eds) *Social Policy Review 4*, Canterbury: Social Policy Association.

Wilson, E. (1983) 'Feminism and social policy' in M. Loney, D. Boswell and J. Clarke, (eds) *Social Policy and Social Welfare*, Milton Keynes: Open University Press.

Wollstonecroft, M. (1792/1985) *Vindication of the Rights of Women*, London: Penguin.

Young, I.M. (1987) 'Impartiality and the civic public: some implications of feminist critiques of moral and political theory' in S. Benhabib and D. Cornell (eds) *Feminism as Critique*, Cambridge: Polity Press.

Young, I.M. (1989) 'Polity and group difference: A critique of the ideal of universal citizenship', *Ethics*, no. 99, pp. 250–74.

Young, I.M. (1990) *Justice and the Politics of Difference*, Oxford: Princeton University Press.

Yuval-Davis, N. (1991) 'The citizenship debate: women, ethnic processes and the state', *Feminist Review* no. 39.

Yuval-Davis, N. (1992) 'Women and citizens' in A. Ward, J. Gregory and N. Yuval-Davis (eds) *Women and Citizenship in Europe*, Stoke: Trentham Books and European Forum of Socialist Feminists.

3 Economic Citizenship: Reflections through the European Union Policy Mirror

Barbara Hobson

Gender research on citizenship and welfare states has made visible the ways in which gender alters the narrative of welfare state formation, the dimensions for measuring inequality, and the mechanisms of exclusion and inclusion within welfare state institutions. Much of this research has focused on the gender logics in welfare states, how women and men are encoded in different policy frameworks that support or weaken a male breadwinner wage, and what policies compensate women for their care work. These studies have extended theories of citizenship by including new dimensions that take into account paid and unpaid work (Hobson 1990; Lewis and Ostner 1995); reproductive rights (Shaver 1993); public care services for children and the elderly (Knijn 1994; Ungerson 1994).

Missing in this discussion of welfare states and gender logics are the direct and indirect pressures from supranational policy influences. In this context one can not ignore the European Union (EU) and its potential to impact political and social citizenship within member states. Louise Ackers (1996) has coined the apt phrase of 'policy incursions' to capture the ways in which EU law and policy introduces notions of citizenship that construct conceptions of family, work and social protections. In this chapter, I accept the idea in principle of incursions, or more precisely potential incursions, that EU policy and law can have on the institutional structures of welfare states. I am concentrating specifically on institutions that concern gender relations in the workplace, family and politics. When addressing gender, the logical place to begin is the European Court of Justice (ECJ) and its role in defining the parameters of EU intervention in policy that shape gender relations.[1] Court decisions take precedence over any contradictory national provisions.[2] Though the EU structure reserves wide areas of decision-making authority to the member states, member states are bound by the Court's interpretations of principles derived from Article 119 of the European Community treaty and specific Directives and Regulations.

The growing influence of transnational policymaking bodies and global economic processes in shaping the lives of citizens opens up new theoretical discussions about citizenship rights across policy borders (Daly 1997; Borchost 1994). Given the potential impact of monetary union on both the possibilities for employment and the conditions of work (Gönas 1997; Montanari 1995) it is useful to begin conceptualizing economic citizenship. Not to be ignored in this discussion are the growing number of women in paid work and the care deficit that has followed their movement into the labour market. Both of which suggests the need for developing theories that include economic citizenship as a dimension in the feminist project of gendering citizenship.

Clearly there are vast differences in expectations about the positive and negative consequences of the European Court and its affect on women friendly policies in member states. At one end of the spectrum, we find prophecies of doom – the end of gender equality as we know it – often found in the Scandinavian debate. At the other end of the spectrum, we find optimism in the ability of the Court to end gender discriminatory practices and to increase women's influence in policymaking. The latter is the stance taken by feminists in societies where women have few social rights, a weak position in the labour market and minimal representation on political bodies.

Before we consider these contested positions, particularly the women friendly or unfriendly potential of EU,[3] it is useful to take a step back from these debates and return to fundamental principles and concepts; the framing of gender equality itself. To do this we might begin by looking at the EU through the policy mirror of other welfare regimes. Sweden with its recent entry in the EU, is an interesting case from which to view the ways in which the European Court has interpreted gender equality. It exemplifies the Social Democratic welfare regime (Esping-Andersen 1990), with its redistributive benefits and universalist policies to protect the citizen worker. Thus, it appears as the country most likely to lose its generous benefits and services through integrationist policies in the EU as a result of direct or indirect pressures to adopt minimal standards and social spending levels of countries with lower taxes and social costs (Drangert and Nyberg 1996). Further integration in EU for member states also weakens the important role of Swedish women as political actors; politics matter in a society where women comprise over 40 per cent of the parliament, have an equal number of cabinet ministers, and have positions in key policymaking roles. Finally, Sweden has been projected as the watchdog for gender equality in the EU. Catherine Hoskyns opens her book on the history of women, law and politics from the Treaty of Rome to the present with a reference to former European Commissioner, from Sweden, Anita Gradin, who when first appointed expressed dismay at the overwhelming number of "grey-suited men" in the upper echelons of the European commission.' (Hoskyns 1996 p. 1).

Sweden also is a logical case to explore economic citizenship. In the Swedish welfare state women's attachment to paid work has been the cornerstone of the policy of gender equality. Policy initiatives over the last two decades have sought to promote women's participation in paid work (Hobson and Takahashi 1996).

My purpose in this chapter is twofold : (1) to lay the groundwork for constructing a gender sensitive model of economic citizenship; (2) to analyze the constraints in the EU framing of gender equality where the market is the main sphere of policymaking. I reflect on the Court's framing of gender equality and rulings in cases involving economic citizenship through the policy mirror of the Swedish welfare state.

By using the metaphor of policy mirrors, I want to suggest two things. First, this article does not presume to be a comparative analysis of the EU and Swedish gender equality policy. These are two different entities: a supranational body with limited jurisdiction over national policymaking, and a national body, a welfare state with law, policies, and norms rooted in a specific history and politics. Second, I am concerned with the general principles and assumptions in the construction of gender equality of policy.

In the first part of the chapter I lay out the contours of economic citizenship within the framing of gender equality in the

European Court, bounded by a treaty in which rights are derived from a treaty developed around the organization of a common market designed to enable the free movement of capital, goods, services and labour. Then I turn to the Swedish case and consider the implications of these rulings through the Swedish gender equality model where the focal point has been the care sector; equality initiatives have sought to increase women's participation in paid work through family policies.

ECONOMIC CITIZENSHIP

In many countries women have not had the possibility to combine paid work with their caring responsibilities, a point made by many feminist researchers who have criticised Gösta Esping-Andersen's measure of the empowerment of the worker/citizen (Lewis 1993; Hobson 1994, 1997; Orloff, 1993). He refers to this process as 'decommodification'; the extent to which a worker's dependence on the market is undercut by social policies (Esping-Andersen, 1990). In the recent feminist scholarship on gender and citizenship, care has been theorized as a dimension of social citizenship (thematic issue: *Social Politics*, 1998) This encompasses both public care services for children, the disabled and the elderly; payments for informal care (Ungerson chapter 7 below) and social support for those with caring responsibilities who are not employed or who work part-time.

Feminist scholars of the welfare state have posited an alternative to construction of social citizenship (decommodification) based upon a gender neutral worker citizen; women's ability to form independent households without the risk of poverty. This gendered dimension of social citizenship reflects exclusionary processes: women's dependency in marriage and poverty after divorce, women's weak position in the labour market, and the failure of policymakers to compensate women for their care work (Hobson 1994; Lister 1995; Orloff 1993). The right to form an independent household (the exit option in marriage or the right to have children outside of marriage) should be a basic social right for mothers. Yet it is only half a loaf if we are talking about economic citizenship. Even if we take this supposition further, the right to combine paid work and family life and access to income outside of marriage (Orloff 1993), this gender-sensitive measure of citizenship rights does not substantially alter the gendered distribution of power in the spheres of politics and labour markets.

That we can now think about economic citizenship in gender terms is a reflection of the growing numbers of women who are in paid work and the increasing role of global economic pressures on welfare states. Moreover at this historical moment, it is useful to conceptualize economic citizenship within the widening policy role of the European Union in which all discussions of equality are placed within the framework of the market. Finally, as the result of economic pressures both from without and within welfare states in this period, and the tendency in all welfare states to reduce public spending, policy-makers appear less and less willing to support benefits for mothers to remain at home as full-time carers (Taylor-Gooby 1996; Knijn 1997).

By incorporating the dimension of economic citizenship in the analyses, I acknowledge the importance of social and demographic processes, such as dramatic shifts in family patterns and assumptions about gender roles, the increased activity of women in the labour market – particularly those with young children. The instability of marriages, and the growing number of solo mothers who are often the only or main breadwinners in their families.[4]

Conceptualizing economic citizenship through a gendered lens looks beyond rights and protections in employment, often referred to as Workplace Democracy, that is, protections and security against arbitrary dismissals; control over one's work environment. But it embraces rights, that enable women to be full participants in work and family life. The right to return to one's job at the same status and pay after interruptions to care for family members, as well as benefits and services such as the right to child care places for children and paid parental leave benefits. It also includes laws and policy to end discriminatory practices at work, such as gender inequality in wages and working conditions, that is, sexual harassment at work. Gendering economic citizenship involves inclusionary strategies, proactive policies to remedy histories of discrimination against women, such as preferential treatment in hiring and promotion, wage equity policies, and interventions against sexual harassment. Gendering economic citizenship implies changing the conditions in the workplace to accommodate care work in families and recasting the definitions of what is a typical worker or a full-time working week that have been based on a gender neutral male worker.

Here it is useful to consider the exclusionary mechanisms that reproduce gender inequalities. The exclusionary mechanisms that reproduce gender inequalities involve the interplay of social actors and institutions. Figure 3.1 illustrates this. Dominant or privileged social actors in policymaking are those who write and implement the rules and those who have the discursive power to define what is reasonable and equitable. Institutions which are the frameworks for citizenship rights and obligations: institutions set the parameters for articulating claims and challenging dominant norms and practices include courts, executive and legislative branches of government, corporate boards, unions, employer organizations, and so on, as well as legal frameworks for rights and protections (formal constitutions, case law, treaties). Through institutions – and the social actors within them – inequalities are perpetuated, re vealed in daily practices and norms, as well as the long term processes and policy feedback effects which reproduce the exclusion of individuals because they belong to a social category.

As Figure 3.1 illustrates, there are two interlocking dimensions: *redistribution* – access to economic, political, social citizenship rights (redistribution of social goods); and *recognition* – a group's difference without devaluing or essentializing difference. It assumes a model of gender equality[5] that (1) offers protections against discriminatory practices and exclusion in law, that is equal treatment, no adverse treatment and (2) acknowledgement of asymmetries among privileged and deprivileged groups in order to recognize the processes that perpetuate discrimination against a group who have been socially and historically devalued (Sheppard 1993).

By bringing together in one model of gender equality (see Figure 3.1), the dimensions of recognition and redistribution, I seek to develop a framework that goes beyond the unresolvable dilemmas connected with a feminism of gender difference and feminism of gender sameness. The model acknowledges that removing inequalities and changing discriminatory patterns involves respect and recognition of the values, capacities and

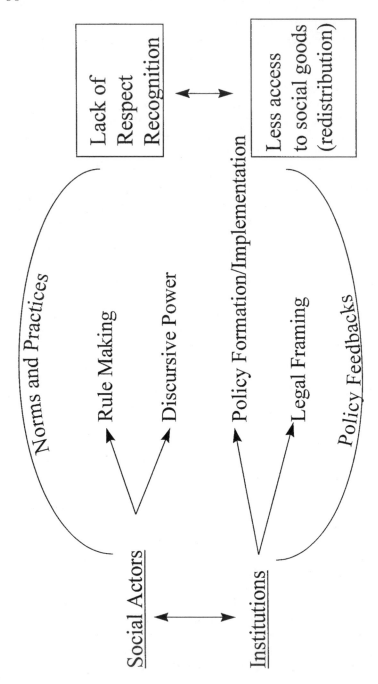

Figure 3.1 Gendered Mechanisms of Exclusion

experiences of subordinate groups. Nevertheless, the right to have one's differences acknowledged and accommodated in laws and polices does not mean creating special protections that limit access to rights and opportunities. Here we can cite numerous examples in past and recent history in which women have been excluded from education, jobs and pensions. These were 'special protections' that were traced to biological and social roles.

The cases analyzed in this chapter demonstrate the ways in which gender neutral frameworks of equality can have exclusionary effects. They do not recognize the power of privileged groups and institutional structures to set standards and norms that are embedded in gender neutral categories such as a typical worker, someone with full-time continuous employment (male patterns of work), versus atypical workers, those with part-time, interrupted employment (female patterns of employment) (O'Connor 1996). Consider definitions of skilled work, most often applied to occupations that are male dominated, versus unskilled work, most often applied to female dominated occupations (Cockburn 1983; Reskin 1986). We can also cite examples of concepts with specific gendered subtexts, such as 'dependent' citizens, those responsible for care work in families, mothers who are doing unpaid work; and 'independent' citizens, those who provide economic resources in families, male breadwinners (Fraser and Gordon 1994; Knijn 1994; Hobson 1994; Saraceno 1994).

Applying the premises in the model to empirical analyses to the gender equality frameworks, we can ask the following questions: how have gender neutral norms reproduced the privilege of dominant groups? Who is being compared to whom and on the basis of what criteria? More specifically to gender inequalities, we have to address the spheres of life that demarcate women's and men's experience.

Spheres of Intervention

A guiding principle in EU policymaking is that of subsidiarity, which has many meanings and levels (Peterson 1994; Spicker 1994), but basically reflects a stance in which intervention at higher levels has to be seen as subsidiary to smaller units, that there is balance between authority levels. In the EU context this refers to the principle of decentralization, ensuring that political decisions are not taken at any higher level than they need to be. This can be understood both in terms of the limits placed on the EU, but also national governments are supposed to devolve powers whenever possible. In comparison to other member states in the EU, one could say that the Swedish case is furthest removed from the subsidiarity principle, particularly in the realm of gender and family policy. Gender equality policy emerged as part of a unified and consistent set of initiatives to increase the birth rate and to shape the choices of families around paid and unpaid work.

For the purposes of analysis, we might consider the different spheres of intervention using the institutional triangle in comparative welfare state research: the state (or in the case of the EU, the suprastate), the market and the family triangle (Esping-Andersen 1990; Taylor-Gooby 1996). In order to capture the sets of relations within the family side, we have to introduce the domestic triangle into the analysis to illustrate the dynamic relationship between policy interventions in the institutional triangle and their impact on relations within the family, among husbands and wives and parents and children.[6] How the sets of relationships in the two triangles are interconnected shape women's participation in economic and political life in crucial ways.

If we refer to the state–family axis (see Figure 3.2), we can see that policies can strengthen the dominant position of the male breadwinner through tax incentives, for instance. Or they

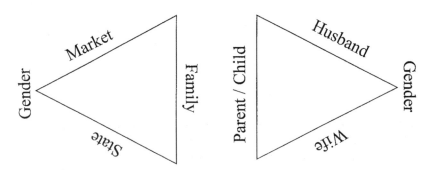

Figure 3.2   Modified Policy Triangles

can encourage women's labour market participation through publicly funded care services; benefits for care that allow women to combine paid work and family responsibilities. Hence they weaken a woman's dependence on her husband's income, that is, shift the balance of power in the domestic triangle (Hobson 1990, 1997).

Moving along the state and market axis, we can see how gender neutral policies can operate as mechanisms of exclusion. Such policies often assume normative definitions around what is work, what is a working day, who is a full-time worker, all of which tend to advantage men as workers. Connection to the labour market as the essential channel to equal treatment limits the whole range of women's claim making and protections from risk that 'normal workers' are entitled, which often means full-time workers.

Because unpaid work, caring work, is not counted as work, women workers lack economic citizenship in systems where the calculation of benefits is based upon working status or contributions of employers.

Thus the ways in which gender is encoded in the institutional triangle reflects different forms of exclusionary mechanisms. The shading out of family as a sphere of policy intervention in the interpretations of gender equality in the ECJ, which divorces what happens in the family around paid and unpaid work from what happens in the market and vice versa, the framing of gender equality as equal treatment in law (in both the EU and Sweden) also excludes all forms of discrimination of individuals as members of social groups that are deprivileged. Equal treatment assumes individuals are treated as like each other. Thus inequality exists when those similarly situated are treated differently. (Sheppard 1990). This principle fails to recognize the patterns of discrimination against women as a group who have been socially and historically devalued (the low wages accorded to occupations that are dominated by women and the so called sticky floor for women in the organization hierarchy).

GENDER EQUALITY FRAMING IN EUROPEAN LAW

The foundation for gender equality policy in the EU is enshrined in Article 119 of the Treaty of Rome

Each Member State shall during the first stage ensure and subsequently maintain the application of the principle that men and women should receive equal pay for equal work.

Any analysis of the EU and its treatment of gender equality can not ignore the fact that European Union law is market law and that market derived rights shade out large segments of women's unpaid work. Legal theorists, such as Hervey and Shaw (1996); Scheiwe (1994), and Moore (1996) have underscored the ways in which gender neutral formulas perpetuate false distinctions between public and private. The failure of the Court to acknowledge the interplay between women's employment opportunities and access to rights and their caring responsibilies, according to Scheiwe, reproduces gendered norms and standards and creates false boundaries between subsystems of law and social spheres (1994: p. 253). Ostner and Lewis (1994) in their analysis of social policy have emphasized the limitations of EU gender equality policy and use the metaphor of the eye of a needle to describe the difficult and narrow passage that all policy innovations must pass which does not allow for any discussion of the interdependencies between outcomes in paid work and the division of unpaid work.

Not to be forgotten in this discussion is that the foundation of gender equality policy in the EU came into being – not because of feminist pressure – but to avoid 'social dumping', or unfair competition, due to lower paid female work, based on a assumption of gender difference (Hoskyns 1996). The underlying assumption behind the Article's creation was that women were workers with less bargaining power and lower standards in respect to pay and benefits. Interested in gaining support and legitimacy for the EU, leaders turned their attention to the social policy dimension (Meehan 1991).

Following the 1972 Paris Summit, the European Commission drew up the Social Action Programme to further the goals of equality between men and women. During the 1970s and 1980s five equality directives were introduced: equal treatment: in wages, in employment, in social security, in occupational pensions, and pregnancy leave (noted as improvements for the safety and health at work of pregnant workers or workers who have recently given birth or are breast-feeding).[7]

The most recent directive, the Parental Leave Directive, on gender equality issues was passed in June 1996. It gave fathers and mothers the right to a minimum of three months benefit on the birth or adoption of a child.[8]

The Parental Leave Directive modified an earlier decision of the Court, which did not recognize father's right to parental leave. The rationale for the earlier decision was based upon the Court's repeated insistence that questions of family organization are matters that are outside its sphere of intervention.[9]

There are numerous ways in which the family-state side of the triangle has been embedded in the EU law and policy, despite the Court's official statements disavowing intervention in the family. Two examples are: (1) the interpretations of discrimination related to pregnancy and childbirth; (2) the exclusion and inclusion of cases that acknowledge the male breadwinner wage as the norm, most blatantly in the treatment of migrant workers.

Pregnancy and Childbirth

In the groundbreaking Dekker case,[10] the Court was unequivocal in its interpretation that dismissal of a pregnant women was direct sex discrimination. In several different cases, the Court claimed that such action could not be justified on the basis of the financial costs, which maternity leave would entail for the employer. Even when a woman had been hired to replace another pregnant woman who was to take maternity leave, the Court ruled that availability for work was not a valid reason for sex discrimination based on pregnancy.[11] However the Court left open the possibility that protections against dismissal for pregnancy might not apply to women on limited contracts.[12] Not addressed was the issue that many employers do not hire young women on long-term contracts because they do not want to bear the potential economic costs of pregnancy and care of infants. Thus, the treatment of pregnancy in EU law represented a departure from the equal treatment principle, but it did not reach the broader terrain of discriminatory practices that result from women's caring responsibilities.

That dismissing a woman because of her pregnancy is sex discrimination was a recognition of gender differences among workers, a break with the equal treatment principle. There was no male comparator (men did not become pregnant). Yet it was a recognition of gender difference that was based on biological differences. Pregnancy was not like other absences from work, a point made by the Advocate

General in his written Opinion, where he rejected the comparison made between a woman on maternity leave and a man unable to work because he was to take part in a sporting event, even if it were the Olympic Games.

> Other considerations apart, a sportsman even a champion (whether a man or a woman) is confronted with a normal choice reflecting his needs and priorities in life; the same cannot be reasonably said of a pregnant woman, unless the view is taken – but it would be absurd – that a woman who wishes to keep her job always has the option of not having children. (C-32/93)

The tendency of the Court in the treatment of pregnancy has been to divorce having children from caring for them. The very construction of the first maternal leave provision as a 'risk' attached to childbirth (the first fourteen weeks after birth) suggested the essentialized view of parenting. This was evident in the case brought by a German father, claiming his right to be the caring parent on leave, challenging the German maternity leave policy. The Court maintained that it was not 'designed to settle questions concerned with the organisation of the family, or alter the division of responsibility between parents'. With the Directive on parental leave passed by the Council of Ministers in June of 1996, there is a recognition of the rights of fathers to leave (the policy is gender neutral). However, unlike laws in Norway and Sweden that mandate fathers take some of the leave, the EU Directive does not propose any proactive strategies to involve fathers. The Directive does not tamper with the negotiations within the family, but undermines laws that prohibit men's participation in parenting leave.[13]

Migrant Workers

Feminist legal scholars have questioned the Court's insistence that it is not prepared to intervene in the division of labour in the family (Ackers 1996; Scheiwe 1994). There is a policy logic around family questions, what Kirstin Scheiwe refers to as a 'selective logic with a gendered dimension'. (p. 247). This selective logic is visible in what policy areas are included as well as excluded. Here one can recognize the unstated norms and assumptions of the male breadwinner wage and how they continue to shape the scope of interventions and the justifications for them. Take for example the case of migrant workers in which the ECJ has intervened in a myriad of ways.

The Court's activism around family issues (children's education, child allowance and social security benefits) is justified on the ground of the free movement of workers (embedded in Article 48–51 of the Treaty of Rome). The male breadwinner ideology underlies the rationale for this type of intervention; there are specific references to *men's* families in various Regulations and Court decisions (see articles 1.12 Regulation 1612/68). The Court has extended it's jurisdiction in these cases to questions of family and social policy by granting benefits to migrant workers' families not residing in the host country. These were controversial cases that challenged the basis of entitlements around citizenship and residence.[14]

According to Louise Ackers (1996), EU Regulations and ECJ decisions, which have afforded the migrant worker extended social rights, are founded upon an 'ideologically loaded conception' of marriage and families. One has to be formally married to be entitled as a spouse, through derived social rights. Clearly this interpretation of families is at odds with laws and norms in Scandinavian countries (which give the same social rights to cohabitant couples as married). Such an interpretation limits the free movement of partners in countries that do not have traditional norms around marriage, which are more likely to be found in societies with more equal gender relations in the family. But beyond this formal technical barrier, there are the structural constraints inhibiting the free movement of dual-earner couples, that is the paucity of care facilities outside the home and the lack of public funding for care of children and elderly in many member states. The hidden assumption in this lack of intervention is that child care is a private matter and not a hindrance to employment. But one could make a strong case that women's economic citizenship is dependent on public provisioning of child care. In fact, lack of child care and elderly care are obstacles that inhibit the free movement of women workers (Scheiwe, 1994) since women provide the main source

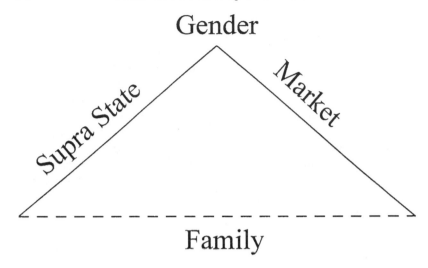

Figure 3.3   Fragmented Policy Triangle

of unpaid care labour in nearly all Western societies. For women workers in Scandinavian countries, where a highly developed public provisioning of child care exists, the lack of public funding for child care in many European countries is an impediment against their free movement across borders.

As Figure 3.3 illustrates, the family has been decoupled from the market and (*supra*) state nexus, that is, the formal parameters of policy. However, this does not mean that family issues were never confronted or totally ignored in ECJ interpretations. To the contrary, assumptions about relations within families and family issues crept into court rationales for rejecting and accepting claims. But what has been and continues to be absent is an explicit recognition of how family policy: (1) can limit women's access to paid work and (2) how gendered power relations in the family reflect and are reflected in discriminatory practices in the labour market, social security and pension schemes, both private and publicly organized.

Paid and Unpaid Work

Claims for gender equality in the ECJ have had to fit into a narrow framework of market derived rights and have not been able to address the way in which gendered mechanisms of exclusion operate in institutions and daily practice. However, in the recent cases on discrimination of part-time workers, there is an implicit recognition of the ways in which gender equality is shaped by the organization of paid and unpaid work in families.

In recent decisions around the rights of part-time workers, the Court acknowledged that women as a group were disadvantaged because they had to reduce their working hours in order to combine employment and family responsibilities. Indirect discrimination is considered to exist when a neutral rule can be proved to affect one sex, the disadvantaged sex, to a disproportionate extent; in the majority of cases it has been applied to women with marital or family responsibilities.

The Court rulings in favour of part-time workers cover a range of issues, such as the exclusion of part-time workers from an occupational pension scheme and access to pay rises, which questioned whether seniority (years spent at job) could exclude part-time workers. In one case,[15] the plaintiff had not been put into a higher salary bracket because she worked part-time hours. In a series of unusual cases,[16] the Court accepted part-time worker's rights to overtime pay for training sessions. These were cases in which part-time workers were denied payment for time spent on special courses, and in each case, there was evidence that part-time workers were women and gender neutral policies disproportionately affected women who were the majority of part-time workers – over 93 per cent.

Where the Court drew the line was around questions of pay and overtime hours because these cases called into question the basic definitions of what is work, and what is considered to be a standard full-time, working week. The case brought by three Dutch women[17] is worth presenting since it highlights the ways in which the ECJ is ultimately locked into the equal treatment standard.

All the plaintiffs were part-time workers who worked in excess of their contractual working week, yet received no overtime pay because they did not spend a full-time work week in paid work. The question before the Court was whether, seeing as the majority of part-time workers are women, that not to give them overtime pay was indirect discrimination; Article 119 requires that time worked in excess of contractual working hours be paid at an overtime rate, as is the case with full-time workers.

However, the Court rejected this argument maintaining that it would be unfair (unequal treatment) to full-time workers to give employees with part-time contracts overtime pay. The Court warned, however, that it would find unequal treatment where the overall pay of full-time employees is higher than that of part-time employees for the same number of hours worked. Nevertheless, the Court concluded that there was no unequal treatment in this case since the part-time workers who worked 30 hours, for example, would receive the same pay as the full-time workers who work 30 hours. The Advocate-General Darmon in his Opinion made this point more forcefully. He claimed that full-time employees with family responsibilities (mainly men) would be discriminated against because they would not receive overtime benefits until they had worked many more hours than a part-time employee.

Here the gender neutral language masked a highly gendered labour market which reflected the gendered division of unpaid work in families. It also masked the long work days that women in 'part-time' work do – reaching over 60 hours a week[18] – if you include hours spent in household work and care. This case illustrates the ways in which exclusionary mechanisms deny women's economic citizenship by disconnecting the institutional triangle, from the domestic triangle disconnecting family decision-making from employment decisions; disconnecting market rights from parental rights.

EQUAL TREATMENT: SPECIAL TREATMENT

To accept the principle of preferential treatment in policy and law is to recognize that there are mechanisms of exclusion in economic and political organizations that are rooted in categorical inequality. This implies that inequality based upon lack of respect and prejudice hinders members of a group (in this case women) from having access to jobs, promotions, training and fair wages. Laws and policies to remedy categorical inequality assume that compensatory measures are needed to correct previous histories of discrimination. However, in an equal treatment framework in which gender neutrality is the governing principle, preferential treatment policy is subject to challenges of reverse discrimination by the dominant group. The ECJ has become a battleground for such cases.

The most well-known of these cases was brought by Eckhard Kalanke, a male candidate who was passed over for job promotion because of a preferential treatment law passed in the Bremen, which sought to recruit members of the underrepresented sex, that is women. The Court ruled in his favour and against gender quotas; and made the following argument: national rules that *automatically* give priority to women who are equally qualified in job sectors where they are underrepresented violate the principle of equal treatment (Szyszczak 1996). The Opinion of the Advocate-General was even more explicit in his rejection of the Bremen law

> A national rule which guarantees women absolute and unconditional priority for appointment or promotion . . . goes beyond promoting equal opportunities and substitutes for it the result of 'equality of representation' which is only to be arrived at by providing such equality.'[19]

Within this interpretation of equal treatment, positive action (preferential treatment) to alter patterns of exclusion was viewed as reverse discrimination against men.

The most recent case on preferential treatment, however, modifies Kalanke. In that case, a tenured male teacher, Helmut Marschall, challenged a regional German law that gave preference to an equally qualified female candidate in order to create a gender balance in promotions. A technical revision in the law (in light of the Kalanke decision) altered the quota system implicit in the earlier law, that the underrepresented group automatically be given preference. More important than the acceptance of preferential treatment in the case, the rationale for the decision represents a departure from earlier rulings since it directly addresses mechanisms of exclusion in employment: that 'men tend to be chosen in preference to women where they have equal qualifications, since they benefit from deep-rooted prejudices and stereotypes as the role and capacities of women.'[20] The judgement highlights the ways in which categorical inequality is perpetuated. Women are excluded from jobs and promotion not only because they do care work in families but because it is assumed that they will interrupt careers more frequently, owing to household or family duties, or that they will be absent from work more frequently because of pregnancy, childbirth, and breast-feeding. This ruling addresses one aspect of categorical inequality, statistical discrimination against members of groups who are labelled as less competent. The case is not a groundbreaking one for the ECJ , but it does open the door for further inroads in preferential treatment. It also puts a damper on reverse discrimination cases based on equal treatment. However, it leaves untouched the Pandora's box of who decides whether a candidate is qualified and on what criteria.

FRAMING GENDER EQUALITY IN SWEDISH POLICY AND LAW

Before presenting the Swedish case, I want to underscore that I am not comparing Swedish gender equality policy to EU policy but considering the similarities and differences in interpretations and spheres of intervention[21] to achieve gender equality, along the different axis of the institutional triangle: state, market and family. Dramatic differences between the two policy frameworks exist in spheres of intervention to promote gender equality. In the EU claims for gender equality have been fitted into the frame of the market. Alternatively, in Sweden family policy (policies relating to care benefits and services) has been a main lever for promoting gender equality.

Nearly all Swedish policies in the 1970s that formed the bedrock of gender equality policy were placed within the institutional box of family policy. Family policy was a distinct area of responsibility with its own Minister of Family Affairs. There was a purposeful approach to family and labour market policy in the 1960s and 1970s; a set of initiatives that sought to alter the patterns of family life so that more women would become labour force participants.[22] The expanded public care facilities provided new jobs for women. A set of coherent policies emerged from political debate, government commissions on individual taxation, family law, parental leave, and day care. From this perspective, one could say that the Swedish case is furthest removed from the subsidiarity principle: forms of intervention were aimed at shaping the choices of families around paid and unpaid work. Individual taxation raised the costs of women's unpaid labour so that families with only a single earner paid a penalty for maintaining a traditional housewife; every kronor a woman earned was extra income for the family: (Gustafsson and Bruyn-Hundt 1992). Generous parental leave and highly subsidized child care and elderly care were the carrots to seduce women into the labour market (Hobson *et al.* 1995).

Policy interventions along the family axis of the institutional triangle have enhanced Swedish women's economic citizenship. These policies have allowed women to be integrated in to the labour market; in Sweden women's labour force participation is nearly equal to men (Sainsbury 1996). Policies, such as social transfers, child allowances, reduced day care costs, advanced payment of alimony, reduce the risk of poverty (Hobson 1997). This is evident when we consider that Sweden has one of the lowest rates of solo-mother poverty among Western welfare states. Nevertheless, though solo mothers are able to combine work and family responsibilities they are highly dependent on social transfers, on average 27 per cent of their income package (Hobson and Takahashi 1996, 1997).

This outcome reflects the gender neutral framing of gender equality in policy and law. The Swedish model of gender equality expects husbands and wives to be equal participants in work and family life. They are treated as individual wage earners rather than family members in tax and divorce law. The assumptions around gender equality are that men and women will participate in employment and family life. Swedish policy has acknowledged the importance of parenting and has compensated parents during periods when they are at home with children. Suppose we return to the two policy triangles: the institutional (state, market and family) and the domestic (wife, husband, parent/child), we can see that Swedish family policy has been connected to labour market policy. However, few policy initiatives sought to disturb or influence the division of paid and unpaid work in the family, the relations in the second triangle and the interaction of the two triangles (see Figure 3.2 above). Various policies that protected part-time workers suggest that there was an assumption that women would take the lion's share of the care work as well as become the employees in the paid care sector (Johansson, see Chapter 10; Sundström 1987).

The gender neutral policies, particularly the parental leave policy, appeared revolutionary in the 1970s; the policy recognized that care work was not just women's responsibility and that parenting included fathers as well as mothers (Hobson *et al*. 1995). That fathers have not taken full advantage of their right to parental leave is a fact that is documented by feminist research (Haas 1992; Näsman 1995) The small proportion of fathers who take more than a few weeks leave reflects the fragmentation between the two triangles, the failure of policy to recognize the dynamic and interactive relationships between state, market and family spheres, that power relations within families shape market behaviours and are shaped by the market. Only recently has Sweden pursued a proactive policy in the form of a 'daddy month': if fathers do not use the month, the couple losses one month of paid leave out of the 12.

Equal Treatment: Special Treatment

Few policies in Sweden have sought to remedy gender discrimination in the labour market through preferential treatment or proactive strategies, such as quotas. The corporatist wage bargaining system has placed constraints on these kinds of initiatives. Even policies involving wage equity (equal pay for work of equal value) have been seen as tampering with the collective bargaining process between unions and employers. Up until 1991, collective agreements superseded any gender discrimination challenge.

It is no secret that Sweden has one of the softest laws against gender discrimination in employment among democratic welfare states.[23] (Eklund 1996; Gelb 1989; Ruggie 1984). Sweden embodies the archetypal gender neutral legal framework, adhering to the principle of equal treatment, which provides individual men and individual women with the same opportunities for claiming gender discrimination. Justice is only guaranteed to an individual who is among the underrepresented sex in a firm; it does not permit group or class actions based on systematic patterns of discrimination (for example female employees in a firm who are systematically passed over in promotions). The law does not require quotas or positive action to remedy categorical discrimination for groups who have been denied opportunities because of pervasive patterns of devaluation and discrimination. In contrast to EJC equal treatment law, the Swedish law does not permit challenges to gender equality measures based upon reverse discrimination.

In response to criticism throughout the 1980s, a revised law came into being in 1991, which allowed gender discrimination cases even when there was union and employer contract. Nevertheless the main contours of the law remained. The parameters for claiming discrimination remain highly circumscribed. The only unlawful sex discrimination exists when an employer passes over an objectively better qualified candidate. Here the burden of proof is on the employer. But if two applicants (male and female) are equally qualified, the employer has the right to decide. When a female applicant who is equally qualified is denied a job, she must show probable grounds that the employer had discriminatory intentions (Eklund 1996). Employers have to find a suitable reason to deny a woman a job, but there are many such justifications.

Equal Pay for Work of Equal Value

Gender discrimination in wages is a question of value attached to jobs (evaluative discrimination, Le Grand 1997) in countries where there are clear laws against direct discrimination.[24] Therefore unless challenges can be made on the grounds of equal pay for work of equal value, gendered differences in pay remain outside the scope of the law. This was not a formula in Sweden's anti-discrimination, but equal pay for work of equal value is part of EU law.[25] Since Sweden's entry into the EU, recent pay discrimination cases before the Swedish Labour Court have taken up the question of equal pay for work of equal value.

One of the most widely discussed was a case brought by the Equality Ombudsman that involved a midwife and the local Örebro county council (Case 153/95). As all cases must have a male comparator in the same organization, this case compared a midwife who was paid 4000 kronor a month less than two technicians employed in the medical technology department. The job titles themselves are suggestive. Midwifery – which requires many years of education in Sweden (one has to become a professional registered nurse and training beyond) – is a profession which retains its earlier associations with a non-professional naturalized gender role (midwives historically have been pitted against those with scientific and medical expertise).[26] The term clinical engineer is associated with expertise, training and skilled.[27] Throughout the case the Equality Ombudsman gathered statistics and job descriptions that underscored the technical and specialized nature of a midwife's tasks and the high demands placed on her in relation to the health and safety of the mother and unborn child.

In the final judgement, the Labour Court concluded that the evaluations of the two jobs were faulty and misleading, and not objective. An important consideration was the evaluations of experts who disputed the claim that midwives had a high degree of responsibility over the life and death of babies and mothers; that they often gave doctors essential advice and instructions for the treatment of patients. Rather the experts dismissed these claims and maintained that it is the ward doctor who has ultimate responsibility. Here all the forces of stereotyping within gender segregated occupations came into play – in defining what was competence, skill and authority.[28]

Though not noted in the final judgement, a significant part of the discussion in the case revolved around gender segregated occupations. Evidence was given that showed there was no shortage of clinical engineers (in fact there were four to five applicants for every vacancy). In the case of midwives, the supply of midwives seem to be of little consequence in setting wages.[29] However, this argument did not appear in the decision of the Labour Court.[30]

The midwife case highlighted the ways in which gender segregation reflects women's weak economic citizenship, even in a country where women's labour force participation has nearly reached levels of men's. Female dominated occupations are accorded less value in the market (with lower wages) defined by the dominant culture as non-technical, non-professional and non-competitive. There is circular logic operating: women tend to enter jobs that are gender differentiated. Because it is a job women do, it is devalued with lower pay and less status, therefore men do not enter it. Because it is a gender segregated occupation, it is defined as having less value and skill and requiring less remuneration to attract the most competent workers.[31] The process is revealed in studies of occupations that become feminized or the reverse pattern (a critical mass of men entering an occupation) (see Reskin 1986; Cockburn 1983).

Because of the highly developed care sector in which the state was and is the dominant employer, Sweden has one of the most gender segregated labour markets (Gonäs and Spånt 1997; Le Grand 1997). Much of the discourse on gender equality in the workplace has been aimed at encouraging women into traditional men's jobs, but given the organization of work in the private sector, and the growing pressures to put in longer hours on the job, this is not a feasible or likely scenario (Hoem 1995).

Only recently has the question of gender equality and economic power come onto the agenda in Sweden with a full-scale government commission in 1994 addressing the unequal division of power between men and women ('om fördelning av ekonomisk makt och ekonomisk resurser mellan kvinnor och män' (commission concerning the division of economic power and resources between men and women)).[32] The conclusion to the Commission reports suggested a multi-causal set of structural conditions that reproduce the unequal gendered redistribution of economic resources, such as sex segregation, organization of work, the low value placed upon paid care work and devaluation of women's capacities. One study was devoted to decision making in the family over resources, time and money, which had not been treated as a policy issue in the past (SOU: 1997: 139). This represented a recognition of the dynamic relationship between the institutional and domestic triangle. An underlying theme in nearly all the reports was the recognition that discrimination and devaluation of women's capacities was pervasive in Swedish institutions, in both the private and public sector, though more so in the private sector. One member of the committee concluded in a wry tone that women who wanted to increase their wages should not change occupation but change sex.

REFLECTING THE EU THROUGH THE SWEDISH POLICY MIRROR

What are the constraints and possibilities for women's economic citizenship in a policy context that cuts across national borders? For some European countries, the decisions in the ECJ have expanded women's economic citizenship, particularly those societies where women have marginal status on the labour market; where part-time work contracts have excluded them from unemployment benefits, pension schemes or pay rises; or countries where no minimal standards for parental leave were in place. Seen through the lens of the Swedish policy mirror, the European Court's interpretations of gender equality would represent a loss of economic citizenship. Suppose we consider the general contours of economic citizenship I defined at the outset of this discussion: (1) the organization of benefits and social services that enable women to combine paid and unpaid work, (2) the proactive policies and laws that seek to redress and compensate women for their discrimination in employment.

Table 3.1   Gendered Aspects of Economic Citizenship

	Sweden	*EU (ECJ Interpretive Frame)*
Unemployment insurance	definite and indefinite contracts part-time, full-time	indefinite contracts part-time, full-time
Parental leave	women and men (1 year) definite and indefinite contracts	women and men (min. 3 months) indefinite contracts
	conditional upon labour force activity for higher benefit (75 per cent of income) universal minimal benefit not conditional	conditional upon labour force activity no minimum amount set
Job security	job security guaranteed	some exceptions
Sickness and invalidity job protections/ payment	definite and indefinite contracts part-time/full-time	indefinite contracts part-time/full-time
Pensions	part-time/full-time leave for care included in calculation of benefit	part-time-full-time

As Table 3.1 illustrates, in nearly every category, Swedish policy toward benefits and services attached to work represent a deeper and more extensive formula for economic citizenship. This is evident in forms of compensation for unemployment and early retirement, sickness and invalidity, old age, and pregnancy/parental care of new-born children. Part-time workers and those on temporary contracts are not excluded from benefits. Furthermore, one finds gender sensitive measures as to what counts as work in the calculation of benefits. Thus parents who take leave from their jobs to care for children are registered as in the labour market in official statistics. Certain other aspects of policy that enhance women's economic citizenship. Paid months taken off for caring for children are counted in pension points. In the new reform unpaid leave will be counted as well. These policy innovations represent an indirect recognition of unpaid care work as work. Still, the norms defining what is work remain intact; and many of the policies that Swedish women have benefited from assume attachment to paid work. Parental leave benefits are calculated on percentage of earnings, for example.[33] Swedish women who work over 60 hours a week, both in paid and unpaid work, and have a part-time work contract for 20 or 30 hours, are not given overtime pay when they increase their paid work. This was the challenge made in the ECJ by Dutch part-time workers without success.

We can see that the ECJ has actually extended the framework of Swedish gender equality by recognizing indirect discrimination and preferential treatment in hiring and promotion. These have opened up new strategies and legal claim making in Sweden. But whether preferential treatment that reaches into the institutional status quo can be incorporated into the Swedish model is difficult to gauge. Antidiscrimination law in Sweden has been soft legislation, that is, not binding (see Sections 3–12). Under the current law all employers have to do surveys of gender differentials in wages and have to propose plans that 'shall promote an even distribution of men and women in types of work and with different categories of employees.' Or to 'make special efforts . . .' to increase the proportionality of underrepresented gender (quoted in Eklund 1996). The vagueness of the law allows for innovative kinds of preferential treatment by employers and unions, but does not penalize or pressure recalcitrant employers.

Neither the ECJ nor the Swedish gender equality policies disturb the mechanisms that deny women full economic citizenship. Preferential treatment that reaches into the institutional status quo has not been incorporated into either model, apart from affirmative action in its narrowest sense of integration of some persons formerly excluded. The principle of equal pay for work of equal value, which has the potential to remedy gender inequalities in wages is constrained by a market exception clause in ECJ law, 'what the market will bear'. In the Swedish context, market exceptions are contained in the phrase, 'what is reasonable to promote efficiency'. EU policy that decouples the family (how paid and unpaid work are organized) from the state/market policy triangle, inhibits active strategies toward removing institutional barriers that perpetuate gender disadvantage. Swedish gender equality policy has not adequately acknowledged the dynamic relationship between family and market behaviours. The only exception is the 'daddy month',[34] which does not alter the way in which life course decisions are made and care responsibilities allocated.

CONCLUSION

A model of economic citizenship that would empower women would have to address the dynamic relationship between the institutional triangle (family, state and market) and the domestic triangle (man/woman and parent/children). Thus policies would go beyond gender neutral policies offering men the opportunity to participate in care work, but provide incentives and penalties for men who do not do care work. This approach would challenge the conventional explanation that women are not integrated into the labour market on equal terms with men because of their caring responsibilities. Rather it would turn this proposition on its head and argue that men are not integrated into the caring sphere and that care work is not taken into account in the organization of work. A gendered model of economic citizenship also would have to confront discrimination in wages between men and women workers, reflected in gender segregated occupations and workplaces, and more generally expressed in devaluation of women as a category of worker, as less skilled or less committed to employment. The low wages accorded to care sector occupations is the most visible and pervasive expression of the lack of recognition of women's training and education.

Finally a gendered model of economic citizenship would imply changing the rules of the game and developing inclusionary strategies that alter the redistribution of power. This is not merely a question of who makes the decisions around hiring, promotions and wage scales, which have the potential to alter institutional arrangements and rule-making in particular work organizations.[35] But more broadly, it concerns the power to influence basic institutional structures, discourse and practices that address what is work; what is a working day; what are the responsibilities of individuals as citizens, workers and family members? In effect, this would lead to a linking of social, political and economic citizenship.

NOTES

I am grateful to Alice Kessler-Harris for her discussions with me during her visit to Stockholm in 1997 concerning the use of this concept, which she has employed in her historical studies.

1. Researchers disagree over whether the Court has been consistent or inconsistent in its treatment of gender equality issues (Hervey and Shaw 1996). There also is disagreement over whether the ECJ is proactive or reactive (Lenaerts 1992; Leibfreid and Pierson 1992; Richmond 1996). However, little disagreement exists over the policy impact of the Court.

2. For a fuller discussion of this principle of direct effect and supremacy: see Moore, 1993 in Hervey and O'Keefe.

3. Helga Hernes (1987) coined this term to refer to the ways in which social policies in Scandinavian countries have increased women's participation in different spheres of family, work and politics. Women's participatory citizenship, according to Hernes, did necessarily lead to power, but there is a potential for influence and power in women friendly societies.

4. From comparative research (Hobson 1994; Hobson and Takahashi 1996), we know that solo mothers have a much lower risk of poverty in societies that have developed enabling policies for women to enter paid work.

5. Anglo-American feminists have used the term equity ('the state, ideal, or quality of being just, impartial, and fair') as a concept that offers a way out of the dilemma of difference and equality (see Fraser 1997: Lister 1995). This concept has different meanings in European legal frameworks. Therefore I am using gender equality not as a dichotomous variable (gender difference versus gender equality), but as a concept that embraces justice and fairness (see Gerhardt 1997).

6. I am indebted to Trudie Knijn who first presented this variation of the welfare triangle at a planning meeting, January 1996.
7. Directive 75/117 equal pay for work of equal value (OJ 1975 L45/19); Directive 76/207 equal treatment in employment; Directive 79/7 equal treatment in social security; Directive 86/378 equal treatment in occupational pensions; Directive 86/613 equal treatment for self employed women; Directive 92/85 pregnancy leave.
8. No fixed base amount or proportion of income is noted in the Directive, but there is a recommended minimum equivalent to sickness insurance. Questions of social security benefits while on leave, part-time or full-time leave, and period of employment before the leave were left up to the member states (Equal Opportunities For Women, Annual Report, 1996).
9. Hofmann, C-184/83; Bilka-Kaufhaus, C-170/84; Helmig, C-399/92.
10. Elisabeth Johanna Pacifica Dekker *v* Stichting Vormingscentrum Voor Jong Volwassenen (VJV-Centrum) Plus, C-177/88.
11. See: Elisabeth Johanna Pacifica Dekker *v* Stichting Vormingscentrum Voor Jong Volwassenen (VJV-Centrum) Plus, C-177/88; Habermann-Betterman C-412/92; Webb C-32 93.
12. See: Elisabeth Johanna Pacifica Dekker v Stichting Vormingscentrum Voor Jong Volwassenen (VJV-Centrum) *Plus*, C-177/88; Habermann-Betterman C-412/92; Webb C-32 93.
13. U. Hofmann *v* Barmer Ersalzkasse (1984), ECR 3047.
14. Some of the most notable cases involved are child allowances and child benefits that required residence: see Athanasopoulos et al. *v* Bundesanstalt fur Arbeit, Bronzinov. Kindergeldkasse and Hughes *v* Chief Adjudication Officer.
15. Nimz *v* Freie Hansestad Hamburg, Case C-184/89,
16. Arbeiterwohlfahrt Der Stadt Berlin E. *v* Monika Bötel: Case C-360/90; Kuratorium fuer dialyse und nierentransplantation c. V. *v* Johanna Lewark, C-457/93.
17. Stadt Lengerich and Others *v* Angelika Helmig and Others: Joined Cases C-399/92, C-409/92, C-425/92, C-34/93, C-50/93, C78/93.
18. This is true also in Sweden where men tend to contribute more hours to unpaid household work than in other countries: see Flood and Gråsjo 1995.
19. Eckhard Kalanke *v* Freie Hansestadt Bremen, C-450/93.
20. Judgement C-409/95.
21. There are of course differences in the scope of intervention (areas of policymaking and levels of benefits). Except in cases where the Court has set minimal standards (pregnancy leave) or where the commission has proposed soft guidelines on day care, much of the content of policy is left to the individual states (Hoskyns 1996).
22. It is a debated question in the research on the Swedish welfare state whether the main reason for the emergence of Swedish gender equality policy was a function of the shortage of labour. This author takes the position that there was a complex set of conditions and social actors in-

volved in the construction of policy (feminists, Social Democratic politicians – women and men – and union leaders).

23. Even Ruggie (1984) who championed the Swedish model and the gains
women made in the citizen worker model views the law as toothless.

24. In a recent study, Petersen, Meyerson and Snortland (1996) found
almost no gendered wage gap in Sweden because they compared men
and women in the same job categories. This is not surprising since employers know the equality law and rarely pay women less than men
doing the same job.

25. See Article 2 section 1 of the Equal Treatment Directive.

26. For analysis of the historical development of midwifery in Sweden: see
Lisa Öberg, *Barnmorskan och Läkaren: Kompetens och Konflikt I svensk förlossningsvård. 1870–1920.* (Stockholm 1996).

27. The male comparator had less advanced education. He completed four
years of gymnasium (high school) and then he subsequently took some
supplementary university courses and shorter courses . He first took a
job as a technician and has been employed as clinical engineer since
1978.

28. The description and analysis of this case was provided through
Jämställdhets Ombudsmannen. I am deeply grateful to Lisa Bergh for
this material.

29. According to the Equality Ombudsman, when there was a shortage of
midwives or nurses, the policy was not to raise wages, but rather to intensify recruitment campaigns, or the last resort, was to close the wards
(Jämställdhetsombudsmannen (1996), p. 16).

30. Had this been a case brought to the ECJ, radical pay differentials might
have been justified on the grounds that there was an alternative job
market for engineers but not for midwives (Enderby, C-127/1992).

31. Le Grand (1997) in his analysis of gender segregated occupations in
Sweden found that after controlling for a range of variables found that
women in occupations with 90 per cent males received 9 per cent higher
wages per hour than women in occupations where there were 90 per
cent females. When he excluded social class and industry, the net effect
was even higher, 14 per cent.

32. Referred to as the Commission on Gender and Economic Power, the
Commission produced 12 books.

33. There is a minimal base amount for parents who have not had earnings
for the past year.

34. The statistics suggest that fathers tend to take these days during
summer holiday (*Riksförsakringsverket* 1998 p. 11).

35. Here I would cite the empirical analysis of Hultin and Szulkin (forthcoming), which examines the process by which dominant groups reproduce themselves. They refer to this as active discrimination, the
tendency of male managers to place a higher value on men's performance and potent than women's. From their analysis of Swedish work
organizations, they find that those with a higher proportion of male supervisors have a greater wage gap than those with female.

REFERENCES

Ackers, L. (1996) 'Citizenship, gender, and dependency in the European Union: women and international migration' in (eds) T. Hervey and D. O'Keefe, *Sex Equality Law in the European Union* New York: John Wiley and Sons.

Arbetsdomstolens domar, (1996) January s. 257–300.

Arbetsmarknadsdepartementet (1997) *Kvinnor och män på arbetsmarknaden: Den flexibla arbetsmarknaden.* Stockholm: Arbetsmarknadensdepartementet.

Borchost, A. (1994) 'Welfare Regimes, Women's Interests, and the EC' in (ed.) Diane Sainsbury. *Gendering Welfare Regimes*; London: Sage.

Cockburn, C. (1983) *Brothers, Male Dominance and Technological Change*, London: Pluto.

Commission of the European Communities, (1994) 'Memorandum on Equal Pay for Work of Equal Value', COM (94) 6 final, Brussels, 23 June.

Daly, M. (1997) 'Social Security, Gender, and Equality in the European Union' European Commission, Employment, Industrial Relations and Social Affairs. V/D 5

De Swaan, A. (1999) 'The Prospects for Transnational Social Policy – A Reappraisal' in Michael Hannagan and Charles Tilly (eds) *Recasting Citizenship*, Boulder, Colorado: Rowman and Littlefield.

Drangert, P. and A. Nyberg, (1996) 'Underlag till remissvar på betakandet Statens offentliga utredningar: SOU 1996: 158).

Eklund. R. (1996) 'The Swedish Case – the promise land of sex equality?' in T. Hervey and D. O'Keefe (eds) *Sex Equality Law in the European Union*, New York: John Wiley and Sons.

Esping-Andersen G. (1990) *The Three Worlds of Welfare Capitalism*, New Jersey: Princeton University Press.

European Parliament session documents A4–0338/95, 21 December 1995.

Flood, L. and Gräsjo, U. (1995). 'Changes in Time Spent at Work and Leisure: The Swedish Experience' Paper presented at Conference on Work and Family in Two Welfare Regimes. Stockholm, 13–14 September.

Fraser, N. (1996) 'Multiculturalism and Gender Equity' *Constellations: International Journal of Critical and Democratic Theory.* Vol. 3: no. 1.

Fraser, N. (1997) *Justice Interruptus: Critical Reflections on the Post-Socialist Condition.* New York: Routledge.

Fraser, N. and L. Gordon (1994) '"Dependency" Demystified: Inscriptions of Power in a Keyword of the Welfare State' *Social Politics: International Studies in Gender, State, and Society.* 1: 1: 4–32.

Gustafsson, S. and M. Bruyn-Hundt (1992) 'Incentives for women to work: A comparison between the Netherlands, Sweden, and West Germany' *Journal of Economic Studies*: 18.

Gelb, J. (1989) *Feminism and Politics: A Comparative Perspective*. Berkeley, CA.: University of California Press.

Gonäs, L. (1997) 'Towards Convergence? Some comments on economic integration and women's employment' in EC Programme, 'Gender and Citizenship: Social Integration and Social Exclusion in European Welfare States Seminar 3'. Alborg, Denmark.

Gonäs, L. and A., Spånt (1997) 'Trends and Prospects for Women's Employment in the 1990's' *Arbetslivsinstitutet*. no. 4.

Haas L. (1992) *Unequal Parenthood and Social Policy: A Study of Parental Leave in Sweden* Albany, NY: State University of New York Press.

Handbook on Equal Treatment for Men and Women in the European Community (1995). Luxembourg: European Commission.

Hernes H. (1987) *Welfare State and Woman Power: Essays in State Feminism*. Oslo: Norwegian University Press.

Hervey, T. K. and D. O'Keefe (Eds) (1996) *Sex Equality Law in the European Union*. New York: John Wiley and Sons.

Hervey, T. K. and J. Shaw (1996) 'Women, Work, and Care: Women's Dual Role and Double Burden in EC Sex Equality and Law' *Engendering Citizenship, Work, and Care*, EC Programme, 'Gender and Citizenship: social integration and social exclusion in European Welfare States', Seminar 1 Aalborg, Denmark.

Hobson, B. (1990) 'No Exit, No Voice: Women's Economic Dependency and the Welfare State', *Acta Sociologica*, Vol. 33, s: 235–49.

Hobson, B. (1994). 'Solo Mothers, Policy Regimes, and the Logics of Gender' in Diane Sainsbury (ed.) *Gendering Welfare Regimes*, London: Sage.

Hobson, B. and M. Takahashi, (1996) 'Care Regimes, Solo Mothers, and the Recasting of Social Citizenship Rights' *Engendering Citizenship, Work, and Care*, of the EC Programme, 'Gender and Citizenship: social integration and social exclusion in European Welfare States'. Seminar 1 Aalborg, Denmark.

Hobson, B. and M. Takahashi (1977) 'The Parent-Worker Model: Lone Mothers in Sweden' in Jane Lewis (ed.) *Lone Mothers in European Regimes: Shifting Policy Logics* London: Jessica Kingsley.

Hobson, B. *et al.* (1995) 'Gender and the Swedish Welfare State.' *Comparative Studies of Welfare States* London: British Social Policy Association.

Hoem, B. (1995) 'The Way to the Gender Segregated Swedish Labour Market' in Karen Oppenheim Mason and Ann Jensen (eds) *Gender and Family Change in Industrialized Countries*. Oxford: Oxford University Press.

Hoskyns, C. (1996) *Integrating Gender: Women, Law, and Politics in the European Community*. London: Verso.

Hultin, M and Szulkin, R. (forthcoming) 'Wages and Unequal Acess to Organizational Power: An Empirical Test of Gender Discrimination'. *American Science Quarterly*.

Jamstalldhetsombudsmannen (Equality Ombudsman) 'Jämställdhetsombuds-mannen, Lena Svenaeus mot Örebro läns landsting' *Arbetsdomstolens Domar*, Vol. 1, 1996: Judgment no. 41/96. Case no. A 153–195. Translated by the office of Jämställdhetsombudsmannen.

Knijn, T. (1994) 'Fish without Bikes: Revision of the Dutch Welfare States and Its Consequences for the (In)dependence of Single Mothers', *Social Politics: International Studies in Gender, State, and Society*. 1: 1: 83–105.

Knijn, T. and M. Kremer, (1998) 'Gender and the Caring Dimension in Welfare States: Towards Inclusive Citizenship' *Social Politics: International Studies in Gender, State, and Society* 4:3:328–361.

Le Grand, C. (1977) 'Occupational Segregation and the Gender Wage Gap in Sweden' Work-Organization-Economy Working Paper Series: no. 50 Stockholm University.

Lenaerts, K. (1992) 'Some Thoughts About the Interaction Between Judges and Politicians in the European Community' *Yearbook of European Law* Vol. 12, no. 2.

Leibfried, S. and P. Pierson, (1995) European Social Policy: *Between Fragmentation and Integration*. Washington DC: Brookings Institution.

Lewis, J. (1993) *Women and Social Policies in Europe: Work, Family and State*. Aldershot, England: Edward Elgar.

Lewis, J. and I. Ostner (1994) 'Gender and the Evolution of Social Policies.' ZES-Arbeitspaper. no. 4/94. Bremen Germany: Centre for Social Policy Research.

Lewis, J. and I. Ostner (1995) 'Gender and the Evolution of European Social Policies' in Stephan Leibried and Paul Pierson (eds.) *European Social Policy*, Washington D.C.: Brookings Institute.

Lister, R. (1995) 'Dilemmas in Engendering Citizenship' *Economy and Society*. 24: 1: s.1–40.

Majury, D. (1991) 'Strategizing In Equality' in M.A. Fineman and N.S. Thomadseh (eds) *At the Boundaries of Law*. New York: Routledge.

Marshall. T.H. (1950) *Citizenship and social Class and Other Essays*. Cambridge, England: Cambridge University Press.

Meehan, E. (1991) 'European Social Citizenship and Social Policies' in U. Vogel and M. Moran (eds) *Frontiers of Social Citizenship*, London: Macmillan.

Montanari, I. (1995) 'Harmonisation of Social Policies and Social Regulations in the European Community' *European Journal of Political Research*. 27: 1:. 21–45.

More, G. (1993) 'Equal Treatment of the Sexes in European Community Law: What Does Equal Mean?' *Feminist Legal Studies*. 1:1. 45–74.

Näsman, E. (1995) 'Time, Work, and Family Life' in B. Arve-Perez (ed.) *Reconciling Work and Family Life – A Challenge of Europe?* Commission of European Communities. Stockholm: Norstedts.

Nyberg, A. and E. Sundin (1997) *Ledare, makt, och Kön*. SOU. 1997: 135 More, G. (1993) 'Equal Treatment of the Sexes in European Community Law: What Does Equal Mean? *Feminists Legal Studies*. 1:1. 45–74.

Moore, S. (1996) 'Enforcement of Private Law: Claims of Sex Discrimination in the Field of Employment,' in *Sex Equality Law in the European Union*, eds. T. Hervey and D. O'Keefe. New York: John Wiley and Sons.

Öberg, L. (1996) *Barnmorskan och läkaren: kompetens och konflikt i svensk förlossningsvård, 1870–1920*. Stockholm: Histriska Institutionen.

O'Connor. J. (1996) 'Labour Market Participation, Gender, and Citizenship' in 'From Women in the Welfare State to Gendering Welfare State Regimes'. *Current Sociology*. 44: 2: 78–100.

Opinion of Advocate-General Jacobs. (1997) Case C-409/95. Helmut Marschall *v* Land Nordhein-Westfalen, delivered on 15 May.

Orloff, A.S. (1993) 'Gender and the Social Rights of Citizenship: The Comparative Analysis of State Policies and Gender Relations.' *American Sociological Review*. 58: 15: 303–28.

Pateman, C. (1989) *The Disorder of Women: Democracy, Feminism and Political Theory*. Stanford, CA: Stanford University Press.

Petersen, T., E.M. Meyersen and W. Snartland, (1996). 'The Within-Job Gender Gap: the Case of Sweden' Working paper no. 470, Stockholm: *Industriens Utrednings Institutet*.

Peterson, W. (1994) 'Subsidiarity: A Definition to Suit any Vision?' *Parliamentary Affairs*. 116–32.

Pierson, P. and S. Leibfried (1995) *European Social Policy: Between Fragmentation and Integration*. Washington DC: Brookings Institution.

Reskin, B. (1986) *Women's Work, Men's Work: Sex Segregation on the Job*. Washington DC: National Academy Press.

Richmond, A. (1996) 'The Politics of Social Law: The European Court of Justice and the Social Dimension' paper presented at the American Political Science Association, San Francisco, 29 August–1 September.

Riksbörsakringsverket, Statistikinformation is-1. 1998.

Ruggie, M. (1984) *The State and The Working Woman: A Comparative Study of Britain and Sweden*. Princeton: Princeton University Press.

Sainsbury, D. (1996) *Gender Equality and Welfare States*. Oxford: Oxford University Press.

Saraceno, C. (1994) 'The Ambivalent Familism of the Italian Welfare State' *Social Politics: International Studies in Gender, State, and Society*. 1: 1.

Scheiwe, K. (1994) 'EC Law's Unequal Treatment of the Family: The Case Law of the European Court of Justice on Rules Prohibiting Discrimination on Grounds of Sex and Nationality' *Social and Legal Studies*. 1: 3: 243–65.

Shaver, S. (1993) 'Body Rights, Social Rights and the Liberal Welfare State' *Critical Social* Policy, 39: 66–92.

Sheppard, C. 1990 'Recognition of the Disadvantaging of Women: The Promise of Andrews v. Law Society of British Columbia' *McGill Law Journal*. 35: 207–34.

Sheppard, C. (1993) *Study Paper prepared on Litigating the Relationship Between Equity and Equality*. Ontario Law Reform Commission. Canada: Ontario.

Siim, B. (1997) 'Towards a Gender Sensitive Framework for Citizenship: Implications for Comparative Studies of Welfare States in Transition' *Engendering Citizenship, Work, and Care*, EC Programme, 'Gender and Citizenship: social integration and social exclusion in European Welfare States'. Seminar 2 Aalborg Denmark.

Social Politics: International Studies of Gender, State, and Society (1997) Thematic issue on Care. 4:3.

Spicker, P. (1994) 'The Principle of Subsidiarity and the Social Policy of the European Community' *Journal of European Social Policy*. 1: 1: 3–14.

Statens offentliga utredingar, (SOU): (1997) Rapport till Untredningnen om fördelning av ekonomiska makt och ekonomiska resurser mellan kvinnor och män: numbers 83, 87, 113, 117, 135.

Steiner, J. (1996) 'The Principle of Equal Treatment for Men and Women in Social Security' (eds) T. Hervey and D. O'Keefe in *Sex Equality Law in the European Union* New York: John Wiley and Sons.

Sundström, M. (1987). *A Study in the Growth of Part- time Work in Sweden*. Stockholm: Arbetslivsentrum.

Szyszczak, E. (1996) 'Community Law on Pregnancy and Maternity' (eds) T. Hervey and D. O'Keefe in *Sex Equality Law in the European Union* New York: John Wiley and Sons.

Taylor-Gooby, P. (1996) 'The Response of Government: Fragile Convergence?' (eds) V. George and P. Taylor-Gooby in *European Policy: Squaring the Welfare Circle* Basingstoke: Macmillan.

Ungerson, C. (1994) 'Caring and Citizenship: A Complex Relationship' (ed.) Joanna Bornal et al. in *Community Care: A Reader*. Basingstoke: Macmillan.

4 Abstract Citizenship? Women and Power in the Czech Republic

Hana Havelkova

The tensions in the dialogue between Western and Eastern European women are rooted in the problems of the direct application of Western feminist theory to post-communist reality. The differences between the realities in Eastern and Western Europe require closer specification to recognize the possibilities and limits of the applicability of existing theories. In this Chapter, I will discuss two of the most common false assumptions about Eastern European women: that they are second-class citizens and that they are conservative. I analyze two aspects of women's position in Czech society that appear to support these assumptions: women's absence from leading political roles and the conservative gender rhetoric in the mass media. In the first case, the argument starts from specific phenomena arising in a transforming society and suggests the introduction of the concepts of abstract and concrete citizenship to explore the 'woman question' under these conditions. In the second case, the connotations of 'conservative' are addressed, since in post-communist societies it can mean the opposite of that implied in established Western democracies. Two as yet open questions are the extent to which such phenomena are transitory in nature, occurring before a stable democracy is established, and to what extent such phenomena represent a persistently different structure of gender relations, thus presenting a challenge to the universalism of feminist theories. I argue that with respect to these specific conditions, the dimension of time must play a more central role in local feminist reflections. So must the general context of the region in terms of the historically perpetuated poverty of its societies as compared to the West, which makes a difference in a theoretical starting point as well as in the structure of the problematics.

WESTERN THEORY, EASTERN REALITY

The reflections on women's situation in Central and Eastern Europe after the disintegration of the iron curtain have not been thoroughly questioned. On the one hand, there is a reality in post-communist countries that requires theorizing; on the other hand, there is a ready-made, imported theory to analyze this reality – namely, Western feminism.[1] Since this theory already exists, it is impossible to ignore it completely in analyzing women's situation in Eastern Europe. Nonetheless, there are numerous pitfalls when applying this theory directly to the Eastern European situation.

Intuitively protecting themselves against the inappropriate application of Western feminist theory to Eastern European women, women from the region have emphasized what is called the 'different experience' or the 'specificities' of their situation. They have also drawn attention to a different hierarchy of values in their societies, which places the family high on the value ladder. Moreover, these attitudes in women seem to correspond with the representations of women's roles in popular political discourse. Together, these two factors reinforce what has been termed a 'conservative' picture of female roles. Consequently, some enthusiastic Western feminists have seen their role as developing enlightened activism in Eastern Europe by challenging such assumptions and values, a focus that has provoked Eastern women's resistance.

In this chapter, I abandon this vicious circle, thus shifting the definition of the problem. If there is on the one hand a reality without a theory, I can also say that, from my point of view, there is on the other hand a theory without reality, meaning the universalist tone of Western theories that constantly speak about 'a man' and 'a woman' without situating them in a concrete social context. At every meeting of women from Eastern Europe and the West, women from post-communist societies try to contextualize their theoretical views, to explain, to translate. Women from the West never feel the need to translate or explain why an American feminist sees the gender relationships as she sees them, because she has grown up and lived in the US. American women's 'reality' is simply taken for granted and thus as the impetus of theoretical concept it remains only implicit. Others cannot distinguish which parts of the theory are 'tailored' to the US context and which are not. Therefore, despite Western theorists' verbal acknowledgment of Eastern differences, the dialogue will remain asymmetrical unless Western theorists begin to translate and explain such differences.

In other words, before we can know which aspects of Western feminist theories can be applied to Eastern European realities or whether feminist concepts should be reformulated entirely before being applied there, it is necessary to delineate the differences between Western feminist theories and Eastern European realities. This has not yet been done. I believe that Eastern European women tend to overemphasize the differences between Western theories and post-communist realities, both taking insufficient account of the transitoriness of their situation and attempting to protect their own authentic experiences against the invading feminist theory.

Moreover, because interest in feminist theory in the Czech Republic is growing, it is important to analyze its impact. This task is twofold. First, we must describe the specificities of post-communist Eastern Europe that make women's experience different there and therefore rethink the universalist claims of the theories developed outside Eastern Europe. Second, we must develop an understanding of 'difference' in this context. It is not enough simply to add new dimensions in the same way that concepts such as class and race are now used to view our societies, because in the case of Eastern Europe this does not work. Some differences may be transitory while others may be more entrenched and may modify gender relations in a particular country irrevocably – something that needs a fuller theorization.

Therefore, my methodological imperative is to keep working with the consciousness of difference between Western and Eastern European experiences, even though more generally I deeply believe in basic commonalities in gender relations between the Czech lands and Western culture. I also believe that it is not possible to work with commonalities in a theoretically 'clean' way unless we understand the extent to which the differences may matter.

On the example of Czech women in politics and massmedia discourse, I want to demonstrate, first, how the situation of a society in transition can conceal many things and, second, how difficult it is at the same time to decide what is transitory and what is more permanent. I believe that methodologically this example transcends the Czech specificities as such. My argument is concentrated on both practical and theoretical meanings of transitional processes, and therefore I will work not only with the concept of societal transition but also with the description of its stages, each of which implies a different constellation of values, attitudes and priorities. Only in this framework can women's situation be analyzed to show the plurality of factors at stake as well as the various levels of possible interpretation.

In the first part of this article, I focus on the problem of women in politics in order to indicate the limitations of a feminist perspective as well as to analyze the character of politics during the phase of building democracy. In the second part, I focus on the gender discourse in Czech mass media after 1989 to argue that a conservative rhetoric can in fact be based on deep emancipatory convictions. It is a question of understanding the configuration of layers of historical experience and their meanings with respect to concrete time and space for concrete actors. Again, it is shown that some apparently transitory phenomena are supported by deep and underlying structures, stereotypes, and mentalities that can create a relatively persistent difference from the Western experience – a conclusion that also has theoretical consequences.

ABSTRACT AND CONCRETE CITIZENSHIP

After the 1992 democratic elections following the Velvet Revolution (the first were in 1990), women's retreat from politics was complete. Although there was one woman in the previous federal government, one in the Czech government, and the president of the Czech parliament was a woman, we now have no woman minister, and the percentage of women deputies dropped from 10 to 8 percent. This alarming situation seems to correspond to the character of public discourse concerning gender and women's issues, a discourse that tends to be rather conservative.

The temptation to interpret these two public phenomena as two sides of a sharply conservative turn and a trend toward clearly gendered power relations is great indeed. Although I agree with those who regard the absence of women in politics as shameful and scandalous, at the same time I realize that to follow this temptation is to yield to an oversimplified and ideologized view of the situation. Therefore, I prefer to avoid starting with this interpretation, albeit it is one to which Western feminist theories seduce us, and instead begin by understanding these phenomena in all their complexity.

We face not only the problem of the transfer of theories rooted in totally different social contexts. We must also recognize that these theories' contexts were and are, despite all their diversity, stable political situations. I will concentrate on phenomena that are occurring in the midst of the thorough transformation of Czech society. Perhaps the more that Eastern European societies stabilize, the more Western feminist theories may be applicable to them. But at present nobody can say what kind of societies they will become, so I will confine myself to what we have evidence for at the present time.

Let me demonstrate this through the concept of citizenship. Zillah Eisenstein uses her concept 'second-class citizenship' only 'in terms of job opportunities and pay' (1993, 303) and then in connection with statist protectionist policy toward women in socialist countries. In common with some other theorists who deal with Eastern Europe from a distance (for example, Wolchik 1979), Eisenstein makes a fundamental mistake, namely, she limits her evidence to an analysis of the official policies of the power elite – which also limits her concept of citizenship. Therefore, although her analysis of communist gender politics is compelling, it is not very helpful in understanding women's strategies after the collapse of communism. She ignores the fact that the rigidity of the 'statist feminist' framework had both negative and positive effects (for example, it also helped to break some gender stereotypes), but above all, it was becoming more and more an empty shell that was filled with specific, 'private' contents. Some theorists speak of the 'colonization of the state by the family' and of a disappearance of the state as related to an individual's everyday life (Mozny 1992). Eisenstein's thematization is too one-dimensional: she only emphasizes the 'conflict between the individual and the patriarchal, totalitarian state.' (1993, 303)

The same kind of objections apply to her treatment of contemporary sources. Focusing on Mikhail Gorbachev's or Václav Havel's opinions, Eisenstein fails to ask whether and in what sense their utterances may be relevant or what is actually the status of the immediate postcommunist rhetoric. Not only have neither of these two men lived like the majority of their fellow citizens but both of them played a rather abstract part in re-binding the individual to the new political order. Under communism, most people tried to live as if apart from the politics, whereas Havel lived in a permanent confrontation with the communist elite (knowing sometimes little about average people's daily lives), and Gorbachev was always one of those elite.

With respect to both phenomena I want to address here (the retreat of women from top political roles and the conservative rhetoric), it is obvious that in the case of Czech society they both result from men's actions and mirror women's attitudes. Therefore, women claim to be both uninterested in pursuing power and more interested in the family as a matter of their own free choice. Or to put it differently, women's attitudes conceal what men would do if women opened the 'power' issue in the classical feminist sense. Not only are themes such as oppression and discrimination never raised, but the existing situation is perceived as a result of women's conscious decisions. Without wanting to minimize the question of consciousness-raising, I believe that it is senseless to introduce such concepts before we know what is rational, conscious, or mature (in the sense of conscious personal decisions) in women's attitudes under the given conditions. Women's own desires and their experience of social transition must first be understood.

Therefore, instead of speaking of second-class citizens in the context of the transition processes, I find it more useful to work with the terms 'abstract' and 'concrete' citizenship. By abstract citizenship, I mean an image of the system into which certain ideals are projected. By concrete citizenship, I mean the attitudes that are rooted in the concrete knowledge and experiences of the individual within a particular social or political system. During transformation processes, citizens encounter unknown conditions into which they project their concrete experiences from the past and their abstract ideals about the future.

These terms enable us to grasp the relationship of a person to civic and public life and to transcend the horizon of power elite policy. The other benefit of utilizing these concepts is that the basic feature of the period of transition is its openness: nothing is settled, nothing is 'for sure', and no social relationship is yet entirely transparent or delineated. Under these circumstances, women relate in a concrete way to their past mode of citizenship. In the Czech case, this relationship is ambivalent: they are critical of it but at the same time build upon specific women's 'strengths' inherited from socialism. However, they relate only in an abstract way to their future citizenship, which connects only in an abstract way to politics in which they do not actually participate. They nurture both hope and illusions with regard to their individual situations and to gender relationships generally – they hope it won't be necessary to break the solidarity of sexes. It is important to note that Czech women do not as yet feel like victims of oppressive patriarchal relations and that this period of transition is one in which to display new forms of female achievement. Therefore, the period of transition deserves further elaboration. The question is, of course, how long women will want to be able to hold this 'abstract citizenship' and to what extent it contradicts their inherited notions of concrete citizenship.

The two phenomena under question must then be theoretically separated. Although women's absence from politics is undoubtedly connected with the somewhat conservative atmosphere at the moment, the connection is less direct than it might seem. With regard to women's attitudes, concrete citizenship is connected with a widespread view that gender representation in top political roles is not particularly relevant for most women (Siklova 1992). Thus, their absence is treated with a certain unconcern or lack of motivation. Abstract citizenship is on the contrary characterized by positive projections of what matters, of human values, and a process of rediscovering one's own identity.

WOMEN AND POLITICS

As to the factors of women's unconcern with gender representation in politics, I make a further distinction between factors concerning the situation of women's issues and those resulting from the very character of transitional politics. Unlike in Poland or the former GDR, in the Czech Republic there is at the moment no significant women's issue that could ignite women's collective action or motivate them to lobby politically. A liberal abortion law has been in place since 1957. A recent amendment introduced a fee for abortions performed after the sixth week of pregnancy to encourage more 'responsible' behaviour (that is, to encourage the woman who was going to have abortions to do so before the sixth week, when the procedure is less harmful to the woman's body). But a woman's desire to have an abortion remains a sufficient condition even after this amendment. In the Czech Republic, the average unemployment rate (including women's) is still very low and is increasing only slowly: from 2.6 per cent in 1993 to 3.5 per cent in 1994. In Prague, unemployment is almost nonexistent. In terms of legal and social protection, Czech women are convinced that the law is in their favour: about 27 per cent of women think that they are better protected than men and the majority of women believe that legal protection is the same for both sexes (Cermakova and Gatnar 1992). In sum, thus far there is no pressing political issue that would put the gender neutrality of political practice into doubt.

The quota system of gender representation, well known in all the former communist regimes, was also used in the Czech Republic but was regarded as purely formal tokenism. In this case, time also plays a certain role. Since the revolution in 1989, when the abolition of the quota system was part of the anticommunist reaction, the attitude has been changing gradually. More and more women and men (over 60 per cent) would welcome the reimplementation of this system. Yet due to the lack of issues around which to mobilize, their arguments for women's presence in politics are still abstract and vague: for example, they mention women's interests, women's practicality, women's sensitivity, and so on as factors that make the situation of women in politics different. They do not therefore see women's representation in conventional politics as an urgent need – at least so far. Under these circumstances, the traditional electoral pattern has continued. Evidence suggests that neither women nor men vote for women parliamentary candidates. Distrust and self-censorship are also factors that prevent women from entering politics, but these factors are intermingled with the others mentioned above.

In summary, women generally hold three stances toward political power that seem contradictory at first glance: (1) a lack of concern as to the gender of the politicians who represent them, (2) an abstract conviction that women's presence in politics makes sense but is not perceived as an urgent issue, and (3) a certain scepticism as to the likely success of women in politics at the present time.

The third stance testifies clearly to a high level of acceptance of the traditional division of gender roles and might allow us to characterize this set of attitudes as conservative. Yet the actual social status of Czech women contradicts such a simplistic conclusion. Since at least the late 1960s women have not derived their social status from their husbands. Five years after the launch of the economic transformation in 1990, women still represent about 44 per cent of the total workforce. According to Marie Cermakova, less than 5 per cent of women have lost their jobs, while 10 per cent have considerably improved their status (1995, 14). As compared to some Western countries, Czech women are well represented in some prestigious jobs, for example, as lawyers and doctors (54.7 per cent of all doctors are women). The education of women does not differ dramatically from that of men: 7.9 per cent of women and 12.2 per cent of men graduate from a university, while the percentage of high school educated women exceeds that of men (*Statisticka* 1994, 190). A similar situation exists in the new enterpreneurial elite where the female elite comprise 5.5 per cent of the female population of productive age as compared to 12.8 per cent of men (*Statisticka* 1994). Cermakova estimates that, while about 15 per cent of women possess the qualifications to be in politics (including such characteristics as a high degree of charisma and aspirational capital (that is, the level of will and energy to make a career)), only 2–3 per cent proclaimed their desire to be in politics (1995, 4). What I want to point out is that the reasons for women's lack of interest in power must also be sought in the specific character of politics in the actual process of a particular society's transition.

Politics during the Transition Process

Two aspects of the transition in Czech society are gender relevant. The first one is the belated reconstruction of the social dimension of politics and with it of what I call concrete citizenship as compared to the reconstruction of political institutions and abstract citizenship. To explain this shift requires an examination of the several phases of the communist period. The point at issue is a gradual decline of the perception of the 'societal' as a public matter during Czech socialist history. Briefly, in Czech society, socialism was launched under the political precondition of democracy and was initially understood as a social rather than political arrangement. The disappointments of the 1950s led to the politicization of all societal phenomena in the 1960s (that is, overpoliticization of the societal life and the deterioration of social issues). The 1968 Soviet invasion brought a civic trauma on account of which both the social and the political became irrelevant for everyday life, and the private sphere became almost the only social reality – in other words, political consciousness survived in the form of a memory and an abstract ideal but the social dimension almost vanished. This hierarchy fashioned the character of the events of 1989; the dominance of political claims over social ones more or less persisted through momentum in the years that followed.

In connection with the 'postinvasion' period (1970s and 1980s), I would suggest that the social be regarded as a split concept. As a social (that is, political) concept, it has lost its personal relevance. As a set of concrete social roles and positions, the social was more and more adopted, privatized, and 'instrumentalized for private interests and private loyalties' (Tatur 1992), which in fact meant a further stage of the alienation of the social.

No wonder that the social dimension of politics is now being reconstructed in reverse order. First, society became politicized again and relearned the democratic 'basics'. The transformation of social politics is just beginning. A new social structure has not yet crystallized, and social arrangements consist on the one hand of the old official familiar framework and on the other hand of family solidarity on account of the adverse financial impacts of the political reform, making the family even more important than before. Since women are relatively well protected by official legislation and at the same time play a dominant role in organizing private social life, their public solidarity will in the near future probably also be subordinated to two 'superior' interests: of the successful transformation of the political 'base' and of private, family interests.

Since the reestablishment of official political structures and a legal system more or less accomplished before the second democratic elections in 1992, the main focus of politics since then – and in fact the main subject at issue in the 1992 elections – has been economic reform. In other words, the economy became a central issue of contemporary politics to such an extent that politics has been reduced to economics. Under these widely known – and accepted – circumstances, this very political period is a male matter par excellence. Not only is the national economy a traditional realm for men, but the concrete scenario of economic reform was prepared long ago by a group of male economists who took the responsibility for its later realization: people simply agreed, 'Let them do it.' Typical of this perspective is the declaration of one of the leading activists of the women's initiative called 'New Humanity' and one of the best known Czech feminists, Alexandra Berkova: 'Politically conscious women must stand on the political right, i.e., they must first of all support economic reform.' (Berkova 1993)

This example of how a conscious, abstract citizenship makes women refrain from political engagement has its counterpart in how women test their ability to compete with men in the labour market, which is women's main public activity. Sociological research has repeatedly confirmed that the vast majority of Czech women (despite the conservative rhetoric already mentioned) want to keep or improve their labour market position and that they fear unemployment, as documented above. This is an area where women know they could lose out – as compared to political engagement that 'can wait'. Due to the fact that everyone's right to work was removed only after 1989, the situation of gender competition in the labour market is a unique context for both sexes, and it is first of all a unique test of an individual's abilities. This is the time for identity seeking and individual empowerment, and women want to keep their financial independence. This has to do with concrete citizenship, which now requires a lot of courage and effort to maintain. Many Czech women believe they will make it on their own and so far do not see lobbying for women's interests in public politics as important or useful. Hence, the kind of organizations they join are those such as the Association of Women Entrepreneurs and Managers. Will the lack of political representation serve eventually to undermine women's labour market position and to dent their confidence in their own position?

Another important aspect of the relationship between politics and the dominance of the economy in the Czech society is the conviction that existing women's problems, such as the double burden of employment and domestic work, can be solved primarily through the improvement of the economic situation and especially by better services, rather than politically.

In summary, women's contemporary absence from the Czech political scene does not need to be ascribed only to a rigid, unchangeable division of power between the two sexes. Although it is true that Czech men eagerly reoccupied their traditional realm, their active discrimination against women seems to be less evident than women's hesitation to enter this old–new male arena. Some of women's reasons for refraining from politics may be only temporary and pragmatically dependent upon the eventual changes in the character of politics. In any case, Czech women (including theorists) hesitate to interpret this situation univocally in terms of discrimination.

Conservative Rhetoric

With respect to women and power, a major question arises: to what extent does the conservative rhetoric express a real tendency in the society to prescribe women's role and to force them into this role, that is, to limit their choices? This issue includes several smaller ones: what is the status of this rhetoric given the context of transition? What are the characteristics of the rhetoric? Can it really be called conservative? What is its role in constructing gender roles?

Answering the question concerning the status of the conservative rhetoric is not simple. This issue is connected with the post-1989 dynamics of who captures the attention of the mass media. In general, immediately after 1989, the voice of those who were most silenced under the communist regime naturally dominated. It was above all former dissidents, Christians, and exiles who became prominent. In these three groups, the gender rhetoric tends to be conservative but for different reasons. Among dissidents, conservative gender attitudes were a part of their radical antisocialist speech, of their emphasis on the superiority of political and civic rights over social and economic rights, and of their abstract moralism. This group was committed in the closest way to political – rather than social – identity and addressed themselves primarily (albeit in a negative way) to political elites. The connection between Christianity and the emphasis on the role of women in the family and on morality is well known. In addition, some of the older exiles lean toward anti-feminist rhetoric. There are two reasons for this. First, their commitment to the superiority of the political was precisely the reason for their exile; second, their personal experience has led them toward an aversion to the formalism of the communist egalitarian rhetoric. That is why they were not able or willing to accept Western feminism, whose rhetoric resembled the communist stance.

It is important to note that these groups are not identical with the intellectual elite as a whole; they represent only a part. After some time, these voices generally retreated and were replaced by those who advocated that to throw away all our 'socialist' past would be unsound because, they argued, 'Well, it was none the less our lives and we do not know anything else.' (for example, Vaclav Jamek) In both sociology and history, the discussion continues about how to characterize the current changes. Is it a transition or a transformation? Can we simply transfer 'universal' standards from an 'average' model of Western democracy or must we develop a more long-term strategy of building upon the structures and values inherited from the past? The pro- and anti-feminist discussions are part of this changing discourse in the mass media. Moreover, the initial conservative rhetoric is not stable, rigid or constant. Here, time is again an important factor. The initial aversion of the public toward feminism seems to be gradually changing, too – especially among students. Therefore, in connection with the status of the conservative rhetoric we can state, without underestimation, that due to the post-revolutionary atmosphere, conservative rhetoric cannot be regarded as completely representative of public or intellectual opinion.

What are the characteristics of this rhetoric? As a matter of fact, openly stated demands for women's retreat from the public sphere and return to the family are uttered quite rarely and with some diffidence. For example, even when the more conservative political parties included this issue as part of their electoral programme, it was only a very minor element of their campaigns and was reduced to an emphasis on the role of the family in society, which was expressed in vague, abstract terms. Nor did the Christian party, although part of the government coalition, even attempt to open an anti-abortion campaign. Due to the very low religiosity of Czech society, such views are not influential. Moreover, the prestige of the church continues to decline still further.

'Conservative rhetoric' addresses gender roles and gender identities without using terms like oppression, discrimination, male domination, or patriarchy. There are exceptions: speakers who go so far as to plead for family patriarchy in a positive sense (Pokorny 1992) and women who make hyperbolic statements, such as 'Our society is rather "matriarchal".' (Hauserova 1992) These discussions circle around the positive values of women's roles and utilize vocabulary such as gender solidarity, family solidarity, 'the humanizing role of a woman in the society', moral values, the role of the mother, and so on. The issue of equality is mostly thought to be one that has already been overcome or is of little importance, whereas sexual and gender differences and the complementarity of sexes are stressed. Despite what I have said about the status of the rhetoric, we must not minimize its importance, for it has also emerged in some women's initiatives established since 1989. Only one of the 40 new initiatives included gender equality as a priority in their programmes. Some initiatives stress a humanitarian mission. Some lean toward an anti-abortion position (Altos and Sopranos 1995). It is interesting that among these 40 organizations there are three men's initiatives whose goals include, for example, the equality of parental rights after divorce and the promotion of the consciousness of fatherhood. Paradoxically, women advocating these positions seem to be the most radical feminists. Their claim is that in the public sphere, every position should be opened to the most qualified, competent women but, in return, men who have skills in bringing up children should also have the opportunity to do so.

Nevertheless, both the rhetoric of conservatism and its manifestations in social movements and programmes is limited. The membership of the aforementioned 'humanist' initiatives is small and more or less limited to Prague. About half of the new initiatives are in fact not ideologically based – they concentrate on concrete and pragmatic goals, such as cleaner air in Prague

(Prague Mothers), legislation for single parents (Single Mothers), and training for women managers (Association of Women Managers and Entrepreneurs).

In other words, the conservative rhetoric can hardly be characterized as a new social ideology or as massive political traditionalism. Yet on a cultural level, the mentioned values predominate over liberationist values. Again, the question is whether conservatism is the right term to use for such ideologies and movements.

This question opens two others. First, how deeply conservative is the articulation of these values? Second, to what extent is the articulation of these values legitimated by the depth of the impact of phenomena to which they are opposed? In other words, is conservatism simply a reaction to the false radicalism represented by the former communist regimes?

A third question underlying these two concerns proportions. What is in fact presupposed when one pleads for idealized femininity and masculinity, or how nice it is to be a mother? I believe that underlying such rhetoric is an assumption of gender equality that is deeply held but taken for granted and therefore never needs articulation.

The first question is one of understanding the cultural and historical context of a particular society. To put it simply, in traditionally strong patriarchal societies the conservative talk means something other than it does in societies that are traditionally more gender liberal. In this respect, the difference between Czech society and other East European societies can affect the different theoretical status of the term 'conservatism'. While detailed historical comparisons are not yet available, some points are clear. During the nineteenth century, Czech society underwent a rapid modernization and democratization process to become (after its declaration of independence in 1918 and its joining with Slovakia) one of the strongest industrial countries, with one of the strongest economies, and the most stable democratic state in Central Europe – and its constitution included women's rights. 'Czechoslovakia's record in the field of women's rights was better than that of most other European countries and certainly outshone that of the other successor states of the Habsburg monarchy', states Karen Johnson Freeze (1986, 51). This was possibly due to several factors. In a perceptive analysis, Katherine David writes,

There is no single answer to the question of what made the Czech piece of the Central and Eastern European mosaic more amenable to women's emancipation than its neighbours – as it indeed appears to have been. The Bohemian Lands' relatively high levels of economic development and education and the Czech's ambivalence about the Catholic Church register as significant factors. The fluid class structure and predominance of the bourgeoisie and petty bourgeoisie, as opposed to an aristocracy, in Czech society engendered practicality rather than deference to ancient social mores. Fear of depopulation or 'race suicide', which caused a backlash in other industrialized countries, did not trouble the Czechs, whose population remained proportionally stable *vis-á-vis* the Germans. Strong patriarchal traditions, upon which so many Slavic women's movements faltered, were absent. (1991, 40)

While the last statement is probably too strong, there is something that makes us assume gender-connected cultural patterns here as significantly different from those in other Eastern European countries.

Since little is known about Czech women's history, I will provide a summary. Since the early nineteenth century, women's liberation and especially educational advancement formed an integral part of the Czech national movement. Basic school literacy was almost 100 per cent for both sexes at the end of the nineteenth century. Secondary girls' schools opened in the 1860s and 1870s. Women gained access to universities in the 1890s. They were publicly active above all as writers and journalists. The first women's journal was published in 1876. For comparison, in 1908 the Czechs published seven women's periodicals, the Germans four, and the Slovenes one, while Polish women did not have a separate journal even as late as 1913. The Social Democratic, Progressive, National Socialist, and various minor parties welcomed female members and advocated full legal equality for women. These political parties joined with the Committee for Women's Voting Rights in 1911 to hold a major demonstration in Prague for equal suffrage and civil rights. A year later, the woman writer Bozena Vikova-Kuneticka was elected deputy of the Bohemian Diet (but she was prevented from holding the office by Austrian authorities).

Fully equal civic rights were embodied in the first constitution of independent Czechoslovakia, created in 1918 and enacted in 1920. Equal rights in the labour code, insurance system, and so on followed during the next decade. The last remnant of the patriarchal legal code, the formulation about gender roles within the family designating the 'head of the family', was removed shortly before the communist takeover in 1948. During the 1920s, women advanced rapidly in education, the professions, and politics. By the beginning of the 1930s, women constituted 30 per cent of the labour force and 25 per cent of the university student body. The number of women in parliament was not very high, about 10 per cent, but women's partisan activity was much higher. Legal norms and the social insurance system were considered to be some of the most progressive in Europe at that time (Garver 1986; David 1991). Interestingly, nobody knows how much this past has actually influenced the current situation. Would women start resisting vigorously if some of their 'self evident' civic rights, achieved in the past and now firmly established and taken for granted, were threatened?

My second subquestion concerns the reactive character of the conservative rhetoric, that is, the way in which it is a response to some of the specific conditions of transition, a 'backlash' without feminism. It is important to be aware of two facts: the communist gender arrangements had held sway since the 1950s – more than 40 years. As such, they brought about a sense of women's liberation based upon access to work. This is a much deeper, longer experience than the current backlash against it. Although this is one of the most frequently discussed themes among Eastern European and Western feminists, feminists have failed to ask themselves to what extent the experience of socialism could be compared to the first wave of Western feminism and in which sense the contemporary emphasis on the maternal role and on gender differences is analogous to the second wave of Western feminism. What is certainly confusing is the total absence of a feminist discourse under communism. However, I feel justified in asking whether in communist countries the two waves were not 'lived in reality', though tested under somewhat harsh conditions. The second fact of which we should be aware is that the conservative turn in Czech society started not after 1989 but in the early 1970s as a reaction to the 20-year communist practice of women's liberation and co-incided with the post-invasion retreat into the private sphere. Some theorists (for example, Wolchick 1979) argue that this turn was also brought about by the power elite to prevent population decline. This is only partly true. In fact, the changes in official ideology paralleled trends from below. The new legislation from the 1970s, enforcing the protection of motherhood, was not connected with any restriction of women's public advancement. Indeed, we can argue that in contrast to this elite-dominated perspective, the conservative trend in gender relations was not resisted by the population after 1989; on the contrary, the rhetoric was articulated as an anticommunist position.

What was the conservative rhetoric directed against? Generally speaking, it insisted that women should not have responsibility for too many things – for caring roles (which were assumed to be 'natural' under socialism), financial contribution to the family budget (that is, wage labour), and contraception. Czech women work because it is the social norm and because everyone expects women to contribute to the family finances while free abortion makes contraception a woman's responsibility. In other words, women's freedom to work outside the family and to decide about their bodies was turned partly against them in the sense that they took on employment as a duty (which their husbands would expect them to do) and that the men often rejected responsibility for contraception, for example in the use of condoms. In other words, the conservative rhetoric expresses the need to first of all correct the other extreme, unknown in the West, the caricature of freedom, which preceded it. An important part of this rhetoric is to challenge men's lack of responsibility. The idea is to liberate women in terms of giving them much more scope to develop what is believed to be their human potentialities, including tenderness, specific kinds of women's wisdom, and so on. Of course, there are also the so-called 'interests of society', meaning that many negative social phenomena like criminality, licentiousness, and a high divorce rate are ascribed to the suppression of feminine potentialities under communism. Women's 'abstractly civic' attitude in this connection is that they believe that to follow the interests of society includes, or at least does not exclude, women's deeper and truer liberation.

Nonetheless, when considering the possibilities of plausible feminist enlightenment in the Czech Republic, Joan Scott's (1990) notion of unmasking the power aspect in the reproduction of the binary opposition of equality and difference is applicable. In addition, we need to understand the pattern of thinking in a society where the private sphere and the family had and still have a specifically high status and are not seen as simply backward or conservative. In this respect, for example, Jean Elshtain's ideas on the reconstruction of the public and private – and in particular of the private – worlds can be very helpful (1981; cf. Havelkova 1993a; 1993b; 1995).

CONCLUSION

In countries such as the Czech Republic, two dramatic historical shifts – toward and then away from communism – structure the present reality in a multilayered, dialectic, often paradoxical way. We could say that these historical shifts have created two additional dimensions of each social phenomenon that must be taken seriously in theoretical attempts to grasp women's situation. Yet there is another message: these dimensions, particularly in the constellations in which they appear in Czech society, also obscure gender conflict and, moreover, allow women themselves to obscure and postpone conflict. This postponement can be both productive and counterproductive. With the emergence of more stable and transparent capitalist conditions and with the maturing of a new generation of young women who have experienced only the new conditions, Czech women will, no doubt, confess their thus far hidden feminist convictions. Nevertheless, their theoretical and practical struggles to find a new place for women will bear much of the legacy of the past, thus making the situation of Czech women and gender relations in Czech society retain some very specific and unique features. Generally speaking, this is true of all the post-communist countries in the sense that the configuration of their pre-communist, communist, and post-communist social patterns is unique for each and should not be automatically expected in the others. Theorists must not confuse the commonalities in power elite policies among these countries with the variety of life arrangements in them.

NOTE

1. In this connection, Western feminists often stress that there is not one but many feminisms. Though it is true that the knowledge of feminist theories is low in Eastern Europe, in the reluctance to accept 'feminism', there is a resistance against common features of all the feminisms, namely, against starting any analysis with a gender focus.

REFERENCES

Altos and Sopranos: A Pocket Handbook of Women's Organizations. (1995). English version, (ed.) Laura Busheikin and Amy Kolczak. Prague: Prague Gender Studies Centre.

Berkova, Alexandra (1993) 'Women on the Left? What Do You Say? Why?' *Reflex*, p. 65 Prague.

Cermakova, Marie (1995) 'Women in the Czech Society: Continuity or Change' in Marie Cermakova (ed.) *Women, Work and Society.* Working Papers pp. 1–17 Prague: Sociologicky ustav AV CR.

Cermakova, Marie, and Gatnar Lumir (1992) *Zeny v socialni strukture*, 1991 (Women in the social structure, 1991). Prague: Institute of Sociology of the Czechoslovak Academy of Sciences.

David, Katherine (1991) 'Czech Feminists and Nationalism in the Late Habsburg Monarchy: "The First in Austria"' *Journal of Women's History* 3, no. 2: 2645.

Eisenstein, Zillah (1993) 'Eastern European Male Democracies: A Problem of Unequal Equality' in N. Funk and M. Mueller (eds) *Gender Politics and Post-Communism* pp. 303–17. New York: Routledge, Chapman and Hall.

Elshtain, Jean Bethke (1981) *Public Man, Private Woman: Women In Social and Political Thought.* Princeton, N.J.: Princeton University Press.

Freeze, Karen Johnson (1986) 'Medical Education for Women in Austria: A Study in the Politics of the Czech Women's Movement in the 1890s' in Sharon Wolchik and Alfred Meyer (eds) *Women, State, and Party in Eastern Europe* pp. 51–63 Durham, N.C.: Duke University Press.

Funk, Nanette and Magda Mueller (eds) (1993) *Gender Politics and Post-Communism: Reflections from Eastern Europe and the Former Soviet Union.* New York: Routledge, Chapman, and Hall.

Garver, Bruce M. (1986) 'Women in the First Czechoslovak Republic' in Sharon Wolchik and Alfred Meyer (eds) *Women, State, and Party in Eastern Europe*, pp. 65–81 Durham, N.C.: Duke University Press.

Havelkova, Hana (1993a) 'A Few Prefeminist Thoughts' in (eds) N. Funk and M. Mueller *Gender Politics* and Post-Communism.

Havelkova, Hana (1993b) '"Patriarchy" in Czech Society' *Hypatia* 8, no. 4: 89 96.

Havelkova, Hana (1995) 'Family and Gender in the Changing Relationship between the Public and Private Spheres in Modern Society' in Marie Cermakova (ed.) *Women, Work and Society* Working Papers. Prague: Sociologicky ustav AV CR.

Hauserova, Eva (1992) 'About the Perspective of Feminism in Czechoslovakia' Unpublished manuscript.

Mozny, Ivo (1992) 'Can a State Work before Society Exists? (The Welfare State and State Skepticism)' in Leiv Ellingsen and Ulf Torgersen (eds) *What Kind of Safety Net? The Welfare State in Norway and Eastern European Countries* pp. 3249 INAS Rapport 92:6. Oslo: Institute for Applied Social Research.

Pokorny, Martin (1992) 'Obhajoba manzelstvi' [A defense of marriage]. *Prostor* 5, no. 20: 18–21 Prague.

Scott, Joan W. (1990) 'Deconstructing Equality versus Difference: Or, the Uses of Poststructuralist Theory for Feminism.' pp. 134–48 in Marianne Hirsch and Evelyn Fox Keller (eds) *Conflicts in Feminism*, New York: Routledge, Chapman and Hall.

Siklova, Jirina (1992) 'Zeny a politika' [Women and politics]. *Prostor* 5, no. 20: 23–9, Prague.

Statisticka rocenka Ceske republiky: Statisticky urad [Statistical yearbook of the Czech Republic: Office of statistics] (1994) Prague.

Tatur, Melanie (1992) 'Why Is There No Women's Movement in Eastern Europe?' in Paul G. Lewis (ed.) *Democracy and Civil Society in Eastern Europe: Selected Papers from the Fourth World Congress for Soviet and East European Studies, Harrogate, 1990* pp. 61–75 Macmillan: Basingstoke.

Wolchik, Sharon L. (1979) 'The Status of Women in a Socialist Order: Czechoslovakia, 1948–1978' *Slavic Review: American Quarterly of Soviet and East European Studies* 38, no. 4: 583–602.

5 Migrant and Ethnic Minority Women: The Effects of Gender-Neutral Legislation in the European Union

Wuokko Knocke

As the European Union continues to establish itself, though not without difficulties and under protest mainly from women and other subordinated groups, we are also witnessing the growing importance of questions related to immigrants and immigration. Among these, the securing of borders is a topic of high concern for all member states, while many issues relating to the social situation and rights of settled immigrants and minorities remain unresolved, especially where women are concerned. I will begin this article by pointing to some of the conceptual problems in this complex field and will then address some of the specific difficulties encountered by women. In particular, I will focus on the effects of legislation that regulates rights of settlement and work. A major question is whether existent formal processes contribute to the marginalization of immigrant and ethnic minority women in the EU.

CONCEPTUAL PROBLEMS AND MATTERS OF DEFINITION

There is to my knowledge no common agreement as to the appropriate *concepts for naming or categorizing* different groups of women migrants, either within or across countries. The first step is therefore to clarify which group of women we are referring to. Are they migrant, immigrant or ethnic minority women? Do we speak of the women who came, sometimes by themselves but mainly as wives or family members, in the wake of recruitment of a country's male workers, when the Western European economies had a shortage of unskilled labour? Do we also speak of political and humanitarian refugees, who are in need of shelter for some period of time? And do we speak of those who are leaving economic misery, demographic over-crowding, and political unrest in their home countries to find a livelihood in our welfare states, many of whom, with current re-strictions on immigration, are turned into 'illegals' and thus criminalized? Finally, in the context of the European Union, is the real dividing line between EU-nationals and nationals from outside the EU?

When speaking of names and categories, we must remember that the naming and categorizing is done by representatives of the 'host' countries, since in most countries immigrant popula-tions have no voice or public representation. Feminist scholars argue that the possibility of representing oneself and one's in-terests is a matter of having access to power (Jenson and Mahon 1992). Naming is also a way of exercizing power in that it socially defines and situates powerless groups in society (Knocke 1991). Moreover, as Barbara Czarniawska-Joerges (1994, 96) points out, 'people are helpless in face of the main instrument of power: language'. Yet, she adds, all hope lies in language, quoting among others a passage from Bronwyn Davies:

> Language is both a resource and a constraint. It makes social and personal being possible but it also limits the available forms of being to those which make sense within the terms provided by the language (1989:1; also in Czarniawska-Joerges, 1994:96–97).

Although the list could be considerably longer, the following dis-cussion provides a few examples of naming and categorizing. In the European or international discourse the most commonly used concepts are 'migrants' and 'ethnic minorities'. The first concept normally refers to persons, in this case women, who move from one country to another, not necessarily with the in-tention to settle permanently in that country (Wilbers 1990). But original intentions often change and those who came as mi-grants turn into immigrants, who settle permanently (Castles *et al.* 1984; Knocke 1986). The term ethnic minority women usually refers to women who are either born in the country of residence or who for other reasons have the nationality of that country but who are of different ethnic origin than the majority population. In some cases (for example Britain), 'ethnic' is in popular and even official discourse often identical with black or any shade of colour darker than white. Often in Europe, however, women belonging to an ethnic minority are born in a former colony of the 'mother country' or they are women belonging to an indigenous ethnic minority. The latter are by definition neither migrants nor immigrants.

Concepts used in both official and everyday discourse often reflect historical ties or the dominant ideological view of a country in relation to either its immigrant population or specific groups in that population. In Germany the term *Gastarbeiter* was introduced and is especially reserved for workers recruited from the Mediterranean countries in the 1950s and 1960s, and it underlines ideologically the temporariness of their stay. Even today, with a settled immigrant population of approximately 6.5 million persons, Germany denies being a country of immigration. In France, the term *immigré/es* is mainly used for immigrants originating in the Maghreb-countries (Algeria, Morocco and Tunisia), which are either former colonies or so-called protectorates of France. *Étrangers* or *Ausländer* are otherwise the most frequently used terms in France and Germany, respectively. The English equivalents (for example, foreigners or aliens) are also used in juridical contexts or demographic statistics to refer to persons who do not have the nationality of the country of residence (Wilbers 1990).

In summary, there is no unanimity in definitions or consistency in naming populations of migrants or those of different ethnic origins, either within or across countries. This obviously creates problems for data collection and research, especially for comparative analyses. International discussions of the immigration issue are difficult and will continue to be unless countries can agree on a common language.

In addition, most of the concepts still in use were developed during the period of post-World War II labour migration, which came to an end by 1974 in all Western European economies. In the 1990s, the motives for immigration and the composition of migratory flows are different. Migration issues in the present

European context therefore need reconceptualization. EURO-STAT, a data collection service, has started to produce statistics on immigrant populations and divides foreigners into two major categories, depending on whether or not they are nationals of a EU-country (OECD, 1991).

A more detailed and relevant categorization suggested by Marijke Wilbers (1990) includes five classifications:

1) EC/EU migrants/immigrants
2) non-EC/EU migrants/third-country nationals
3) ethnic minorities
4) refugees and asylum seekers
5) undocumented (so called illegal) migrants.

Inherent in Wilber's categorization are differences in legal rights with regard to entrance, settlement, access to the labour market, social rights and the right to free movement inside the European Union (as it is called since the Maastricht Treaty).[1]

EC/EU-MIGRANTS AND THIRD-COUNTRY NATIONALS

Since 1968, free movement of citizens of EC member states across community country borders has been a right for workers and their families. With the introduction of the Single European Market in 1992, the rights of EC/EU migrants and their families have been strengthened with regard both to work and social protection by Regulations and Recommendations from the Council of Ministers. The situation is different for third-country nationals. Free movement of citizens inside the EC/EU and migration from outside the member states or of third-country nationals between EC/EU member states are legally and politically different phenomena at EC/EU policy level. The Treaty of Rome limits EC/EU-Commission competence to the freedom of movement of EC/EU nationals, while the Commission is neither responsible for activities relating to safeguarding external borders nor for the 'harmonizing' of asylum and immigration policies between member states. In 1991 the European Council of Maastricht confirmed that only visa policies are to be determined by the Commission.[2] Currently, intensive talks are going on at intergovernmental ministerial levels are attempting to establish joint long-term objectives for immigration policies, 'to ensure that uncontrolled mass migration would not occur' and to come to a common policy with regard to asylum seekers and family reunification (Widgren 1993).

With the exception of free movement of EC/EU-citizens, migration issues have not been regulated at EC/EU-level. These questions are regarded as falling under the sovereignty of each member state. Neither is a migrant's worklife and social situation considered an issue to be regulated by the EC/EU. It is significant that migrants, immigrants and ethnic minorities are not even mentioned among the groups who are covered by the Social Charter for the protection of workers' rights. It was only after protest from immigrant populations that the following statement was included in the Charter's preamble:

> Whereas it is for the member States to guarantee that workers from non-member countries and members of their families who are legally resident in a Member State of the European Community are able to enjoy, as regards their living and working conditions, treatment comparable to that enjoyed by workers who are nationals of the Member State concerned.

Immigrant populations and the Migrants' Forum of the European Communities have expressed their concern that the rights of non-EC nationals are left entirely to the discretion of each individual member state. A host of empirical evidence indicates serious shortcomings in most member countries with regard to equality in social, political, economic and cultural rights between migrant and ethnic minority populations and the indigenous population. These concerns are therefore more than justified.

Some Facts and Figures

Before proceeding, it would be useful to consider some background statistics on immigrant women in the Community. At the end of the 1980s almost 6.5 million women of foreign nationality and/or women born outside their countries of residence were living in 11 of the 12 community countries. Spain is not included in these figures, but OECD (1991) reports for Spain the presence of 63 000 legally settled women in 1990, which corresponds to 0.3 per cent of the total population. Of foreign-born women in the EC almost 37 per cent came from other community countries, including the former labour exporting countries Spain and Portugal, who did not join the community until 1986. From non-EC countries, women from Turkey and the former Yugoslavia consituted the largest groups. Both countries had provided the economically developed parts of Europe with labour. The majority of women from non-European countries were from North-Africa, India and Pakistan, Indonesia and the Middle East.

These statistics were presented at a seminar on migrant women and their working lives, which summarized the combined efforts of the European Network of Experts on Women and Employment, (COM, V/1955/88). It is important, however, to emphasize that the figures do not represent the entire female population of migrant origin. Women who have acquired the nationality of the host country or women born in former colonies or territories are not included, nor are their children. Even less is known about the number of undocumented or so called illegal immigrants in the member states. Estimates, or rather guesstimates, indicate that there are several hundred thousand such persons – and probably more. Exact numbers are not available, nor is it known how many of them are women. A study conducted for the ILO reports growing numbers of 'illegal' women in unprotected domestic work, especially in Spain and Italy (Weinert 1991). There is also an increasing number of women among the undocumented migrants from the Eastern European countries to Germany (Morokvasic 1992).

Women's Derived Rights

Policies and regulations relating to the rights of migrant or immigrant populations vary among the member states. Yet, the effects of these regulations have much in common when it comes to women. The majority of legally settled women have lived and worked in their country of residence for many years, but surprisingly little is known about their living and working conditions. The lack of empirical data is deplored in reports produced at EC-level (COM, V/1955/88); my own experience, when trying to map their situation, confirms the absence or scarcity of data (Knocke 1994). Two reasons, connected but of different character, explain the lack of concrete data and analyses: (1) differences in methods in the collection of data and in the definition of the immigrant populations; (2) the invisibility and marginalization of migrant/immigrant women in the receiving countries.

I will comment particularly on the second point, since the first one is to a great extent a logical outcome of the second. Apart from negative attitudes and cultural stereotyping, a crucial way to understand the situation of women immigrants is to look at formal rights and legislation. Legal frameworks regulating immigration are in themselves gender neutral. In principle, they apply equally to women and men. In reality, the outcome differs greatly for the two sexes. This has been pointed out in research (for example Phizacklea 1983: 2; Morokvasic 1992) and is been confirmed in a Communication from the EC commission:

> The existing legislation on migrants has been drafted on the assumption that, generally, migrant workers are men, and tends to see migrant women as dependent spouses. Women arriving in their host countries as dependents following family reunification, experience greater problems than their husbands already settled in the country in procuring work permits, and in extending these to the full range of occupations (COM (88) 743, 1988).

Women migrants are simply not considered independent legal subjects, nor are they counted as an active part of the immigrant population. Migration to the Western European economies was initially mainly male, since men were recruited and welcomed as workers. Contrary to popular beliefs, many women also arrived as independent migrants, for example, Irish women to England and Finnish women to Sweden. Although most women travelled to join their husbands in the framework of family reunion, they came with their own emancipatory project, namely to become wage earners (Morokvasic 1983; Knocke 1986). Yet in most countries (Sweden being an exception), male migrants, as first arrivals and workers, received a residence and work permit, while women were only given derived rights with regard to residence and work. Annie Phizacklea (1983) and Shirley Dex (1983) issued 'early warnings' of the inferior position of immigrant women, due partly to the definition of them as primarily wives and mothers, dependents of the male breadwinner. More recent research has shown that the ideological notion of the male-breadwinner model still determines the position and legal status of immigrant women (Pillinger 1992). Although entire volumes of scholarly journals and books have been dedicated to immigrant women's labour market participation (for example Phizacklea 1983; IMR 1984; Simon and Bretell 1986), the economic activity of both single and married immigrant women is still considered a marginal and accidental phenomenon.

Legislation not only creates difficulties for women looking for jobs on the open labour market. The fundamental right of family reunion is often provisional, surrounded by a web of regulations (for example long waiting periods, access to suitable housing, dependent on the number of years married and the number of years at work for the first arrived), all of which delay or make it difficult for women to join their husbands. Consider just a few examples. In Germany, a waiting period lasting of from one to three years is imposed before the spouse (usually the wife) can join the first-arrived, economically active partner. Since December 1981, the spouse of a second generation immigrant can immigrate only if the first arrived has been settled for eight or more years and the couple has been married for at least one year. For a work permit, four years of settlement by the first arrived are required before the spouse may join. The period may be shortened to two or three years, depending on the labour market situation and the economic sector in which work is sought.[3] Waiting periods for a work permit also differ depending on country of origin. For Turkish spouses the waiting period is still three years. The waiting periods of eighteen months for Greek and three years for Spanish spouses were abolished when the countries joined the European Community (COM V/676/86–FR).

In the Netherlands one year of settlement and work are required before the spouse can join the first arrived. On the other hand, suitable living quarters are required before reunification is permitted and the suitability of living quarters is judged by the local Dutch authorities. In the Netherlands, the employer must be licensed to hire foreign workers, and the foreign worker is tied to a specific employer unless an exemption is granted. The work permit of the wife depends on the type of work permit that has been issued to the husband. If the husband has been granted exemption, she too has free access to the labour market, otherwise she is tied to a specific employer (COM V/676/86).

Unlike the other European countries, until 1992 Denmark had allowed immediate entry to the country for the spouse and children up to 18 years of age. The joining spouse was also entitled to a work permit, and the permit was not dependent on the status of the first arrived. Since 1992 non EC/EU nationals must have been settled in Denmark for five years before the spouse can join. The first arrived must also prove able to support economically the joining spouse.[4] There is now no special waiting period imposed for a work permit. Second generation immigrants, both women and men, have the right to be joined by their foreign partners. Irrespective of sex, they are also entitled to their own work permit, which allows them to look for jobs on the regular labour market.

The legal frameworks that regulate immigration and the rights of immigrants rest more or less implicitly on the ideology of the male breadwinner model. Male migrants, who normally were the first arrived, received a residence and work permit. Since women are only granted *derived* rights of settlement and work, they have ended up in socially invisible and economically vulnerable, marginalized positions, which is also reflected in the absence of data. Thus, even though the legislation is gender neutral for example, in the use of the term 'spouse'), in practice the legislation promotes *indirect discrimination* against women. In the event of a divorce or the death of the husband, a woman has no access to the open labour market to earn a living for herself and her children and she runs the risk of losing her right of residence, even after many years of settlement.

Low-wage Jobs and Unprotected Women

Due to their secondary legal status and the absence of a work permit, even legally settled immigrant women are often compelled, at least initially, to accept whatever employment they can find. They work in low-wage, undeclared jobs in the black economy – for example, in the domestic service industry, in catering, cleaning, and homeworking in the clothing industry –

where many of them get trapped. They find themselves in jobs that are not covered by social protection or labour legislation. They are not registered in any labour market statistics. The confinement of women to such jobs is confirmed in a report to the EC Commission, which states that 'restrictions on lawful entry to the labour market do not have the effect of preventing activity, but rather of making it illegal and of confining it to those sectors in which illegal work is easiest.' (COM, V/902/1988:15)

I will now turn to some aspects of immigrant women's work situation by first presenting labour market participation rates for foreign women in selected countries of the European Community.

Table 5.1 was presented by the EC Network of Experts on Women in Employment, who met at a seminar in Brussels in August 1987 to summarize country reports on migrant women's working lives.[5] This table resembles a beautiful Swiss cheese that, when you cut it up, is full of holes. Yet it illustrates several important facts.

First, data about foreign women's labour market participation by nationality and/or by other relevant categories are either not collected or are scarce in many community countries.

Second, for five member countries no activity rates are presented at all. Data for Denmark and France cover the full range

Table 5.1   Economic Activity Rates of Foreign Women; Selected Nationalities. Early 1980s, percentages

Settled in	All Foreign	Turkey	Morocco EC, Total	Yugoslavia	Foreign	Italy	Cap Verde
Belgium	22.5	13.3	10.3	25.2	—	26.9	—
FRG	52.5	43.6	—	70.3	—	55.3	—
Denmark	60.0	61.4	49.0	74.1	58.6	48.3	—
France	33.1	18.9	20.5	63.9	43.5	26.3	—
Italy	27.2	—	—	31.0	—	—	—
Netherlands	—	40.1	16.0	—	—	—	—
Portugal	—	—	—	—	—	—	32.5

Source: COM V/1955/88; figures are for different years in the early 1980s and for different age groups or unspecified age groups.

of nationalities or categories mentioned. Denmark keeps accurate statistics, as apparently does France. We should keep in mind that certain nationalities may not be present at all or only in very low numbers in some countries, which may explain their absence from the statistics; for example women from Cap Verde are typically present – or presented – only for Portugal, because Cap Verde is a former colony of Portugal.

Third, in countries where legal access to the labour market is difficult, women who have resorted to jobs on the black market remain invisible in the statistics. Available statistics therefore give only an indication of the minimum number of migrant women in the labour force. The exception is Denmark, where legal access to the labour market is relatively easy.

A final interesting observation in relation to this table relates to cultural stereotyping. Immigrant or ethnic minority women's low activity rates are often explained by pointing to their cultural background. I do not suggest that culture, correctly defined, does not matter. It is difficult to explain, however, why cultural background would matter so much for Turkish women in Belgium and France, where participation rates are very low, while their cultural background would seem to be less important in the Netherlands and Germany and not at all important in Denmark. Similar discrepancies are evident in Moroccan women's patterns of work and, more surprisingly, for women from the former Yugoslavia, who with the exception of Belgium and Italy, have the highest participation rates.[6] I would argue that cultural background determines foreign female labour activity less than factors in the host country. In other words, factors such as structural labour market needs, negative attitudes, stereotyped images and discrimination against women as *foreigners* in combination with general attitudes towards *women's paid labour* seem to have greater bearing. Where national women have high labour market participation rates, immigrant and ethnic minority women also have high rates. Since migrants come in two kinds, women and men, the working of gendered ideologies and the sex segregation of the labour market are simultaneous phenomena that add to the difficulties encountered by immigrant and ethnic minority women.

Thus, neither employment nor unemployment statistics tell the whole story of immigrant and minority women's labour market situation. Unemployment rates are misleading, for

Table 5.2 Unemployment Rates of Foreign Women Compared to all Women. Early 1980s, percentages

Settled in	All Women	All Foreign women	EC, Total	Turkey:	Suri-nam	West-Indian, Guyana	India, Pakistan, Bangladesh	Cap Verde
France	11.4*	20.0	—	—	—	—	—	—
Belgium	—	27.4	—	39.7	—	—	—	—
FRG	10.6*	16.9	—	—	—	—	—	—
Denm.	13.5	23.8	16.0	41.1	—	—	—	—
Netherlands	—	—	—	27.0	30.0	—	—	—
Portugal	11.8	—	—	—	—	—	—	—
UK	10.5	—	—	—	—	16.6	20.8	—

Source: COM V/1955/88

*Except foreign women. Rates refer to different years between 1981 and 1984. Unemployment for Turkish women in Denmark had risen to 55.7 per cent in 1991.

when women wish to work but do not have work permits, they may not register as unemployed – nor do they qualify for unemployment benefits. Moreover, there is little information on legal or 'illegal' women who work in undeclared jobs in the black economy. Unemployment statistics therefore do not reflect their labour market situation or the true demand for work from jobless immigrant women.

Table 5.2 also illustrates the lack of statistics. Where comparative figures exist, unemployment rates for foreign women are always higher and often substantially higher than for national women. The summary report on the worklife situation of migrant women, from which the table is derived, restates the earlier point: statistical data deal very little or not at all with the situation of employment, unemployment, incomes and education of migrant and ethnic minority women (COM V/1955/88, 28).

CONCLUSION

While awareness of cultural diversity and different social realities is growing in the European Union, important questions remain about old and new patterns of segregation. In their book *Woman, Nation, State* Nira Yuval-Davis and Floya Anthias (1989) argue that an understanding of how national and ethnic processes intersect is relevant not only in relation to subordinate collectivities, since, as Yuval-Davis and Anthias argue, 'they constitute a feature of social processes in general, and are therefore relevant to the discussion of majority dominant collectivities' as well. For example, a theoretically interesting question in the current context of the EU is what immigrant and ethnic minority women's position and function will be in the social formations and labour markets and how national women's increasing entry into the labour market intersects with the position of immigrant women. Which economic sectors and what kinds of jobs are immigrant women needed for? Previously the demand was for female workers for unskilled, low-paid industrial jobs that now are disappearing. Immigrant women were also needed in service jobs such as in hotel and catering, as cleaners and kitchen aids, in low-hierarchy caring and hospital jobs. This is still partly the case, although cut-downs and economic saving plans are increasingly turning into a threat to their employment in these sectors.

Where are the new job openings for immigrant women at present? Over the two last decades, more and more national women in the EC/EU-countries are entering the labour market, while social support structures for working mothers (for example, child care provision, care of the sick and elderly, paid parental leave) are still very underdeveloped, except in Denmark and Sweden. Figures from Spain and Italy indicate that growing numbers of migrant women, both legally settled and 'illegal', women, are employed as domestic workers, in other household-oriented services and as childminders. A great number have neither been given residence rights, a work permit or a work contract with the employers. Even when legally settled, many are paid at rates below the national minimum wage, they are not covered by social security, by labour legislation or against health hazards. Present trends indicate that they are increasingly becoming part of the support structure, which allows national women to take on regular (better paid) jobs in the open labour market. There is, it seems, a link between national women's growing economic activity and the labour market function of migrant and immigrant women.

Migrant and immigrant women are replacing the kind of social services that in Denmark and Sweden have been offered by the welfare state through public sector provision. It is only recently, and often still reluctantly, that women and feminist scholars in Europe have started to recognize the truth of the argument made by women of colour in North America, namely, that women participate in the oppression and exploitation of women from other ethnic groups as well as from other economic classes (for example hooks 1984; Bannerji 1987; Yuval-Davis and Anthias 1989; Knocke 1991)[7].

This development points to the the the risk that we are witnessing the growth of a new ethnically defined female underclass. Most welfare states in the EU are still reluctant to develop support structures for working women. Unless women of the dominant majorities start locating their interests in a more long-term inter-ethnic and cross-class perspective, they will contribute to the exploitation of immigrant and ethnic minority women. I argued earlier that immigrant and minority women's dependent and secondary legal status is to a large extent the result of the male breadwinner doctrine. In the European Union, the ongoing struggle of women and women's networks for individual social rights, instead of family or household based rights, is basically a struggle against the male breadwinner doctrine, since deficiencies in social support structures and welfare state provisions can be traced back to this ideology. In this struggle, majority and minority women's interests intersect, despite different social realities and origins. Therefore, to avoid the creation of a new ethnically defined female underclass, the common struggle should focus first and foremost on dismantling the ideology of the male breadwinner, because it places all women in a secondary status and makes them dependent on men (Borchorst 1991).

NOTES

1. I will use EC/EU to indicate that processes described are essentially the same both before and after Maastricht.
2. The listing of countries used by the Commission to determine visa-requirements, comes from the Schengen group, which is now installing an elaborate data base system for border control of foreigners. Only Denmark, Ireland and the UK are today outside the Schengen group.
3. Within this general framework, the different Bundesländer can have their own provisions.
4. This provision does not apply to refugees.
5. More precise figures on activity rates are available for EC and non-EC women thanks to a special analysis of EUROSTAT data for 1987 by the OECD (1991) for six countries (B, F, D, L, N, the UK). When activity rates are controlled for by age, the analysis shows that foreign women from EC-countries have in general higher activity rates than other foreign women. In all countries the rate for non-EC foreign women is considerably lower than the rate for both EC-women and national women.
6. In Sweden too, women from ex-Yugoslavia have until recently had among the highest activity rates among foreign nationals, 77.5 per cent in 1988. The present recession and industrial restructuring has over the last few years reduced their activity rate to 54.3 per cent in 1993.
7. Feminist scholars have noted the objections by black and coloured women against the universalization of white women's realities to women in general (for example Harding 1986). A warning against the institutionalization of scientific 'truths' on the basis of feminist research has also been issued by Dorothy Smith (1987).

REFERENCES

Bannerji, Himani. (1987) 'Introducing racism: Notes towards an Anti-racist Feminism.' *Resources for Feminist Research: A Canadian Journal for Feminist Scholarship*, Vol. 16, no. 1:10–13.

Borchorst, Anette (1991) 'Europaeisk integration, konsarbejdsdelning og ligestillingspolitik' Netherlands Aarhus universitet: Institut for Statskunskab.

Castles, Stephen, Heather Booth and Tina Wallace (1984). *Here For Good. Western Europe's New Ethnic Minorities*. London: Pluto Press.

Czarniawska-Joerges, Barbara (1994) 'Editorial: Modern Organizations and Pandora's Box', *Scandinavian Journal of Management*, Vol. 10, no. 2: 95–8.

Davies, Bronwyn (1989) *Frogs and snails and feminist tales. Gender and preschool children*. Australia: Sydney: Unwin and Allen

Dex, Shirley (1983) 'The Second Generation: West Indian Female School-Leavers' in A. Phizacklea (ed.) *One Way Ticket. Migration and Female Labour* pp. 53–71. London: Routledge & Kegan Paul.

European Community Commission (1986) 'Les Discriminations et Difficultés Juridiques pour l'Emploi des Femmes Étrangères' V/676/86–FR. Rapport élaborée par IRFECD * Europe, Brussels: EC Commission.

European Community Commission (1987a) 'Migrant Women and Employment' V/902/88. Brussels: EC Commission.

European Community Commission (1987b) 'Migrant Women in the European Community with Particular Reference to their Working Lives' V/1955/88. Summary report on the situation in the Member States. Copenhagen.

European Community Commission (1988) 'The Social Situation and Employment of Migrant Women' (88) 743. Communication from the Commission, Brussels: ECC.

Harding, Sandra (1986) *The Science Question in Feminism*. Milton Keynes: Open University Press.

hooks, Bell (1984) *Feminist Theory: From Margin to Center*. Boston: South End Press.

International Migration Review (1984) *Special Issue: Women in Migration*. Vol. 18, no. 4, Staten Island, N.Y.: Center for Migration Studies.

Jenson, Jane, and Rianne, Mahon (1992) 'Representing Solidarity: Class, Gender and the Crisis of Social Democratic Sweden' Paper presented at Eighth International Conference of Europeanists, Chicago, Illinois.

Knocke, Wuokko (1986) *Invandrade kvinnor i lönearbete och fack*. Stockholm: Arbetslivscentrum.

Knocke, Wuokko (1991) 'Women Immigrants – What is the 'Problem?'', *Economic and Industrial Democracy*, Vol. 12. n. 4: 469–486.

Knocke, Wuokko (1994) *Tendenser och utveckling på kvinnornas arbetsmarknad inom den europeiska gemenskapen*. Working paper, Stockholm: Arbetslivscentrum.

Morokvasic, Mirjana (1983) 'Women in Migration: Beyond the Reductionist Outlook' in A. Phizacklea (ed.) *One Way Ticket*. pp. 13–31 London: Routledge & Kegan Paul

Morokvasic, Mirjana (1992) 'New Dimensions of Migration in Europe and Gender' Paper presented at the conference 'Mass Migration in Europe', Vienna.

Organization for Economic Cooperation and Development (OECD) (1991) *Continuous Reporting System on Migration*. SOPEMI 1990, Paris: OECD.

Phizacklea, Annie (ed.) (1983) *One Way Ticket. Migration and Female Labour*. London: Routledge & Kegan Paul.

Pillinger, Jane(1992) *Feminising the Market. Women's Pay and Employment in the European Community*. London: Macmillan.

Simon, Rita J. and Caroline B. Bretell (eds) (1986) *International Migration. The Female Experience*. Totowa, NJ: Rowman and Allanheld

Smith, D. (1987) *The Everyday World as Problematic: A Feminist Sociology*. Boston, Mass.: Northeastern University Press.

Weinert, Patricia (1991) *Foreign Female Domestic Workers: Help Wanted!* Working paper, Geneva: International Labour Organiztion.

Widgren, Jonas (1993) 'The Need for a New Multilateral Order to Prevent Mass Movements form Becoming a Security Threat in Europe' Paper presented at the conference 'New Mobilities. Element of European Integration' Berlin.

Wilbers, Marijke (1990) *The Labour Market and Housing Situation of Migrants and Ethnic Minorities in Europe*. Maastricht: European Centre for Work and Society.

Yuval-Davis, Nira and Anthias Floya (eds) (1989) *Woman, Nation, State*. London: Macmillan.

6 Patriarchies and Feminisms: The Two Women's Movements of Post-Unification Germany

Myra Marx Ferree[1]

In the nearly five years that have passed since the Berlin Wall was opened with such initial hope and joy, there have been many accounts of the enormous problems that have swept now-unified Germany. Unemployment and anomie in the East (ex-GDR), higher taxes and greater competition in the West, and a resurgent racism on both sides of the former Wall have tempered the mood of celebration. Although many did foretell the costs, particularly for women, the extent of these problems has been sobering for all. The phrase that 'women are the losers of the unification' has become virtually a cliché, reflecting the reality that women have an official unemployment rate (over 20 per cent) that is virtually twice as high as men's, that rises in the cost of living and the end to subsidies for basic goods have widened the gap in standards of living, leaving those with lower incomes (often women) relatively worse off, and that benefits such as childcare leave and kindergarten subsidies have been slashed (Bialas and Ettl 1993), not to mention the change in abortion law that has cost ex-GDR women their prior right to abortion on demand in the first trimester (see other articles in this book).

In this painful situation, feminists both in the East and West have been actively drawing attention to women's problems, but have found it surprisingly difficult to establish a common ground from which to combat them. This chapter attempts to analyze certain aspects of these problems of mutual understanding that have arisen between East and West German feminists in particular and East and West German women more generally. It argues that some of these tensions and incomprehensions may have their roots in the different structures of state policy in the two post-war Germanies and the resulting differences in women's experiences and collective identities. In this sense, the conflicts between East and West German feminists can be understood as a specific case of a more general problem of feminist identity. Other conflicts over feminist identity – such as those between White and Black feminists in the United States or between First and Third World feminists globally – may both illuminate and be illuminated by consideration of the dynamics of this specific case.

I suggest that these broader questions of conflict over interpretations of feminism may often be rooted in different experiences of women with the state. States and state policies play a major role in systematically shaping women's experiences of paid work, marriage and motherhood. Their effects may be seen in part in the interpretations of oppression and freedom that women construct based on such personal and deeply felt experiences.

It is important to make clear at the outset that I am not arguing for a simplistic translation of women's experience into the politics of feminism in general, or in either portion of Germany specifically. In both East and West, there has been a complex process of debate both among feminists and between feminists and others that has contributed to shaping the understanding of what goals the women's movement stands for and what means it wishes to employ (Hampele 1993; Gerhard *et al.* 1990). In each locus of debate there arises what I call a 'collective self-representation' of feminism, that is, a shared and yet personal sense of what a collective identity as a feminist means. Such a collective identity links an interpretation of the past – what are women's experiences – to an interpretation of the future – what are women's aspirations. Collective identity is thus neither just a reflection of past experience nor independent of it, but an actively constructed interpretation of shared history (Melucci 1988; Taylor and Whittier 1992).

Such collective self-representation of feminism is different in important ways in each portion of Germany, I contend, and some of these differences arise from the nature of women's experiences of patriarchy when there were still two different countries. At the root, each system was organized around a fundamentally different sort of patriarchy. Following the lead offered by some feminist theorists of the welfare state (Siim 1987; Brown 1987; see also articles in Jonasdottir and Jones 1988 and Sassoon 1987), I distinguish between what has been called public and private patriarchy. At an abstract level, most analysts of gender oppression would agree that patriarchal power is both private and public and that both intrafamilial relations and state politics are arenas in which women's subordination is constructed and male domination exercised on a daily basis. At a practical level, however, one or the other form of patriarchy may dominate certain women's concrete experiences and thus carry a disproportionate weight in the explanations of oppression and aspirations for freedom that these women develop for themselves – what Mansbridge (1994) calls the 'street theory' of feminism and that I refer to as their collective self-representation.

My core argument is that such practical feminisms arising in the two post-war Germanies reflected women's efforts to interpret experiences that were fundamentally different because they were predominantly structured by a different type of patriarchial state system: one that reflects principles of public or of private patriarchy. Because of this, mutual incomprehension, misunderstanding and recriminations have become commonplace among feminists in the united Germany (cf. Holland-Cunz 1990; Helwerth and Schwarz 1993; Rohnstock 1994). Even when there is a shared self-identification as 'feminist,' there is often a different interpretation of what this term means. Some of the sources of these unanticipated misunderstandings and difficulties in communication arise from experiences of domination, competition, or recriminations in the period after unification; while these are also important, they are not my focus here (see Ferree 1992 for a fuller examination of these issues). In this paper, I limit my consideration to factors that were already there before the Wall ever fell, differences that arise from the different structures of state policy in each country, and the resulting differences in women's experiences and collective identity.

THE TWO GERMANIES AND THEIR POLICIES

The distinction between public and private patriarchy rests fundamentally on the role of the state as either supplanting or supporting the conventional authority and practical power of the individual male as head of household. The state socialism of the GDR supplanted the individual male head and so embodied principles of public patriarchy; the state policies underpinning the social market economy of the FRG are, in contrast, strongly oriented to sustaining private patriarchy. The issue defining this distinction is not whether the state is more or less influential in women's lives, but rather the nature of the effects that it strives for and accomplishes.

In the GDR state policy tended to diminish the dependence of women on individual husbands and fathers but to enhance the dependence of women as mothers directly on the state (Ferree 1993; Bastian, Labsch and Müller 1990). In the FRG state policy follows the principle of subsidiarity and actively encourages private dependencies. In particular, it has a mandate to preserve 'the family', which it understands primarily to be the husband–wife relationship as a context in which children can be raised (Moeller 1993; Ostner 1994). Thus, overall, the nature of the state's role in public patriarchy is to emphasize the direct relationship of mothers to the state, and the nature of the state's role in private patriarchy is to encourage the dependency of wives on husbands and children on parents. In turn, this means that in public patriarchy, women experience their oppression as mothers, and as more directly connected to the activities of the state as patriarch; in private patriarchy, women experience their oppression as wives, and as more directly connected to their individual dependency on their spouses.

To make these abstractions more concrete, compare the nature of women's ordinary life experiences in the two systems. In the former GDR, approximately a third of all babies were born outside marriage, virtually all women were in the labour force and worked essentially full-time jobs, where they earned 40 per cent of the family income on average. Out-of-home child care for children aged under three and kindergartens and after-school care for older children were universally available at low cost (which one should note is an exception among socialist as well as nonsocialist countries). Subsidies from the state for child care, rent and other basic necessities reduced differences in standard of living between single mothers and two-parent, two-income families. Divorce was easy to obtain, women were the ones who primarily petitioned for divorce, and the divorce rate was the highest in the world.[2] Dependence on an individual husband appears to be reduced to a minimum.

By contrast, in the FRG, 90 per cent of babies are born within marriages. Living together is not uncommon, but when the baby comes, so does marriage (87 per cent of cohabiting relationships are childless compared to 18 per cent of marriages). Having a child is structurally inconsistent with having a full-time job, given the short and irregular school hours and scarcity of child care for pre-school children. There are child care places for less than 5 per cent of children under three years old. Of all women aged 30 to 50, only a third have full-time jobs; on the other hand, 15 per cent of women aged 40–50 are childless. A majority of employed mothers interrupt their careers for at least six years; even mothers of older children (15+) are less likely than non-mothers to be in the labour force at all, not even considering the reductions they face in the hours they work or the status of their jobs. Given their restricted labour force participation, it is not surprising that West German women provide on average only 18 per cent of the family income and that the majority of employed women do not earn enough to support themselves independently, let alone raise a child. Tax subsidies such as income splitting further widen the gulf between the standard of living of two-parent families and single mothers; if a mother is confronted with the choice of keeping her job or keeping her marriage, the economic incentives strongly favour the latter.[3] Dependence on an individual husband is strongly institutionalized.

These differences are well-known. The problem of how they play themselves out in feminist identity and analysis is less obvious. There are several distinct areas where I think the differences between public and private patriarchy, and thus the structurally different experiences of dependency and oppression, were expressed in the specifics of feminist consciousness and politics before unification and which still carry a residue into current interactions.

FEMINIST IDENTITY AND STRUCTURES OF EXPERIENCE

The most central difference relevant for feminism may be how women's own identities are shaped in relation to the dominant

form of patriarchy in general and how it has been institutionalized. In the West, there is a conceptual package invoked by the
phrase 'wife – mother'; these two roles are treated as bundled
together and virtually inseparable. This conceptualization does
not carry over easily to the East where motherhood is not so
structurally bound to wifehood. Thinking about mothers in the
FRG shades easily into imagining them only as wives; one needs
to specify 'single mother' and in doing so, one invokes the
image of mothers who are politically and culturally deviant as
well as impoverished. In the East, the imagery of single mother
was not so necessary: women were mothers and workers and
they may or may not have chosen to be or stay married. It is not
an identity that carries a connotation of victimhood, deviance
or struggle.

The imagery of 'woman' is more shaped by the wife role in
the West: both her tenuous connection to the labour force and
her need to attend to her appearance and to the care of the
household, to be sexually attractive to and able to depend on an
individual man is the 'conventional' picture of womanhood.
Women's magazines instruct their readers in how they can
achieve the current style of satisfying their husband's needs.
Identity is expressed in 'lifestyle', which for most women
means the nature of their consumer activities and personal
appearance.

For ex-GDR women, the conventional woman was not at the
disposal of an individual man but instrumentalized by the state
as patriarch. The image of woman is thus the 'worker–mother'
who contributes both reproductive and productive labour to a
collectively male-defined state. The concept of worker–mother
appears to have been as much a self-evident package as the
Western concept of wife–mother; the ability to combine paid
employment and motherhood was hardly more questioned than
the ability to combine wife and mother roles was in the West. In
both the conventional image and the self-understanding of
GDR women, wifeness is much less salient than the fact of
working. Not only did the GDR woman's constant work at home
and in the labour force take precedence over her appearance or
the appearance of her home in the perceptions others have of
her, but she identified her children and her job as her achievements, not her spouse or her home. Consumption was a chore,
not a means to identity and self-expression. That this was an

issue of identity, not merely deprivation of consumer goods is suggested by the collapse of Western-style women's magazines in ex-GDR markets; indeed, the West German firm that bought the largest existing women's magazine in the GDR and tried to use it to market 'glamour' to ex-GDR women after unification largely failed to attract an audience, and within a year the magazine collapsed.

The exaggerations and stereotypes of each version of womanhood are distorted reflections of these differently organized patriarchal demands: on the one side, the wife of leisure working on her appearance waiting for her husband to come home; on the other, the single mother with a career who has the help and support of the state to do it all. Note that from each side, the dependency of the other woman is idealized; husbands support 'their' wives, the state supports 'its' mothers, and neither patriarch asks anything in return. Envy of the 'ease' and generous support offered to women in the other way of life was a theme that could be used politically on both sides of the wall. From inside either public or private patriarchy, it was never so simple, of course. However, the price that was paid for each of these 'privileged' ways of life was more evident to the women paying it than to the women whose personal experience was with patriarchy of a different sort.

In reality, neither public nor private patriarchy constitutes liberation for women, but each does tend to shift the focus of women's attention to different aspects of their oppression. In the context of private patriarchy, the family, sexuality and relations between husbands and wives are initially at the forefront of theorizing (see, for example, Janssen-Jurreit 1976; Millett 1970; Friedan 1963). The initial feminist idea is that if relationships between individual men and individual women could be put on a different footing, this would lead to structural change and vice versa – the structural changes that are sought are those that would change the balance of power within familial relationships. Power relationships within the family are often problematized and are seen as 'spilling over' into the rest of social organization. In fact, rejecting marriage and seeking full-time employment, in the context of private patriarchy, are ways for women to live out a challenge to the status quo.

In the context of public patriarchy, the role of public policy and the state is more immediately central and visible. The male domination of political decision-making in all areas, the role of the state as 'guardian', one who speaks for women rather than allowing them to speak for themselves, the felt absence of collective political voice: these are all aspects of the sense of powerlessness that are directly evident in the experience of women's subordination by collective rather than individual male power. Power relations within the family, if problematized at all, are seen as stemming from more fundamental policies and decisions taken at the public political level. Private relationships – whether lesbian or heterosexual – are experienced as irrelevant or secondary in comparison (see for example documents such as Merkel *et al.* 1990, and accounts of early GDR autonomous feminism in Kahlau 1990; Hampele 1991). The common theme of feminist critiques is that women are 'instrumentalized' by the state, and it is state power that must be challenged.

Neither of these experientially grounded perceptions is wholly wrong. Both the family and the state are arenas in which women's power and self-determination are abridged and where efforts to reconstitute social relations along less patriarchal lines are essential to the feminist project. However, each form of organization of patriarchy tends to encourage one distinctively one-sided form of analysis or the other because each 'fits' and explains certain gut-level experiences of oppression better. What is particularly interesting and instructive, albeit painful, is the collision between these two understandings. The double vision of feminism

Unlike the other Eastern European countries, the GDR in the 1980s had a slowly emerging feminist movement that became mobilized during the course of the transition and played an active political role in the process of its restructuring. This movement largely demobilized as the reform of the GDR was transformed into its absorption into the Federal Republic (Ferree 1994). In West Germany, there has been an active autonomous feminist movement and a variety of local feminist projects since the early 1970s (Ferree 1987). Because of German unification, there are two differently grounded feminist identities that arose in these differently organized social contexts but that now have to share the same political space. Both sides have a tendency to disparage the degree of feminist understanding of the other: backward, hypocritical, arrogant, atheoretical, callous, naive, hypersensitive, know-it-all – the charges and countercharges go on and on, unfortunately cast primarily in terms of the individual or collective personalities of the 'other'. The attempt to define 'better' and 'worse' feminists, and in the process to defend one's own version of feminism as 'more true' ultimately founders however, on the reality of difference.

This reality is that the contexts of public and of private patriarchy, separate national experiences which were being independently theorized and from which two different women's movements emerged at two different times, are in practice differing organizations of oppression. What 'feels true' as a collective self-representation has to resonate with each woman's experience of her own oppression to be accepted, and that feeling depends on this fundamental political structuring of personal experience. Given such different ways of structuring experience as public and private patriarchy, what 'feels true' to a woman raised in one system will be likely to 'feel alien' to a woman whose identity has been formed in the other. Because an authentic feminist politics has to 'feel true', it cannot – and should not – aspire to universal priorities or any single dimension of 'correctness'. Although sustaining a view of feminism as intrinsically multiple in its analyses and emphases is difficult, it enriches and strengthens feminist practice. This argues for attempting to preserve as much of the perspective that arose out of the experience of public patriarchy in the GDR as possible – not only for the insights it generates into the contradictions and identity processes of such a system for women, but also because it offers a form of valuable insight into features of private patriarchy that women who live under it might otherwise tend to take for granted and allow to become theoretically invisible. Moreover, the comparison suggests the extent of analytical problems that East German women will have to overcome as they attempt to grapple with understanding the costs and benefits of the new, imposed status of dependent wife.

Contrasts such as these help to expose the experiential preconditions of feminist theorizing, and thus to broaden and differentiate theories. Western European and North American feminists have already learned much from such critical contrasts drawn by women in Third World countries and from the differences in experience and interpretation between women of dominant and subordinate ethnic and racial groups in the industrialized countries. The common ethnicity and developed industrial economies that existed on both sides of the Wall may have made German feminists underestimate the difficulties of communication and the gulf in experience and identity that was still to be bridged when the Wall fell. The sheer unexpectedness of such fundamental differences blocked many attempts to listen to and learn from theory grounded in a significantly different structuring of women's lives. Nonetheless, the contrast between public and private patriarchy now being painfully articulated between East and West is worth attending to, rather than wishing away, because it may bind together a number of common experiences across specific situations.

One of the most interesting of these potential analogies may be the way in which Black feminist thought has also attempted to come to terms with the greater significance of public patriarchy in African-American women's lives than in the lives of White American women. Using such an analogy should not be interpreted to suggest that African-American women's experience with a racist state is in any way identical to East German women's experience in the GDR, but to indicate that some of the elements that define public patriarchy, especially the direct relation of mothers to the state, may be responsible for similarities in identity and perspective that would otherwise be very surprising. Thus despite dramatic differences in economic opportunity, family poverty and social devaluation, among many other things, there are some points where Black feminist thought touches closely on issues that GDR women have also been attempting to express (the best summary of the diverse insights that characterize Black feminist thought is Collins 1990). Such surprising commonalities need some explanation, and one possibility is that they reflect some general characteristics of difference between public and private patriarchy.

First, there has been a tendency for East German feminists to talk more positively about the family and to see a challenge for feminism in integrating men more fully into family life. In comparison to women under private patriarchy, they did not see men's exclusion from the family as offering a good in itself or define single parenting as freedom from male oppression – but they were also not so willing to marry, unless men met their expectations for family participation (see first person accounts in

Rohnstock 1994, for example). Men's relationship to children was something that women valued and that the state ignored and actively marginalized. These are experiences on which Black American feminists have also had to insist and about which White feminists have been sceptical (Collins 1990).

The experience of family as a support system in a stance of opposition to the culture at large, of withdrawal into the family as a form of privacy from the state is another theme that presents family in a positive light in Black feminist writing that are echoed in some of the descriptions of the role of the family in state socialism in Germany and elsewhere (for example Einhorn 1993; Funk and Mueller 1993). Because private patriarchy is not so dominant in the experience of Black women or East German women, it may be easier for them to imagine bringing men more centrally into families without conceding patriarchal authority to them, than it is for many White American or West German feminists. It seems at least possible that political practices that simply exclude men, as if changing them were either irrelevant or impossible, do not make nearly as much sense from a vantage point of public patriarchy as they do for women whose experiences have been more shaped by domination by individual men.

Second, women's labour force participation is easy to connect to women's liberation in the context of private patriarchy since the extent of a woman's earnings is in practice directly related to her independence from an individual husband. This link is more problematic in public patriarchy, since women's labour is expected, even demanded, in the paid labour force as well as in unpaid domestic work. For Black American feminists, as well as for East German feminists, paid employment provides a self-evident part of their identity as well as a burden – but it is hard to confuse it with 'emancipation'. The conditions of integration into the paid labour force, such as discrimination, rather than the fact of employment itself, tend to draw theoretical attention and need more explanation. For many West German feminists, labour market discrimination is clearly a problem but one that apparently can be explained by women's frequent and extensive exclusion from the labour force in whole or in part when they have children. From this perspective, marginality rather than discrimination is the problem and creating compatibility between paid employment and motherhood is the solution;

from a perspective of public patriarchy, the issue is the conditions under which such compatibility has already been produced and why and how women are made to pay for it. Such ongoing discrimination needs explanation in terms of something other than women's intermittent labour force participation.

For East German women, after unification, the self-evidentness of paid employment was destroyed, but answering the question of what this growing exclusion from the labour force means is an entirely new issue, not a standard part of their feminist repertoire of self-understandings. As long as permanent or quasi-permanent exclusion was simply inconceivable, it did not need to be theorized as a source of oppression. For women under public patriarchy, the idea of paid employment as somehow 'an expression' of feminism does not make much sense, yet is also not experienced as irrelevant to a feminist agenda. It is more the invisible precondition of experience and selfhood, parallel almost to the way literacy is taken for granted in industrialized countries.[4]

Third, within a framework of public patriarchy, it makes little or no sense to talk about politics that remain 'autonomous' by virtue of staying out of the affairs of government for fear of being co-opted, a position that has been popular in West Germany, albeit with declining support in recent years (Ferree 1987). Insofar as it is the state that is directly usurping the right of women to speak for themselves, there is little alternative to challenging this head-on and pragmatically. That means that women can and must find practical ways to restructure the state itself to be less patriarchal. This 'obsession' with formal politics makes much less experiential sense to women in private patriarchy, who perceive more of their lives as being directly shaped by non-state actors and by cultural norms and expectations that are not formally enacted into law. Within the context of private patriarchy, the role of the state is more indirect and so less visible, and the more obvious targets for action seem both more diffuse and more personalized. In the eyes of those accustomed to public patriarchy this can look like too much concern with symbolic issues like language, that are 'trivial' compared to direct confrontations with policymakers.

For women who have lived under public patriarchy, the direct tie experienced between mothers and the state means that the state cannot so easily be felt to be remote and irrelevant. The specific demands levelled at the state will vary with political context, of course. Women of colour in the United States particularly point out the significance of welfare levels, access to health insurance, and affordable housing as feminist issues, of great and burning relevance to their daily lives, and direct attention to state policy in these areas that White feminists can more easily overlook. East German women have raised the position of public child care, anti-discrimination law, and representation in state and national politics higher on the feminist agenda in the post-unification FRG by highlighting the immediacy of their impact. While feminist practice in West Germany even before unification had increasingly emphasized the importance of such state policies, this concern has been greatly accelerated by unification and its aftermath. It remains to be seen whether a national feminist organization, aimed at influencing federal policy, such as the East German feminists originally favoured, will ultimately emerge as well.

CONCLUSIONS

To summarize, the experience of family, paid employment and state politics shows certain common threads between feminist concerns in East Germany and those raised by some women of colour in the US that would otherwise be surprising. These commonalities in theorizing and in critiques of pseudo-universalized theories that fail to reflect their experiences suggest that some common explanation might be sought. Such an explanation may rest in the different purposes that state intervention serves in public and in private patriarchy. It is not a question of quantitative differences in the degree of state activism or state determination of people's life chances overall, but rather of the qualitative differences in the ends that such state intervention serves: either supporting the authority and power of an individual husband as patriarch, or undermining it in favour of the collective authority of the male-dominated state for the benefit of men as a group.

As more Eastern European feminists find a voice in which to articulate their concerns, it may turn out that their collective self-representation of feminism, structured by their experiences of public patriarchy, may be even more different from the feminism arising from private patriarchy than is now apparently the case in the united Germany. What some have advanced as the reasons why there is 'no women's movement' in Eastern Europe may yet become explanations for why the feminism that emerges there will take a distinctive form (Tatur 1992).

The experiences of the feminism articulated from 'the other side' as not 'really' being feminism according to the standards of one's own collective self-representation have contributed to the disillusionment and discouragement of both sides. The early efforts to deny differences, pointing instead to the indisputable commonalities that are always to be found where women are not fully equal, have over the course of the past five years largely been abandoned. The many practical experiences German feminists have had in conferences, workshops, meetings and projects have provided all too much evidence of difference. The model of public and private patriarchy outlined here suggests that the tensions and resentments that often accompany such expressions of difference are built up not just from political competition over scarce resources, new hierarchical relationships, and personal failures of empathy and understanding in the current crisis – important as such experiences also have been – but also from threats to the collective self-representation of feminism itself. These varying self-representations may contain a large structural component reflecting the differently organized forms of patriarchy with which women had experience. Thus different aspects of feminist politics can 'feel true' to women on each side of the Wall, and feminist authenticity for each pushes them to reject and criticize claims that express understandings of what 'women' are and need that are not validated by their own experiences.

Ultimately, however, the reality of such diversity in women's experiences – not just in their interpretations of them – demands a definition of feminism as encompassing difference. What is now being so often expressed as 'better' and 'worse' versions of feminism in Germany today could thus not be understood so much as matters of women being naive or anti-male or careerist or statist – in other words, not as expressions of deficiencies of feminist analysis – but rather as reflections of the differences in the organization of patriarchy and of women's lives. Theorizing difference in this context takes on a new meaning, and a new urgency.

NOTES

1. An earlier version of this chapter was presented at the conference 'Crossing Borders' held in Stockholm, Sweden, in May 1994. The research reported here was conducted with the support of research fellowship 3–53621 from the German Marshall Fund of the United States and a Provost's Award from the University of Connecticut Research Foundation. This paper has benefited from the comments of many of the attendees, too numerous to list here. Still earlier versions of the paper have also benefited from comments and suggestions from Christine Bose, Lisa D. Brush, Irene Dölling, Christel Eckart, Jo Freeman, Ute Gerhard, Carol Hagemann-White, Eva Maleck-Lewy, Natalie Sokoloff, Verta Taylor, Wayne Villemez, Lise Vogel, Jane Wilkie and Brigitte Young. My thanks to all the above, even when I still (perversely) do not accept all the arguments they have offered.
2. For details and statistics on the status of women in the GDR see Einhorn 1993; Helwig and Nickel 1993; Maier 1992; for a history of policy that discusses its objectives and how it has secured these outcomes, see Penrose 1990.
3. For more extensive and detailed data on the status of women in the pre-unification FRG, see Helwig and Nickel 1993; Maier 1992; Kolinsky 1989; for a history of policy that suggests how these outcomes were sought and institutionalized, see Moeller 1993 and Ostner 1994.
4. For differences in specific attitudes and experiences relating to paid work and family relations see Institut für Demoskopie Allensbach 1993. As one illustration of the substantial gulf in expectations between East and West, consider the level of agreement with the statement 'an employed mother can give a child just as much warmth and security as a mother who does not have a job'. While 66 per cent of East Germans agreed, only 39 per cent of West Germans did. In this regard, it is the East Germans who are closer to the European average (61 per cent agreement).

REFERENCES

Bastian, Katrin, Evi Labsch and Sylvia Müller (1990) 'Zur situation von Frauen als Arbeitskraft in der Geschichte der DDR'. Originally published in *Zaunreiterin* (Leipzig), reprinted in *Streit* 2: 59–67.

Bialas, Christiana, and Wilfried Ettl (1993) 'Wirtschaftliche Lage, soziale Differenzierung und Probleme der Interessenorganisation in den neuen Bundesländern' *Soziale Welt* 44(1): 52–75.

Brown, Carol (1987) 'The new patriarchy' in Christine Bose, Roslyn Feldberg and Natalie Sokoloff, *Hidden Aspects of Women's Work*, pp. 137–60, NY: Praeger.

Collins, Patricia Hill (1990) *Black Feminist Thought.* Boston: Unwin Hyman.

Einhorn, Barbara (1993) *Cinderella Goes to Market: Citizenship, Gender and Women's Movements in East Central Europe.* New York: Verso.

Ferree, Myra Marx (1987) 'Equality and autonomy: Feminist politics in the United States and West Germany' in Mary Katzenstein and Carol McClurg Mueller, *The Women's Movements of the United States and Western Europe,* pp. 172–95. Philadelphia: Temple University Press.

Ferree, Myra Marx (1992) 'The wall remaining: Two women's movements in a single German state' Paper presented at conference on German Unification, Western European Studies Program, South Bend, IN: Notre Dame University.

Ferree, Myra Marx (1993) 'The rise and fall of "mommy politics": Feminism and unification in (East) Germany' *Feminist Studies* 19: 89–115.

Ferree, Myra Marx (1994) '"The time of chaos was the best": the mobilization and demobilization of a women's movement in East Germany' *Gender & Society*, Vol. 8, no. 4 December, pp. 597–623.

Friedan, Betty, (1963) *The Feminine Mystique.*

Funk, Nanette, and Magda Mueller (1993) *Gender politics and post-communism.* New York: Routledge.

Gerhard, Ute, Mechthild Jansen, Andrea Maihofer, Pia Schmid and Irmgard Schultz (eds) (1990) *Differenz und Gleichheit.* Frankfurt a/M: Ulrike Helmer Verlag.

Hampele, Anne (1991) 'Der unabhängige Frauenverband' in Helmut Müller-Enbergs, Marianne Schulz and Jan Wielgohs (eds) *Von der Illegalität ins Parlament* Berlin: LinksDruck Verlag.

Hampele, Anne (1993) '"Arbcite mit, plane mit, regiere mit": Zur politischen Partizipation von Frauen in der DDR' in Gisela Helwig and Hildegard Maria Nickel (eds), *Frauen in Deutschland* 1945–1992 pp. 281–320 Bonn: Bundeszentral für politische Bildung.

Helwerth, Ulrike and Gislinde Schwarz (1993) 'Drei Jahre nach der Wende': Zum Stand der Ost-West-Beziehungen in der Frauenbewegung'. Paper presented at the Goethe Institute, New York.

Helwig, Gisela and Hildegard Maria Nickel (eds) (1993) *Frauen in Deutschland, 1945–1992.* Band 318, Studien zur Geschichte und Politik. Bonn: Bundeszentrale für politische Bildung.

Holland-Cunz, Barbara (1990) 'Bemerkungen zur Lage der deutsch-deutschen Frauenbewegung' *Links* September: 35–39. Institut für Demoskopie Allensbach, 1993.

Institut für Demoskopie Allensbach (1993) *Frauen in Deutschland: Lebensverhältnisse, Lebensstile und Zukunftserwartungen.* Cologne, Germany: Bund Verlag.

Janssen-Jurriet, Marielouise (1976) *Sexismus* Cologne, Germany Jonasdottir, München, and K. Jones (1988) *The Political Interests of Gender: Developing Theory and Research with a Feminist Face.* Munich, Germany: Carl Hansen Verlag and London: Sage.

Kahlau, Cordula (ed.) (1990) *Aufbruch! Frauenbewegung in der DDR.* Munich: Frauenoffensive.

Kolinsky, Eva (1989) *Women in West Germany: Life, Work and Politics.* Oxford: Berg.

Mansbridge, Jane (1994) 'What is feminism?' in (eds) Myra Marx Ferree and Patricia Yancey Martin *Feminist Organizations: Harvest of the New Women's Movement*. Philadelphia PA: Temple University Press.

Maier, Friederike (1992) 'Frauenerwerbstätigkeit in der DDR und BRD: Gemeinsamkeiten und Unterschiede' in (eds) Gudrun-Axeli Knapp and Ursula Müller. *Ein Deutschland – Zwei Patriarchate?* Bielefeld pub.

Melucci, Alberto (1988) Getting involved: Identity and mobilization in social movements. in (eds) Bert Klandermans, Hanspeter Kriesi and Sidney Tarrow. *From structure to action: Comparing social movement research across cultures* Greenwich, CT: JAI Press.

Merkel, Ina *et al.* (eds) (1990) *Ohne Frauen ist kein Staat zu machen*. Hamburg: Argument Verlag.

Millett, Kate (1970) *Sexual Politics*. Garden City NY: Doubleday.

Moeller, Robert (1993) *Protecting Motherhood: Women and the Family in the Politics of Postwar West Germany*. Berkeley: University of California Press.

Ostner, Ilona (1994) 'Back to the Fifties: Gender and welfare in unified Germany' *Social Politics* 1(1): 32–59.

Penrose, Virginia (1990) 'Vierzig Jahre SED-Frauenpolitik: Ziele, Strategien, Ergebnisse' IFG: *Frauenforschung*, 4: 60–77.

Rohnstock, Katrin (1994) *Stiefschwestern: Was Ost-Frauen und West-Frauen voneinander denken*. Frankfurt a/M: Fischer.

Sassoon, Anne (1987) *Women and the State: The Shifting Boundaries between Public and Private*. London: Hutchinson.

Schenk, Harrad (1981) *Die feministische Herausforderung*. München: Germany: CH Beck Verlag.

Siim, Birte, (1987) 'The Scandinavian welfare states: Toward sexual equality or a new kind of male domination' *Acta Sociologica*, 3–4.

Tatur, Melanie (1992) 'Why is there no women's movement in Eastern Europe?' in (ed) P.G. Lewis *Democracy and Civil Society in Eastern Europe*, pp. 61–75 London: Macmillan.

Taylor, Verta and Nancy Whittier (1992) (eds) 'Collective identity in social movement communities: Lesbian feminist mobilization' in (eds) Aldon Morris and Carol McClurg Mueller *Frontiers of social movement theory*. New Haven, CT: Yale University Press.

7 The Commodification of Care: Current Policies and Future Politics

Clare Ungerson[1]

This chapter has four themes: an attempt is made to define 'payments for care' using conceptual and empirical evidence; second, the chapter traces the development of these systems of payment both in Britain and elsewhere; third, it outlines why this is a topic of growing importance, and how a politics of payments is likely to develop; fourth, it outlines four streams of thought that are currently making claims for the transformative powers of 'payments for care' and suggests that these claims, made at a high level of generality, need to be considered within political contexts, and sociological understandings of the relationship between carers and users.

DEFINITIONS AND CONCEPTS

The Concept of 'Care'

It is the predominant theme of this paper that the activities of 'informal care' are increasingly being commodified and that there are new issues of social and economic relations that arise as a result. However, the central proposal that care is being commodified runs counter to the conventional definition of what constitutes 'care', particularly 'informal care' within the British literature. For, in that literature, it has become the convention to apply these terms to activities that provide personal services within the domestic domain for people with special needs; most importantly, within the British convention, the provision of these services is *unwaged*. The assumption is that the supply of these domestically based caring services is forthcoming, not because it is paid for, but because its provision fulfils certain norms and obligations arising out of the operation of affect, biography and kinship. This tradition of distinguishing informal care – as distinct from 'formal' care which is essentially *waged* – has had an enormously fruitful outcome, both in policy and in research terms. As far as policy is concerned, it means that needs of 'carers' in the private domain are addressed, at least in the rhetoric of policy documents (see, for example, Griffiths 1988); in research terms, it means that there has been a burgeoning of feminist sociology and social policy analysis that has analyzed the caring relationship within the household (Hicks 1988; Lewis and Meredith 1988; Ungerson 1987; Wright 1986), theorized the concept of care (Graham 1983, 1991) and developed a theory of the origins and practice of obligations to care (Finch 1989; Finch and Mason 1992; Qureshi and Walker 1989).

However, there are now considerable signs that a critique of this dichotomy between formal and informal care is emerging within the British feminist literature. In a recent paper Carol Thomas (1993) argues, using the work of Hilary Graham, Roy Parker and Clare Ungerson, that the British feminist concept of 'care' is broadening to include waged care, although particularly in the case of Graham and Ungerson, their concepts of care are diverging. In recent work, both Hilary Graham and Clare Ungerson have begun to discuss the way in which some care is waged in practice, and/or that the concept of 'care' should not preclude waged care. Graham has discussed waged care within the domestic domain when it is provided by domestic servants (Graham 1991). Ungerson has argued that it is difficult to suggest that formal and informal care are logically and qualitatively different, since they *both* contain elements of labour and love; moreover, to argue that only informal care contains love is to argue that informal care is necessarily better care – and such an argument is dangerous, particularly for women carers in the domestic domain. Hence, Ungerson argues, it is important to try to put formal and informal care together, consider them primarily as work rather than affect, and then think about the implications of a policy to wage all care (Ungerson 1990). In a later paper, written with John Baldock, she argues that there are considerable empirical signs that waged care, in the form of 'paid volunteering', is developing in Britain (Baldock and Ungerson 1991).

Carol Thomas suggests that both the Graham and the Ungerson formulation are deficient or, as she puts it, 'partial'. She argues for a unified concept of 'care' that varies along seven dimensions, of which one is 'the economic character of the care relationship'. In other words, Thomas is suggesting that, in analyzing 'care' within a feminist framework, it is not essential that it be unwaged. The point she makes is a theoretical one rather than one based on *empirical* observation of the way in which care in practice is developing. Thomas's important point is that there is no need for *conceptual* boundaries; in contrast, in the paper here I develop the point that *empirical* boundaries are also breaking down and that we need to consider the pragmatic implications of this breakdown – within a gendered framework.

The Concept of 'Payment'

The empirical developments of 'payments for care' that I wish to discuss take, within the British context, three forms: symbolic payments to volunteers, and two kinds of benefit payment – one directly to carers, the other to care recipients. The pioneering experiment for paid volunteers was set up in the early 1980s by Kent Social Services Department. 'Volunteers' were paid symbolic amounts and contracted to provide services to individual elderly people living close by; such services were absolutely essential if the old people were to remain living in their own homes, rather than in residential care. The payments the volunteers received were nominal and per visit, taking no account of the time they spent with the person they were caring for. The experiment has since been positively evaluated in a number of studies (Challis and Davies 1986) and the motivations and satisfactions – of which there were plenty – of the 'community care helpers' analyzed in a book co-authored by Hazel Qureshi (Qureshi *et al.* 1989). Many schemes like it now exist, organized directly by local authority social service departments or by voluntary organizations, in many parts of Britain (for some descriptions of various schemes, see Leat and Gay 1987; Leat 1990; Leat with Ungerson 1993; Thornton 1989; Tinker 1984). An important feature of such schemes is that the payments that they make look very like wages, in the sense that the payments are *conditional* on evidence that specific work has been undertaken and successfully carried through – a customer has been got out of bed, a meal has been made and fed to the dependent person. It is this element of conditionality that distinguishes these payments from the payments discussed in the immediately following paragraphs – a point that we will return to later.

The second kind of payment consists, in the British system, of a benefit paid for from the social security budget. The 'Invalid Care Allowance' was introduced in 1975 as the result of a campaign for the rights of single women carers (Groves and Finch 1983) and as the result of the recognition, in a government White Paper on 'Social Security Provision for Chronically Sick and Disabled People', of the value and absolute necessity of informal care (Department of Health and Social Security, 1974). It is payable to informal carers who are of working age and not in employment, but are looking after someone in need of care for at least 35 hours a week. Initially, the benefit was payable to a very narrow range of carers falling into very particular demographic groups: they had to be of working age (up to 60 for women, 65 for men); relatives of the person being cared for; they could be single women, single and married men; but married women were excluded on the grounds that 'they might be at home in any event' (the White Paper, cited in McLaughlin 1991). The benefit, which though not means tested nevertheless was subject to very strict interpretations of what constituted income from other paid work and very low earnings disregards, was, without any noticeable fuss, extended to non-relatives in 1981. The exclusion of married women from the benefit led to a vociferous campaign mounted by the Equal Opportunities Commission and carers' organizations to include them, culminating in a successful test case brought to the European Court of Justice in 1986. As a result of the inclusion of married women in the remit of the benefit, the number of successful claimants for Invalid Care Allowance (ICA) grew from less than 5000 in 1981/2 to 155 000 in 1991/2 (Central Statistical Office 1993). Like the payments arising out of 'paid volunteering' schemes, ICA serves directly to increase carers' incomes but unlike those schemes this payment through a benefit system is not based on any contract to carry out certain caring tasks. In this sense, ICA is essentially an *unconditional* payment.

To give this paper a wider comparative focus, it is important to bear in mind that payments to carers through centralized benefit systems are actually relatively rare, apparently occurring only in Britain and Ireland (the Irish system is means tested). Rather more common are benefit systems which give benefits directly to the disabled person. Indeed, this is a feature of the British system, where the Attendance Allowance, the Disability Living Allowance, the Disability Working Allowance and the Severe Disablement Allowance, are paid to the person who is disabled. These benefits are not primarily designed to cover the costs of purchase of personal care (even the therefore oddly named Attendance Allowance) but are rather expected to contribute to the extra costs entailed by disability: for example, to cover extra heating costs, expenses for special diets, additional laundry costs, and there is a specific 'mobility' rather than 'care' component now included in the Disability Living Allowance. Benefits paid directly to disabled people in need of care are also a feature of systems elsewhere, but in many countries the expectation is that the care-recipients will use these monies to purchase care or to reimburse their informal carer. Hence in France, the benefit has the words 'pour tierce personne' included in the title of the benefit, and in Italy the benefit is known as 'indennita di accompagnamento' ('companion benefit'). Austria is currently turning over its entire care system to high cash payments to care recipients in the expectation that they will purchase their own care. The nearest we get in Britain to such benefits are the allowances organized by the Independent Living Fund which can, for longstanding claimants, pay very seriously disabled people up to £560 a week to allow them to purchase their own care – a sum which, since November 1992, has been considerably reduced and circumscribed for new claimants but from which it is still possible to receive up to £300 a week (Robertson 1993).

It is arguable that benefits paid to the disabled person, unless they are specifically designed for the purchase of care, are not payments for 'care' at all. In an earlier paper (Ungerson 1993b) I suggested precisely this, following evidence, from Horton and others, that in Britain at least, benefits paid to the disabled person are used to pay for general household expenses and not for care (Horton and Berthoud 1990; Glendinning 1992). However, in an empirical and longitudinal study of stroke patients and their carers (Baldock and Ungerson 1994) it seems that many households containing a disabled person understand the Attendance Allowance to be a benefit which is to be used to purchase hands on care, and to pay directly a hands on carer. We have instances, in our sample of 32 households, of individuals waiting for the allowances to come through before they feel that they can legitimately offer (and have the offer accepted) payments to kin and neighbours in exchange for the care they are receiving. For example, Mrs Bolton, a stroke patient, was insistent in the first interview that as soon as she got the benefits she had applied for, she would start paying her daughters for their services:

> *Int*: And you haven't been offered any help at home. But if you were, you said you'd sooner have your own daughters do it.
> *Mrs Bolton*: Yeah
> *Int*: Why do think that is ?
> *Mrs B*: Because they have offered. They offered, and I said, 'well if I get some money through, you know, that helps to pay for that doesn't it? For the cleaning and such like?' I said I'd pay them as though I was having somebody in, you know. Naturally they said 'No – you dare mum!'. I said 'well that's what it's for'. Susan said 'Well I wouldn't take it' and Lyn said 'Don't be so stupid, I wouldn't take it'. I said 'Well that's what it's for, that's what I'm getting paid *for*'. You know, for help, 'so you might as well have it otherwise I'd only get somebody else in which I don't want to do'. Sooner have my own family naturally.

Similarly, Mrs Adlington said in the first interview:

> Because you see as it is now, if Linda takes my washing or gets any shopping, I offer her money, she won't take it. If I get attendance allowance, she will. And to me that means more than, well what I say I'm not going to be a burden and of course they say 'well you're not a burden, you're our mother'. So.

By the third interview, when, at long last, she was in receipt of Attendance Allowance, Mrs Adlington was paying her female relatives in cash and in kind:

> *Int*: Now I think you give some money, don't you to your family for the laundry?

Mrs A: Yes, Maureen (daughter) does a lot of the cooking for me so obviously I give her money. If Linda (daughter-in-law) does laundry for me I pay for the powder. They object but I will not be, I will not be dependent on them if you know what I mean?

Other respondents also used euphemisms and linguistic sleight of hand to describe such payments 'for the petrol' or 'for the shopping' but more often than not payments and gifts were explicitly exchanged for the care received. We think that the beliefs about, and actions surrounding, these benefits for disability in Britain are changing for the important reason that, as a result of the new regime of community care currently being introduced, Social Service Departments in Britain are increasingly and quite explicitly explaining to their clients that their disability benefits will be used to pay for the personal social services they are receiving. Thus, in Kent, as soon as clients receive the Attendance Allowance or another disability benefit, the charges for home care are very considerably increased, sometimes by as much as 100 per cent. Dependent people appear increasingly to understand their disability benefits to be the means by which they are expected to purchase personal care. Since the sums involved are small the most typical form of purchase is by largely symbolic payments to people whom they have known for many years, rather than to strangers working at the 'rate for the job'.

Thus it seems to be at least arguable that disability benefits paid to the disabled person constitute the beginning of a chain of payment for care. In Britain we are talking about large and growing sums of money: there were 970 000 people receiving Attendance Allowance in 1991/2, amounting to expenditure of nearly £2 billion in 1991/2 (Central Statistical Office 1993), and the benefit constitutes one of the fastest growing aspects of the British social security system. If, as suggested here, these monies are increasingly accepted in the vernacular and in actuality as the basis for payment for personal care rather than for the extra living costs entailed by disability, then this benefit constitutes a major source of such money flows. These are money flows that are unregulated and informal. Their likely consequences are akin to those already apparent in other countries, particularly countries where money is increasingly attached to disability, namely, the development of a form of 'grey' or shadowy caring labour (discussion at the conference on 'Payment for Care' sponsored by the European Centre, Vienna, July 1992). I am therefore going to take these disability benefits as an embryonic form of payment for care, but one that in some countries is currently much more developed than in Britain.

So far I have identified three forms of 'payment for care': symbolic payments to volunteers, and payments through the benefits system, either to carers directly, or to people with special needs. In the latter case, it may be an explicit assumption that these benefits will be passed on to a carer by the care-recipient; in other cases, such as with the British Attendance Allowance and Disability Allowances, I have argued that behaviour within the care relationship is changing such that, increasingly, the benefit is exchanged for care services. But having referred to all these different forms of cash transfer as 'payment' I could, rightly, be accused of begging the question. It is fairly clear that systems of 'paid volunteering' do actually involve 'payments' in the classic sense that the payment is only made as a consequence of certain tasks being carried out. But it is difficult to argue that *benefits* payable to carers are 'payments' in the same way. This is because these benefits are not conditional on particular aspects of care being carried out, but are usually conditional on proven disability of the care recipient and the proximity (physical and/or familial) of the care giver. Once those minimal conditions are fulfilled, an allowance or benefit, payable to the carer, is put in place, and no further questions asked. In that sense, the 'payment' is not made in exchange for services rendered. Moreover, Eithne McLaughlin has argued that ICA, largely because of its low level, is not a 'payment for care' but rather, an 'honorarium' (McLaughlin 1991 p. 5). (Nevertheless, the majority of recipients of ICA studied by Eithne McLaughlin considered the benefit to be payment for care, and thought it was too low, both in relation to the care work they were undertaking and in relation to the level of earnings they might realistically have achieved had they been in paid work (McLaughlin 1991, p. 48).) There are also the theoretical problems posed by Esping-Andersen's use of the term 'decommodification' to describe, at a highly general level, the way in which benefit systems operate to 'maintain a livelihood without reliance on the market' (Esping-Andersen 1990 p. 22) thus, at one stroke, apparently disqualifying benefits as a means of commodification or 'payment'. But a number of commentators have pointed out that Esping-Andersen's dichotomous formulation of commodification/decommodification and state/market is both too rigid to take account of the unpaid work within the household particularly that is undertaken by women (Lewis 1992), and that it assumes that decommodification is necessarily emancipatory, while commodification is not (Shaver and Bradshaw 1993). As Jane Lewis has pointed out, there is a central blurring that occurs in the lives of women arising out of the domestic division of labour:

> Decommodification for women is likely to result in their carrying out unpaid caring work; in other words 'welfare dependency' on the part of adult women is likely to result in the greater independence of another person, young or old. The unequal division of unpaid work thus blurs the dichotomous divisions between dependent and independent, commodified and decommodified. (Lewis 1992)

Moreover, particularly in the case of benefits conditional upon a relationship of care rather than a status of unemployment or sickness, such blurring inevitably takes place. For neither care giver nor care recipient is wholly within or wholly outside the labour market: the care giver, particularly someone in receipt of a benefit like ICA, may well consider the benefit to be a form of wage and reflect upon its utility in relation to wages in the conventional labour market. Similarly, the care recipient might, as we have argued above, understand their disability benefits to be a means by which the labour of a personal carer can and should be purchased; and in some systems, such as those of France and Italy, the benefit is specifically designed to be spent on the purchase of caring labour. It is for these reasons that I argue that these benefits are a form of commodification of domestic caring labour, and constitute a 'payment'. The conditions under which they are granted are different from the conditions under which symbolic payments are made to 'paid volunteers', but they nevertheless are either conditional on the existence of an extant relationship or, in turn, lead to a commodified relationship, between care recipient and care giver.

In order to keep hold of the specifics of these conditionalities, it is necessary to develop a form of classification. In such a

classification, I would suggest that the term 'quasi-wages payments for care' be applied to the kinds of payment made under
paid volunteering schemes, and to the payments made by individual care recipients, using benefits, to care givers. The use of
the term 'quasi-wage' indicates that many of these payments
are symbolic and unrelated to market levels of wages, but, like
wages, are conditional on certain tasks being fulfilled, and are
subject to formal and informal contract. Benefits paid to carers,
and dependent on the existence of an extant relationship, are
best classified as 'carer-allowance payments for care'.

THE POLITICS OF 'PAYMENTS FOR CARE' POLICIES

There are a number of reasons why it is important to understand payments for care, not least, as I shall argue below,
because these systems are often gendered in conception, and
are certainly gendered in consequence. But it may be protested
that expenditures on them are so small a part of the 'welfare
state' compared to, for example, expenditures on health care or
social security as a whole that they hardly qualify for the effort
of definition and classification outlined above. But it seems to
me that, with one or two national exceptions, they are systems
of support for informal care that are likely to develop into and
beyond the millenium. Most countries of Europe face rapid demographic expansion in numbers of the elderly. At the same
time they are attempting to pursue policies of decarceration
and care in the 'community' particularly with regard to the
elderly, but also with regard to other groups with special needs
such as the mentally ill. The policies of decarceration are partially, if not wholly, driven by the idea that care in and by the
community is likely to be cheaper than residential care. A shift
towards dependence on domiciliary care services provided by
professionalized care givers combined with a growing reliance
on the services of informal carers is visible in most of the countries of Western, and now Central Europe (see, for example,
Baldock and Evers 1992). A further policy trend is also in place:
as part of an economic interpretation of the current recession
that dominates economic thinking in the West, it is now the
case that almost without exception the countries of Europe are
committed to containing public expenditure (although they

start from varying bases). The personal social services are no exception to this concern, and despite visibly growing demand for social services, particularly from the growing numbers of very elderly people in most European populations, most of the nations of Europe are introducing new 'marketized' systems of care designed to tap into private and voluntary sectors of care as well as the more traditional public services funded, organized and delivered by the state (Abrahamson 1991; Baldock 1993). In order to make these new market-orientated systems of care delivery work efficiently, personal care services, even those provided by the public sector, increasingly have prices attached to them which someone – the consumer directly, or the agencies contracted to organize and purchase the services – has to pay. And if the market is to operate at all, then there has to be effective demand arising out of the expenditure of the consumers of care. These 'consumers' are expected to be at least as much the care recipients as the care organizers. Thus the condition of disability will increasingly have to have money attached to it, and personal care services, from whatever source, will increasingly be commodified.

These two policy trends are operating within social and political contexts that are also likely to reinforce their commodifying impact. The social trends are the well established cross-European (with one or two notable exceptions) features of marriage breakdown, geographical mobility, and women's participation in the labour market, all of which are likely to mean that 'traditional' concepts of gendered kinship obligation – insofar as they ever existed – are likely to become looser and looser. The temptation to governments to introduce reinforcements of caring 'responsibilities' through the use of payments to informal carers, or to use symbolic payments for 'paid volunteers', or to leave the entire enterprise to care recipients by giving them allowances with which to purchase care, is likely to be very considerable. Similarly, a politics of payments and allowances for care is already in existence but is also likely to develop further. The politics takes two, often conflicting, forms. In the first case, there are the associations of carers (particularly active and noticeably successful in Britain and Ireland) which argue for carers' rights to, for example, respite care, but, more particularly, for increased benefits while they care and, if they are of working age, protection of pension rights. Secondly, there are the associations of the disabled themselves, who argue for empowerment through the debureaucratization of the allocation of care, and the transfer to themselves of the right to decide on how and when they want their care (Morris 1993). This often takes the form of arguing for cash incomes rather than professionally allocated services – an argument that also has the support of those on the right who support market systems of allocation as more efficient than bureaucratic and managed systems of allocation (Craig 1992; Laing 1991). Thus within this politics, two strands run parallel: the one, from carers, arguing for higher benefits for care work; the other, from care recipients, arguing for cash benefits high enough for them to organize and purchase their own care rather than – somewhat passively – wait for services in kind. In either case, if these political campaigns gain leverage, then payments for care, whether directly to the carer, or using the care-recipient as the conduit for monies which in turn generate a private sector of care, are likely to develop.

The signs are that these developments have already begun. Using data from Eithne McLaughlin and Caroline Glendinning's study of financial support for informal carers in six European countries, it is possible to discern general trends both in systems of payment for care, and in their take-up (Glendinning and McLaughlin 1993a). For example, in 1990 the Irish government replaced a relatively unused Prescribed Relative's Allowance (payable to the care recipient) with a Carers' Allowance paid directly to the carer and at a much higher rate (though means tested). Take up of the new benefit expanded very quickly. Italy has had 'Companion Payments' at least since the 1980s, payable to the care recipient but expected to be spent on the purchase of care, and the level of it (about £75.00 a week) is high enough to do so. In 1990 there were 1.1 million recipients of this benefit. One regional government in Italy (South Tyrol) has recently introduced further payments directly to carers. In France, since 1975 when decarceration policies were introduced, there have been two benefits payable to care recipients – one for those aged 65+ and one for those aged less – but expected to be handed over to care givers. The levels are higher than the British Invalid Care Allowance and Attendance Allowance put together. Since 1990 some French *departements* have introduced payments directly to carers. In

Germany, the subsidiarity principle has until recently largely prevented systems of payment for care developing and the insurance system has been geared towards payment for health care rather than social care. Nevertheless, despite these real obstacles, very recent policy developments are beginning to put payments for care in place. Since 1989, carers have had rights to a 'holiday care allowance' to pay for substitute care for four weeks in the year and since 1991, severely disabled people living at home have been able to claim cash payments or up to 25 domiciliary 'assignments' a month. Most claimants have opted for the cash (£161 per month) and there was very rapid take-up in the first six months of operation. The city of Berlin, along with some other municipalities, introduced payments to care recipients in 1992, and also in 1992, the Federal government agreed in principle that by 1996 a 'care insurance' system should be in place, guaranteeing cash or rights to care for those with special needs.

It is interesting to note that in these countries the idea of 'paid volunteers' does not appear to exist. The idea that there should be 'quasi-wage' payments for care *orchestrated by the state* is anathema in many of the countries of Europe, such as France, Belgium, the Netherlands and Germany, where minimum wage legislation would render such payments for care illegal. But it is also interesting to note that in some of these countries the transfer to care recipients of quite considerable amounts of money set at levels notionally high enough for them to pay market-related wages to their carer/s and specifically intended for them to do so, is likely to lead to the development of symbolic payments *orchestrated by care recipients*. Indeed, given minimum wage legislation, it seems that the governments of these countries may be encouraging care recipients and their care givers to enter into illegal wage relationships, and certainly there is concern among commentators from these countries that there are now in place – and about to be further developed – flows of money that will encourage unregulated and informal 'grey' labour markets (discussions at the Vienna Conference on 'Payment for Care', July 1992).

The countries of Scandinavia have had a much longer tradition of payment for care and within the formal labour market. Sweden, Finland and Norway (this last example from research by Susan Lingsom) have all had in place systems for the full-scale employment of informal carers as municipal home helpers at least since World War II. The Scandinavian model appears to be much more radical in conception than the other developing European systems. These are not systems designed to stimulate private systems of care within the context of decarceration policies. Rather they are systems that accept that in terms of work and in terms of working conditions, 'informal' care is – and ought to be – indistinguishable from 'formal' care. There is some evidence from these countries that this radical version of payment for care is in decline; certainly in Sweden the direct employment and payment of caring relatives on a full-time basis as municipal workers has declined: in 1970, 18 517 family care givers were employed by municipalities and by 1991 the number had decreased to 6500, although a further group are employed on a part-time and hourly basis on the same wage as municipal home helps.

Thus the evidence that these systems are becoming more important across Europe is available. However, the Swedish example of a system in decline may tell us something about counter-pressures. I have suggested above, that movements towards payment for care arise out of policy trends towards decarceration and a reemphasis on maintaining people in their own homes for as long as possible, supported by domiciliary services and informal care. I have also suggested that these policies are driven largely by ideas of reducing expenditure – namely that it is cheaper and more cost-effective to care for people in the 'community'. Payments for care, used within these policies, are seen as a cost-effective way of mobilizing and reinforcing informal and voluntary care within the community; in other words, they can be seen, relative to the fixed costs and formal labour costs of residential care, to be a means of *cost containment*. But clearly payments for care can represent a form of *cost escalation*, in the sense that it is arguable that, particularly where they are paid to informal carers or to volunteers, these payments are being used to generate a supply of care that was 'previously' (perhaps in some mythical golden age) available for free and might, in future, be available anyway. Much of the argument that payments will lead to cost-escalation rather than underwrite cost-containment depends, of course, on the level of payments available and whether it is possible for governments to hold the line that these payments are in some sense symbolic rather than realistically designed to represent, or in turn pay for, market-related wages. The way in which the line can be held is to present the work of care within the private domain as something that differs qualitatively from the work of care carried out in the public domain. In other words, the line is held by maintaining the public/private dichotomy, and presenting care relationships within the private domain as quite unlike those that occur in the public domain. It is at this point that the questions of gender, of marriage, and the public/private dichotomy enter the discussion directly.

GENDER, MARRIAGE AND THE PUBLIC/PRIVATE DICHOTOMY

There are two levels at which discussion of payments for care is permeated by the relationships of the private domain: the conceptual and the empirical. To take the conceptual level first. The drift towards payments has, as we have seen, a number of causes. But at its root, particularly in those countries which perceive payments as the essential lubricant that will ease the transfer of caring responsibilities to the 'community', and hence to a cheaper form of care, payments for care represent an upholding of the public/private dichotomy. The expectation is that there is already, and will continue to be, a pool of labour within the private domain which is subject to the pressures of affect, kinship obligation and duty, reciprocity, biography, altruism and habit, and willing to remain within it. The point of *symbolic* payments is to reinforce these pressures at an ideological level by implicitly suggesting that informal carers undertake care work for 'love' – the common shorthand term for the pressures listed above – and not for money. As innumerable studies over the past 20 years have shown, the people within the private domain for whom those pressures are most telling are women (Finch and Groves 1983; Dalley 1988; Ungerson 1987; Ungerson 1990) and the husbands of disabled wives (Parker 1990, 1993). Thus the assumption behind symbolic payments is that provision of caring resources from particular demographic groups within the private domain has been, and will continue to be, maintained and further, that symbolic payments will themselves be part of that maintenance structure.

However, it might be objected that even symbolic payments, far from representing a reinforcement of the public/private dichotomy, rather represent the blurring of the boundary between these two worlds; that the payments, however low, could become a 'thin end of the wedge' leading to fully fledged wages and employment for workers in the private domain paid for by the state (as is already in existence in the countries of Scandinavia), or the development of cash transfers from the state to allow for the development of a private market for care. Payments for care, once in existence and placed on the policy agenda, will almost certainly lead to a politics concerning the levels of payment and the principles driving the payment systems. Such a politics will be fed by many strands visible in social welfare politics in the late twentieth century: feminist claims for the extension of full citizenship to women (Pateman 1988; Lister 1990; Fraser 1999); carers' claims to rights to support whether in terms of cash or services; and care recipients claims to autonomy and independence. But the other side of that politics will be robustly defended by the cost-containing ministries of government. The argument will be the familiar one that the private domain institutions of 'family' and 'community' have distinct caring qualities – quite unrelated to the cash nexus – which must be maintained. Part of that defence, whether explicit or implicit, will be that women are the 'natural' fount of these distinct qualities of care, and that stabilized institutions of marriage and the 'traditional' family differentially, but successfully, reinforce obligations on both men, as husbands, and women as wives, daughters, sisters and in-laws, to care. Symbolic payments will be represented as 'recognition' – but no more – of the special and desirable qualities of those who care. However, in one sense it is evident that the state also has an interest in blurring the boundaries. This is particularly clear in the British systems of 'paid volunteering' where the idea is that a symbolically paid and contracted volunteer will begin to understand her role and her identity in relation to the person she is caring for as though she were that person's informal carer, and that she will extend her care work into a much broader and deeper caring relationship, even engaging her own family in the care (Challis and Davies 1986). But it is still the case that the nature of the symbolism of the payment is expected to work in much the same way as it is expected to work with informal carers; like informal carers, such 'paid volunteers' are presented with the view that the basis for the work they undertake is, and ought to be, the breadth of love – not the narrowness of money.

The empirical level of the discussion about the provision of care within the private domain and payments concerns the way in which these systems of payment tend to be sexed. This is certainly true as far as Britain is concerned: the people who receive benefits as carers, and the people engaging in paid volunteer schemes tend to be disproportionately women. In the study by McLaughlin of Invalid Care Allowance recipients in 1989, 79 per cent of current carers in receipt of the allowance and 98 per cent of ex-carers were women (McLaughlin 1991, Table 2.1), and in Hazel Qureshi's study of Kent Community Care Scheme 'helpers' all but two of these paid volunteers were women (Qureshi *et al.* 1989). Similarly, in Ireland, in 1991, 2538 women received the Carers' Allowance compared to 817 men (Glendinning and McLaughlin 1993a). The evidence from the rest of Europe is less clear, partially because, as we have seen, many of their systems of payment are characterized by informality at the point of cash exchange and hence the data on who actually receives the money is not available (although this is obviously not true of the Scandinavian systems). However, evidence from those countries which have done studies of informal carers indicate that the large majority of carers (not just those in receipt of payment), just as in Britain, are women (see for example, data on Germany and Finland in Glendinning and McLaughlin 1993a). Hence, not surprisingly, there is evidence that there is a common European culture about informal care that is highly gendered; one would expect therefore, that most recipients of payments for care to be women – whether they themselves are directly in receipt of benefits, or on the receiving end of payments channelled through care recipients, or through employment as 'paid volunteers'.

But cultural determinants are not the only basis for expecting the recipients of payments from whatever source to be female. There are also policy determinants and these largely take two forms. The first policy determinant is that many of the carer allowance payment for care schemes appear to be geared to a notional amount of what is necessary to purchase care, or to pay an informal carer. Although some of these amounts seem high compared to the level of the British Invalid Care Allowance (currently

£33.70 a week but with flat-rate additions for adult dependants and children) – for example, £75.00 a week in Italy – they nevertheless appear to represent very low rates of pay compared to likely prevailing wage rates in these countries. It is not clear from the available data just how these amounts are calculated, but it is probably fair to assume that they relate to a notional minimum amount that policymakers expect will generate a supply of caring labour. Given sex segmented labour markets throughout Europe, it is likely that such amounts are geared to attract labour that has low expected earnings in alternative employment, and that is more likely to be women workers than men.

Secondly, some of these policies, including the British 'paid volunteer' schemes, seem to have implicitly embedded within them the idea that there are certain groups within modern society for whom small amounts of money will call forth particularly large amounts of time. There are a number of groups with apparently large amounts of flexible time resources: the unemployed of working age, pensioners, women who are housewives and are dependent on the resources of their husbands, and students in higher education (perhaps this latter group rather more in continental Europe than in Britain). These groups other than the 'housewives' (and possibly the students) may, depending on the basis on which their income support is provided, lose their major source of income if they enter paid employment; even at very low wages, through the operation of earnings disregards, and/or rules about total hours that can be worked, income maintenance may be reduced or taken away altogether. But 'housewives' dependent on their husbands' incomes are not subject to such constraints. Single mothers, particularly if they are able to operate – just as the other groups identified here might do too – within the 'grey' caring labour market, will find such low additional earnings and flexible time resources might fit well both with their financial needs and with the demands of mothering. In previous work on 'paid volunteering' John Baldock and I argued that the 'paid volunteer' schemes seemed implicitly and sometimes explicitly targeted to recruiting women who needed extra income, but only in small amounts in order to avoid tax and social security thresholds (Baldock and Ungerson 1991). It does seem that there might well be parallel implicit targeting in systems of payment to care developing elsewhere.

One further feature of these systems must be mentioned. If cash is increasingly attached to the condition of disability then the result of this is likely to be the development of relatively unregulated labour markets, where disabled people, and agents acting on their behalf, seek out the most cost effective and flexible labour they can find – even if this implies the use of irregular and 'grey' labour. The source of this labour will not only be women; it is also likely to be women (and some men) who are 'outsiders'. At present, both in Europe and in North America, there are large international migrations of peoples taking place. Particularly in Europe, with the loosening up of borders as a result of the collapse of the old Communist regimes, we can expect these international migration streams to continue into the foreseeable future. Thus there will be available the labour of people who have very limited citizenship rights, and for whom work from whatever source, under unregulated conditions and with limited pay, will nevertheless remain attractive, and who in turn, will be attractive to employers seeking workers who are cheap and flexible. Hence there are issues of race and nationality embedded in these developments as well as gender (for a further discussion of the race dimensions of caring labour, see Graham 1991).

SOCIAL AND ECONOMIC IMPACTS OF PAYMENTS FOR CARE

There are four streams of literature currently in existence that see payments for care as potentially transformative of important aspects of post-industrial society. The first two streams – that coming from the new right and arguing for cash rather than services for users in order to develop more efficient markets for care (Laing 1991), and that coming from the disability lobbies, arguing for the same policy but specifically to empower an oppressed minority (Morris 1993) – have been mentioned above as part of a politics of payments for care that are already 'in place'. Both these streams of thought make large claims for the impact of redirected cash flows, suggesting that cash has enough potential power to chip away at, if not topple, economic and cultural oppressions, and the professionalization, medicalization and bureaucratization of social and personal life. The second two streams – the one derived from a feminist analysis of social policy, the other derived from commitment to welfare pluralism – are presently less noisy on the political stage but becoming louder.

The feminist discussion of payments for care takes place within the context of a larger debate about how to establish women's rights to citizenship in post-industrial society. Unlike the other three streams of thought, it is concerned not with payments to care *users*, but with payments to care *givers*. The central problem in this literature is whether women should be treated as the same and with the same routes to citizenship as men, or whether they should be treated as different, with special claims, as mothers and carers, to full citizenship. This is the problem identified by Carole Pateman as 'Wollstonecraft's Dilemma', indicating its very long antecedents coinciding with industrialization (Pateman 1989). Industrial welfare states drove the problem underground by using the notion of the 'family wage', thus rendering women's work in the home invisible, and elevating their dependency on men into a general principle governing social, economic, political and personal life (Land 1978). But the relative success of the second wave of feminism, and the window of opportunity provided by the fluidity of post-industrialism, have brought the problem to the fore again. As Nancy Fraser has recently suggested, 'a new world of economic production and social reproduction is emerging' where 'we should ask: What new, post-industrial gender order should replace the family wage?'. She goes on to answer:

> Two different sorts of answers are presently conceivable, I think, both of which qualify as feminist. The first I call the Universal Breadwinner model. It is the vision implicit in the current political practice of most US feminists and liberals. It aims to foster gender equity by promoting women's employment; the centrepiece of this model is state provision of employment-enabling services such as day care. The second possible answer I call the Caregiver Parity model. It is the vision implicit in the current political practice of most Western European feminists and social democrats. It aims to promote gender equity chiefly by supporting informal carework; the centrepiece of this model is state provision of caregiver allowances. (Fraser 1999 p. 4)

While the paper by Fraser succinctly lays out the criteria by which we may judge either of these policies, and the advantages and disadvantages of both of them, I doubt whether Fraser is right to posit such a clear distinction between 'US feminists' and 'Western European feminists' or implicitly suggest that, on the European side of the Atlantic, we are all united behind payments for care, rather than labour market participation, as a route to women's citizenship. We are not, and our writing – not least my own – continue to struggle with the old dilemmas (Ungerson 1993a; Leira 1992). As Ruth Lister has recently put it:

> In this contemporary variant of Wollstonecraft's dilemma we are torn between wanting to validate and support, through some form of income maintenance provision, the caring work for which women still take the main responsibility in the 'private' sphere and to liberate them from this responsibility so that they can achieve economic and political autonomy in the 'public' sphere. (Lister 1999 p. 19)

It is largely because it is so difficult to disentangle this conundrum that so many of us write with 'dilemma' in the title, and, except where driven by outrageous circumstance (as when the British Invalid Care Allowance was not made payable to married women on the grounds that they were 'at home anyway'), tend to stand puzzled and reluctant on the political sidelines (or shift the argument away from discussion of cash back to discussion of services (Ungerson 1993a; Lewis 1994). But part of that reluctance stems from the knowledge that the issue of 'payments for care' lies at the heart of the policy implications of the more general discussion of the engendering of citizenship. Hence, just as with the new right and the disability lobbies, feminists, whether they support payments for care or not, expect that such payments would have very powerful transformational properties – for good or ill.

The fourth stream of thought is, like the first and the second, far less equivocal about the merits of payments for care. This is the 'welfare pluralist' argument made, in particular, by Adelbert Evers. He suggests that 'payments for care', primarily to care users, but also to care givers, constitute a path that leads towards a new middle ground, that stands between the polarities of state, family and market. Lying between the land of consumerist individualism on the one hand, and service orientated collectivism on the other, there is a middle ground of solidarity and community which can be rediscovered through the commodification of the care relationship. Thus Evers argues that payments to care users

> strengthen those economies of care which are easily over-looked in the consumerist model . . . the small-scale markets of local neighbourhood help, services offered by charitable as-sociations, co-operatives and small-scale voluntary organisa-tions . . . they have survived and sometimes blossomed because their character seems very well adapted to the balance of needs amongst suppliers and users of care . . . these care services work through trust and unwritten rules quite different from the 'easy in/easy out' norms and values of larger commercial suppliers. (Evers 1994)

At the same time, he suggests, there is a pool of labour involved in 'new volunteering' and 'post-traditional' forms of micro-solidarity and community building, and that people 'have a right to a multi-dimensional life' which can be satisfied by entering commodified caring relationships. (Evers 1994). Such arguments are concerned not with questions of power nor with issues of citi-zenship, but rather with issues of co-operation and social cohe-sion. They are muted as yet, but as leftist parties grapple with new post-industrial realities and variants of social democracy take a hold of one time communist Central Europe, they may move closer to the core of the politics of welfare. Just as with the other three streams of thought, the argument makes major claims for the transformative powers of payments for care.

However, arguments such as these are pitched at a very high level of generality and, in my view, lead to oversimplified claims for the power of cash to transform social relationships in a single and particular direction. It seems to me that the social, political and economic *contexts* in which payments for care operate, and the way in which payments for care are themselves *organised*, are just as likely to transform relationships as the ex-istence of the payments themselves. One of the particularities left undiscussed in these streams of thought is the level of payment, whether to user or carer, they have in mind, and whether they are talking about symbolic amounts, or amounts high enough to guarantee financial independence for the care recipient and care giver. The actual amounts of money involved will radically affect labour market behaviour of potential carers, their relationship to the state and the household, and, last but not least, may have real impact on the prevailing sexual division of caring. It will also affect the types of care relationships that both users and carers can afford to enter, and the mixes of time, personnel, sources of income, and location of care, that carers and care recipients would have to put together. Similarly, with the exception of the disability lobby which has a clear commitment to the style of payment for care operated by the British Independent Living Fund, no thought is given to how such payments would flow, and whether and how the way in which the flow is organized would affect the location of power and decision-making within and beyond the caring relationship. In work undertaken by Diana Leat and myself, we identified six routes of payment, and variants of them, each of which would have very different implications for the locus of power, quality control, employment rights, within the caring relationship and in relation to funding agencies (Leat with Ungerson, 1993). There is considerable evidence that in the non-conditional carer allowance systems like the Invalid Care Allowance in Britain, or the Home Care Allowance system in Finland, both of which 'pay' carers directly, care recipients are very pleased that their carers are in some way being compensated for the work they have undertaken (Leat and Gay 1987; McLaughlin 1991; Glendinning and McLaughlin 1993b; Sipilä 1993). In contrast, one might expect more conditional quasi-wage systems to introduce an element of control, and the possibility of complaint and sanctions, which might make relations between care giver and care recipient much more difficult. In systems where care recipients are themselves using benefits to purchase care, the relationships between care recipient and care giver may come to resemble relations between master and servant. And in quasi-wage systems where social service agencies are using payments to contract care workers and 'volunteers' to provide particular aspects of care, there may well be problems of routinization and confusing divisions of labour which are not necessarily in the interests of care recipients and may be alienating for the care givers (for a further discussion of this last point see Ungerson 1993b).

Moreover, none of the four streams of thought outlined above, with the possible exception of the feminist stream, pay much attention to the working conditions entailed by payments for care. We are talking about work which is very time-consuming and located within the domestic domain. The feminist stream understands that such working conditions have considerable, and negative, implications for the ability of carers, and women in particular, to participate in public life (in other words, that the Marshallian conception of citizenship construed as social rights, runs counter to the republican conception) (Lister 1994). It is also the case, that, typically, existing systems of payment identify only one person to receive the whole benefit or payment and none of the current streams of thought (with the possible exception of the new right) have further ideas on this matter. Hence, a certain loneliness is entailed for the care givers: they are likely to see themselves as the one person mainly responsible for the well-being of the care-recipient, as well as being physically alone with the persons they care for.[2] Some of the existing systems of payment appear to be building in really powerful measures to ensure that carers do work entirely on their own; for example, the developing German system which allows care recipients to opt for *either* cash *or* a limited number of domiciliary visits, seems designed to make certain that carers receive exceptionally limited social service support.

CONCLUDING REMARKS

I am suggesting, therefore, that we need to develop two levels of analysis of 'payments for care' – at a micro as well as at a macro level – and that we have to deal with these two levels *together*. Both levels of thought make claims that payments for care would be transformative of social relations, but we need to be aware of precisely the kinds of transformations we have in mind, and their implications for relationships between carers and users, citizens and the state, consumers and the market.

Moreover, it is important to understand that the way in which the presence of money may determine the nature of caring relationships can also be unravelled within a more conventional sociological understanding of the nature of labour markets and how they are intersected by the independent variables of class, race and sex. In terms of 'class' (very loosely defined) we may be seeing the beginnings of a revival of a form of domestic service, with all the connotations of subservience and unequal work relationships that that implies. In terms of 'sex', payments may represent a form of targeted and because they are generally so low, exploitative, wages for casual 'women's work' and lead to the further sex segmentation of already sexually divided labour markets. In terms of 'race' and 'ethnicity' we may be seeing the beginnings of yet another form of unregulated and grey labour market, where employers, be they agencies or individual disabled people, might feel they can find particularly 'flexible' labour, and to which those with already limited rights of citizenship might well be attracted, particularly if they can resolve their housing needs by moving into a disabled person's household.

There remains a great deal of work to be done to tease out the moral, political and economic implications of the growth, in many developed countries, of payments for care, and the increasing prominence given to the issue in various sets of literature. At the same time there is also work waiting to be done which applies the various social science disciplines to the question. For example, within economics, the issue can be discussed within a discourse of labour supply and its determinants; within sociology, the discourse could focus on the nature of caring obligations, and the way in which informal and volunteering caring relationships are affected by cash exchanges and the existence of implicit or explicit contracts; within social policy, the discourse could focus on the question of regulation of caring relationships, and the rights of both carer and cared for.

NOTES

1. An earlier version of this paper entitled 'Gender, Cash and Informal Care. European perspectives and dilemmas' was published in the *Journal of Social Policy*, Vol. 24, 4, January 1995. This paper is printed with the kind permission of Cambridge University Press, publishers of the *Journal of Social Policy*.
2. It would be particularly interesting to see some Scandinavian research on how relatives employed as municipal home helps feel their relationships with the people they have been caring for have been altered by this fact of full-scale employment, and vice versa.

REFERENCES

Abrahamson, P.E. (1991) 'Welfare and Poverty in Europe of the 1990's: social progress or social dumping?', *International Journal of Health Services*, Vol. 21, no. 2, pp. 237–64.

Baldock, J. (1993) 'Patterns of change in the delivery of welfare in Europe', in P. Taylor-Gooby and R. Lawson (eds), *Markets and Managers: New Issues in the Delivery of Welfare*, Buckingham: Open University Press.

Baldock, J. and Evers, A. (1992) 'Innovations and Care of the Elderly: The Cutting-edge of Change for Social Welfare Systems. Examples from Sweden, the Netherlands and the United Kingdom' in *Ageing and Society*, no. 12, pp. 289–312.

Baldock, J. and C. Ungerson (1991) '"What d'ya want if you don' want money?": a feminist critique of "paid volunteering"', in M. Maclean and D. Groves (eds), *Women's Issues in Social Policy*, London and New York: Routledge.

Baldock, J. and C. Ungerson, (1994) 'Choice and constraint and the welfare mix: the experience of stroke patients' Report to the Joseph Rowntree Foundation.

Central Statistical Office (1993), Social Trends, 23, London: HMSO.

Challis, D. and B. Davies (1986) *Case Management in Community Care*, Aldershot: Gower.

Craig, G. (1992) *Cash or Care: A Question of Choice?*, York: Social Policy Research Unit, University of York.

Dalley, G. (1988) *Ideologies of Caring: Rethinking Community and Collecitivism* London: Macmillan.

Department of Social Security (1974) *Social Security Provision for Chronically Sick and Disabled People*, HC 276, London: HMSO.

Esping-Andersen, G. (1990) *The three worlds of welfare capitalism*, Cambridge: Polity Press.

Evers, A. (1994) 'Payments for care: a small but significant part of a wider debate' in A. Evers, M.Pijl and C. Ungerson (eds), *Payments for Care: the European and North American experience*, Aldershot: Avebury.

Finch, J. (1989) *Family obligations and social change*, Cambridge: Polity Press.

Finch, J. and D. Groves (eds) (1983) *A Labour of Love: women, work and caring*, London: Routledge and Kegan Paul.

Finch, J. and J. Mason (1992) *Negotiating family responsibilities*; London; New York: Tavistock/Routledge.

Fraser, N. (1999) 'After the Family Wage: Gender Equity and the Welfare State' in Hobson (ed.) *Gender and Citizenship in Transition*, Basingstoke: Macmillan Press Ltd.

Glendinning, C. (1992) *The Costs of Informal Care: looking inside the household*, London: HMSO.

Glendinning, C. and E. McLaughlin, (1993a) *'Financial Support for Informal Care: A European Study'* report prepared for the Social Security Advisory Committee, London: HMSO.

Glendinning, C. and E. McLaughlin (1993b) 'Paying for Informal Care: Lessons from Finland', *Journal of European Social Policy*, Vol. 3, no. 4, pp. 239–53.

Graham, H. (1983) 'Caring: a labour of love' in J. Finch, and D. Groves (eds), *A Labour of Love: Women, Work and Caring*, London: Routledge and Kegan Paul.

Graham, H. (1991) 'The concept of caring in feminist research: the case of domestic service' *Sociology*, Vol. 25, no. 1, pp. 61–78.

Griffiths, R. (1988) *Community Care: Agenda for Action*, London: HMSO.

Groves, D. and J. Finch, (1983) 'Natural selection: perspectives on entitlement to the invalid care allowance' in D. Finch, and D. Groves (eds) (1983), *A Labour of Love: women, work and caring*, London: Routledge and Kegan Paul.

Hicks, C. (1988) *Who cares: looking after people at home*, London: Virago.

Horton, C. and R. Berthoud, (1990) *The Attendance Allowance and the Costs of Caring*, London: Policy Studies Institute.

Laing, W. (1991) *Empowering the Elderly: direct consumer funding of the services*, London: IEA Health and Welfare Unit.

Land, Hillary (1978) 'Who Cares for the Family?', *Journal of Social Policy*, Vol. 7, part 3, pp. 257–84.

Leat, D. (1990) *For love and money: the role of payment in encouraging the provision of care*, York: Joseph Rowntree Foundation.

Leat, D. and P. Gay, (1987) *Paying for Care*, PSI Research Report no. 66, London: Policy Studies Institute.

Leat, D. with C. Ungerson, (1993) 'Creating Care at the Boundaries: issues in the supply and management of domiciliary care' report to the Joseph Rowntree Foundation, Canterbury: Dept of Social Policy, University of Kent.

Leira, A. (1992) *Welfare States and Working Mothers*, Cambridge: Cambridge University Press.

Lewis, J. (1992) 'Gender and the development of welfare regimes' *Journal of European Social Policy*, Vol. 2, no. 3, pp. 159–73.

Lewis, J. (1994) 'A comment of family policy and the welfare of women in cross-national perspective' in Linda Hantrais and Steen Mangen (eds), *Family Policy and the Welfare of Women*, Loughborough: European Research Centre, University of Loughborough.

Lewis, J. and B. Meredith, (1988) *Daughters who care: daughters caring for mothers at home*, London: Routledge.

Lister, R. (1990) 'Women, economic dependency and citizenship' *Journal of Social Policy*, Vol. 7, no. 4, pp. 445–67.

Lister, R. (1999) 'Dilemmas in Engendering Citizenship' in Hobson (ed.) *Gender and Citizenship in Transition*, Basingstoke: Macmillan Press Ltd.

McLaughlin, E. (1991) *Social Security and Community Care: The case of the Invalid Care Allowance*, Department of Social Security Research Report No. 4, London: HMSO.

Morris, J. (1993) *Independent Lives: Community Care and Disabled People*, Basingstoke: Macmillan.

Parker, G. (1990) *With due care and attention: a review of research on informal care*, 2nd edn, London: Family Policy Studies Centre.

Parker, G. (1993) *With This Body: caring and disability in marriage*, Buckingham: Open University Press.

Pateman, C. (1988) *The Sexual Contract*, Cambridge: Polity Press.

Pateman, C. (1989) *The Disorder of Women*, Cambridge: Polity Press.

Qureshi, H., D. Challis and B. Davies (1989) *Helpers in case-managed community care*, Aldershot: Gower.

Qureshi, H. and Walker, A. (1989) *The caring relationship: elderly people and their families*; Basingstoke: Macmillan.

Robertson, S. (1993) *Disability Rights Handbook*, 18th edn, April 1993–April 1994, London: Disability Alliance Educational and Research Association.

Shaver, S. and J. Bradshaw (1993) 'The Recognition of Wifely Labour by Welfare States' Social Policy Research Centre Discussion Paper, no. 44, Kensington, New South Wales: The University of New South Wales.

Sipilä, J. (1993) 'Home care allowances for the frail elderly in Finland – a contradictory innovation', in A. Evers, and I. Svetlik (eds), *Balancing Pluralism – New Welfare Mixes in Care for the Elderly*, Aldershot: Avebury.

Thomas, C. (1993) 'Deconstructing concepts of care', Sociology, November.

Thornton, P. (1989) *Creating a Break: home care relief for elderly people and their supporters*, London: Age Concern Institute of Gerontology.

Tinker, A. (1984) *Staying at home: helping elderly people*, Department of Environment, London: HMSO.

Ungerson, C. (1987) *Policy is Personal: sex, gender and informal care*, London: Tavistock.

Ungerson, C. (1990) 'The language of care; crossing the boundaries' in Ungerson, C. (ed.) *Gender and Caring: Work And Welfare in Britain and Scandinavia*, Hemel Hempstead: Harvester/Wheatsheaf.

Ungerson, C. (1993a) 'Caring and citizenship: a complex relationship' in J. Bornat *et al.* (eds) *Community Care: A Reader*, Basingstoke: Macmillan.

Ungerson, C. (1993b) 'Payment for care: mapping the territory' in N. Deakin and R. Page (eds), *The Costs of Welfare*, Aldershot: Avebury.

Ungerson, C. (1995)'Gender, cash and informal care: European perspectives and Dilemmas', *Journal of Social Policy*, Vol. 24, no. 4.

Wright, F.D. (1986) *Left to care alone*, Aldershoopean perspectives and Dilemmas', *Journal of Social Policy*, Vol. 24, no. 4.

Wright, F.D. (1986) *Left to care alone*, Aldershot: Gower.

8 The Rationalized Marginalization of Care: Time is Money, Isn't It?

Trudie Knijn

According to the calculations of the cleaning-company, the cleaning-woman from ex-Yugoslavia, Turkey or Morocco, got three seconds to clean my office-desk.

Civil servants got exactly 170 minutes to deal with the insurance application of a client, including 45 minutes for an interview. There is no time any more to do the usual home-to-home calls or for some extra activities to help clients to refind their way to the labour market.

A friend of mine, single mother of a 13 year-old daughter, had to stay in bed for six months because of a slipped disc. Together with some intimate friends her daughter had to run the household, home help was only available for two mornings a week. When she had to go to the hospital to have an operation, the home help service let her know that there was no possibility to get support for caring for her young daughter.

My daughter was confronted at her primary school with many temporary teachers. Her own teacher had to take care of her older parents who were waiting for a room in a serviced home.

This is only a small selection of my recent experiences with 'daily care'. They show a general 'decline in all kinds of daily care'; cleaning the workplace, guiding the unemployed, helping sick parents and caring for the elderly. All these forms of 'daily care' are subjected to a regime of 'rationalized marginalization'; they are losing their meaning in a process of calculation. The rationalized marginalization of daily care in the public and the private sphere seems to be an ongoing process in all

Western countries. What is the background to this process and what are its consequences for the everyday life of women and for such 'gendered areas' as care and intimacy? Which criteria are available to evaluate the consequences of this process? These are the topics I would like to deal with in this chapter.

PRIVATE CARE; A MATTER OF WOMEN'S TIME, PROXIMITY AND WILLINGNESS

Caring, cleaning and cooking have been viewed as reproductive activities, belonging to the private domain of the family and done, or co-ordinated, by housewives without training. Although there were also some professionals who performed these activities (cooks, nurses, stewardesses, nannies) the major part of the work was – and still is – done by women (wives, daughters, mothers and neighbours) in a personal relationship with the recipients. As long as a majority of women, during some decennia of this century, were available for and felt obliged to care, political and social discussions about personal care concerned the way these women fulfilled this task. In particular 'modern housekeeping' and 'modern motherhood' drew attention.

During the first part of this century 'scientific housekeeping' was put forward. In the United States as well as in Europe housewives and professionals were trained in rationalizing housekeeping and house cleaning in a Tayloristic way. The objective of this programme was to reach efficiency and to discipline the servants. The status of the housewife, the hygiene of the family and their modernity were implicitly connected to the way a housewife succeeded in developing a modern way of housekeeping. With the introduction of 'modern housekeeping' such activities as airing the bedrooms, eating with a knife and a fork, daily bathing, cleaning the windows and so on, became part of the weekly routine of the housewife.

Taylorization of housekeeping therefore was in the first place a matter of 'civilization'; by ranking and ordering the former tasks of the housewife and by adding some new aspects from the perspective of hygiene and public health. (Van Daalen, 1993). In no way was this a time-saving development. In contrast, modern housekeeping consumed the time women did not spend any longer in productive work. Modern housekeeping filled the void which was left since (middle-class) women withdrew from the labour market. It was only in the 1950s and the 1960s that housekeeping started to become less time consuming. With the mechanization of household apparatus – showers, electric washing machines, vacuum-cleaners and central heating – housekeeping became easier and demanded less of a housewife's time. Together with the declining birth rates and the increase of incomes this meant a decline in the time housewives spent on housekeeping from about 60 to 30 hours a week. Housekeeping disappeared as a topic of importance.

The modernization of motherhood was a second theme of debate, especially after World War II. In reaction to the disruption of family life during the war, several, ostensibly contradictory, new child care paradigms developed; the permissive child care paradigm of Spock, the attachment paradigm of Bowlby and the warning against overprotective motherhood (Singer 1989). All these approaches had in common their search for a modern style of child care in which the mother was viewed as the pivot of the inter-familial relationships and the main care giver. In this 'role' she was supposed to create a warm and safe nest, in which the children could develop their individual identities on the basis of a respectful and communicative relationship with the mother. Although the hegemony of this paradigm of motherly personal care of children was not established in all countries at the same time, nor with the same strength, it influenced the thoughts about and the practices of motherhood all over the (Western) world in the post-war years. (Singer 1989) The consequence was that, to a certain degree, the time saved by the introduction of modern apparatus in the house, was directed into the time spent with children; listening, playing and developmental activities were viewed as necessary investments in child development, and it was the mother who was supposed to professionalize her attitude towards the children (Knijn 1994).

Times have changed; giving personal care not only to children but also to other relatives and important others, presumes at least three dispositions; *time, proximity and willingness*. These three dispositions are currently under pressure. Since women entered the labour market their *time* became a scarce resource and spending their scarce time to satisfy real or supposed needs of important others cannot be taken for granted any longer.

Nowadays women sometimes can, sometimes have to, and sometimes cannot choose to give personal care, depending on their workload. Also, *proximity* now offers difficulties, whether because of a woman's own choice to spread her wings and leave her family, or because of economic reasons; the free trade economy forced many women, and/or their male partners to go where the jobs are. Migration, commuter relations and instability of settlement are the consequences of a free market that have an irreversible influence on personal care in families. Only some specific groups, mostly at the lowest level of the labour market, are still living in the neighbourhood of their families of birth. So, a majority of the population lacks, solely because of distance, the possibility to take care of their relatives for a longer period . The last disposition, the willingness to take care, has been discussed by politicians and social scientists for some decennia. Some state that because of individualization, the decline of altruism and a growing narcissism (always with respect to women) the willingness to provide personal care declined (Lasch 1977, Popenoe 1988). Willingness however, is not an unambigious capacity, nor can it be viewed from the perspective of women's behaviour only. Willingness to care is embedded in a social context in which the possibilities of combining care and labour, the relations between the sexes, the quality of institutionalized care and familial attitudes direct and structure the claims women make. If the structure of work is not adjusted to workers with caring responsibilities, women (and men) who are willing to care, do not have the opportunity to act correspondingly. To conclude that they lack the will to care, is a chutzpah. On the other hand, many people appear to prefer caring for their relatives in addition to institutionalized or professional care. But the more care giving becomes a continuous, necessitive and protracted activity, the less satisfying it is and the more tensions it causes, to the carers as well as to the recipients (Qureshi 1990).

The pressure on women's time, proximity and willingness to take care obviously has consequences for the amount of personal care they can and will give. This is also the conclusion of many studies of care in families. Although there prove to be many variations in families in spending time on care, most studies report that women, especially mothers, are confronted with many problems in coping with caring, cooking and cleaning, not to speak of the more emotional aspects of family life, marriage and parenthood. The problems vary from practical problems with the necessary flexible organization of daily life, time schedules which are always disturbed, working double days, unexpected claims on time by the work of children's schools or sporting clubs, to emotional problems such as being exhausted, feelings of guilt towards the children, the partner or colleagues and burn-out (Hochschild 1989; Wheelock 1990; Brannen and Moss 1991, Stacey 1991). Although many working women often think about giving up their job, most of them are eagerly willing to be employed. The causes of the problems working women have in combining care and labour can be summarized in two acknowledged factors: workplaces are still arranged on the assumption of an employee who does not have responsibility for care, and male partners refuse to share the responsibilities and the practical consequences of caring for a family.

Although the causes of women's problems with care giving are recognized, the consequences for family life are seldom disputed in feminist studies. Friedan (1981) and later on Hochschild (1989) were the first to try to get an insight into the consequences of the 'stalled revolution' for family life and personal care. They spoke about an unwanted reduction of care, a family life dominated by time schedules, marital relations continuously operated by negotiations and ten year old children who manage to take over their parents responsibility for care. Those signals have up till now been viewed as the negative consequences of women's entry into the labour market. But that is not what Friedan and Hochschild try to explain. They state that the reduction of personal care is not a women's problem only, it is mainly a social problem related to the undervaluation of care and I think this point has to be taken seriously.

It has to be taken seriously because of the interwoveness of femininity and care. The hierarchical relation between men and women as sexes is, as we know, not limited to their existence as human beings. It is also reflected in the negative appreciation of supposed feminine characteristics, symbols and activities. Care forms a core element in this undervalued conglomeration of femininity. That is why we have to understand the problems of care beyond the context of family life and to analyze the developments in care from a broader perspective.

THE MARGINALIZATION OF CARE

Since the feminist debate focused on care as a core aspect of the definition of women's identity and activities, many descriptions and distinctions have been made between different kinds of care. Ungerson (1983) distinguished the emotional aspects of care ('care about') and the work aspects of care ('caring for'). Waerness (1984) put emphasis on the power relations of care and therefore distinguished care based on a hierarchical social relation ('personal services'), care in a relationship between a dependent and his/her care giver ('care giving work') and reciprocal care ('spontaneous care'). Tronto and Fisher (1990) distinguished various caring activities, each demanding different kinds of involvement and responsibility; the recognition of care ('caring about'), responsibility for the identified need ('taking care of'), direct meeting for care ('care giving') and responding to the care ('care receiving').

The advantage of these feminist conceptualizations of care is that they go beyond the dichotomy of public and private life and beyond the distinction between paid and unpaid work. Although they differ in the accents they highlight, these approaches to care show us that daily care is everywhere in society and not limited to private relationships. In the same way as physical work is not only located in the harbours or the building industry, and intellectual work is not only carried out by employees who are working at desks, care work is not confined to the mother–child relationship or to women working in the service areas. Besides, these recent feminist conceptualizations offer us the tools to analyze the differences and similarities of many diverse caring activities women perform. It teaches us to understand the similarities between women's caring labour as housewives, secretaries, stewardesses, managers, teachers, home helps, cleaners and nurses. Finally these conceptualizations of care are helpful in offering us tools for analyzing the relationship between developments in labour circumstances, professional skills and emotionality with reference to this wide variety of daily care.

I would like to explore the latter in this chapter. The above mentioned reduction of care in the private domain does not come about in isolation. It appears to be less a private problem of working women than an indication of the devaluation and reduction of care in society in general. Besides the changing habits in family life, especially in dual earner families – such as the necessity of using calendars to meet friends, the agenda which regulate our common meals with the children, the impossibility of guiding dying parents or close friends and the poor excuses people need to stay at home when their children are sick – other developments in care are drawing our attention.

TABOOING CARE DEPENDENCY

From a cultural approach we see a change in the meaning of care dependency during the last decennium. Care has a negative connotation which influences the provider as well as the recipient of care. In the Netherlands for instance, since the 1980s there has been a continuous flow of publications which stressed the negative consequences of care dependency (Gordon and Fraser (1994) signalled the same tendency in the US). According to these, care dependency would lead to passivity, tutelage, laziness, a lack of responsibility, a-morality and all other kinds of unwanted behaviours and characteristics (Achterhuis 1980, Adriaansens and Zijderveld 1983, WRR 1990). This redefinition of care, of care dependency created a taboo; the recipient became characterized as a calculating citizen who tries to receive maximum profit from the welfare benefits. The problem with this analysis is that it has equalized in the negative approach all kinds of welfare and care recipients, whether they were really disabled persons, people of old age, single mothers with young children or cohabitants who fraudulently obtained welfare benefits, the un-employed who worked additionally in the informal labour market or partially sick-listed people who received too much allowance. (An exception was made for the care dependent breadwinner, his care dependency was never viewed as problematic.) Instead of stimulating a public debate about new criteria to judge the legitimacy of care, there is an overall tendency to accuse every recipient of care and welfare of abusing welfare benefits. In doing so two transformations take place. The first is an individualization of the problem of dependency: every citizen is expected to be independent, no matter her situation, ability or condition. The proof of being dependent on welfare and care shifts from the (local) government to the citizen. The second transformation is a redefinition of care dependents in a rational – economic vocabulary which refers to the marketization of care. People who are dependent on care and welfare are more and more described as consumers or clients; buyers of care products. In being a consumer a care dependent is supposed to be an active citizen who takes whatever s/he needs, who negotiates the prices of the products of care and is autonomous in her decisions about the character and the quality of care. In other words; in order to maintain their personal dignity, care dependents are increasingly assumed to be clients who make rational choices with respect to all the products available in the supermarket of care.

This image, however, hides two important realities. The first is the – partial – social inadequacy of many of the care recipients, the second is the lack of quantitively and qualitively good care. The senile elderly person who is confronted with the care consultant to discuss her needs, the patient who has to decide about her medical treatment, the psychiatric patient who has to decide about her future form of independent living, the single old person who needs emotional and social care as much as a daily meal and an injection of insulin, all are more or less incapable of making the right decisions. Not only because their care dependency partly results in an inability to make such autonomous decisions, but also because they realize that the offered care does not come at all from a well-filled care supermarket. Although there are great differences between countries with respect to the supermarket of care, the withdrawal of the welfare state shows a continous process of decline in the quantity and the quality of the available care. The taboo on care dependency, however, does not take into account that many people not only are dependent on some standardized care, but that they also are not always able to make the right decisions about the kind of care they need. Recognizing care dependency as a natural state of humanness requires another morality than that which is involved in the rational choice paradigm. It requires attention, commitment, acknowledgement of the other's vulnerability and taking the other's perspective into consideration before making the decisions about the care provided (Sevenhusen 1991).

RATIONALIZING CARE WORK

As far as it is studied and documented, we see an overall tendency in the European countries to reduce the costs of institutional care and care provision. We cannot generalize on this point, because in some countries, especially the Scandinavian countries, the quality of care and the professionalization of caring jobs is much higher than it is in other countries. Nevertheless we can conclude that everywhere caring professions are under pressure or at least are the subject of a heavy political dispute (Waerness 1990). In this process contradictory policies are going on, which only seem to be signalled by those who have knowledge of the role of women in the field of paid and unpaid care (Balbo 1987, Waerness 1990; Ungerson 1990). Feminist studies challenged in the first place the expected assumption that informal personal care can increase to the same degree as professional care is declining. The reason is the paradox of the demand and the supply of care while demographic and medical developments imply that in all European countries the ratio of elderly, and care dependent persons is increasing, while the availability of women who can informally support care dependents is diminishing due to growing labour market participation and migration.

The second feminist argument against the decline of professional and institutionalized care is that sex-segregation in paid and unpaid care has disappeared nowhere in the world. Since care remains a women's activity, cutting down the care provisions especially means the exchange of paid for unpaid care by women. This argument is hidden in the political debate behind the 'costs talk'; the costs of institutionalized care are in most countries experienced as being bound to economic growth. The idea that boundaries of taxes necessary to pay good and professional care have been reached is experienced everywhere, no matter what the percentage of taxes really is

Care remains a women's issue, but this issue now has an extra dimension. Where we once discussed care from the perspective of symmetrical gender-relations, equality and emancipation, now care is becoming an important issue because its availability and quality are under pressure, and since women are the main (and as far as it concerns elderly women, also the main recipients) suppliers of care, women are confronted with the consequences of the marginalization of care. What are these consequences?

First to cut the costs of institutionalized care, a bureaucratic regime arose. Although the rationality of care is different from and sometimes contradictary to scientific and bureaucratic control (Waerness 1984) all kinds of efforts were undertaken to rationalize institutionalized care. In the Netherlands, for instance, two enormous re-organizations took place in home help services. The first was a forced fusion on a national scale of different forms of home help, the second was a very detailed description of all kinds of 'care products' offered by those new home help services, which was accompanied by a new system of indication of the clients' needs. Despite the euphemistic vocabulary used for the introduction of these changes – the government described it as 'towards care at measure' – it became clear very soon that this whole operation implied an enormous reduction of the available home help. The care products were limited to three central forms of care – housekeeping, care and social assistance. The time for each product was limited, a proof of no available relatives who could undertake care was introduced, a distinction was made between home care and home help, and hardly anyone who was categorized as needing home help received the needed help; waiting-lists increased in some municipalities to two years. The result is that at this moment 47 per cent of all elderly women who need help do not receive any form of support. (Tjadens and Woldring 1989)

The consequences on the side of the care workers are twofold. There is an increasing burn-out among care workers, the job became too demanding to do it full-time, workers complain about the reduction of time available to individual clients, and they often leave the care sector for another job or become a housewife again. The other consequence is that young women increasingly refuse to choose a caring job. Overall in professional care there is a shortage of employees, while unemployment among women, and especially among lower educated women is high. (Hattinga Verschure 1981, Beukema 1990)

Second a growing demand for informal care is the second consequence of the reduction in quality and quantity of professional care. In many countries governments introduced a 'back to the society' policy with respect to care. While it was called 'care-in-the community' in Britain (Ungerson 1990), 'community' care in Scandinavian countries (Waerness 1990), it was called 'caring society' and 'care at measure' in the Netherlands. A recent study about informal care in the Netherlands drew some important conclusions about the current state of informal care. One concluded that: disabled people who require care are disproportionally lower educated and also disproportionally living alone, more than half of those with a disability receive informal care, those with high incomes more than those with low incomes, young disabled people in need of care prefer private care services above institutional care and/or informal care, elderly disabled people need more personal attention which cannot be provided by home helps and district nurses, so alternative forms of care such as sheltered housing and group housing must be developed.

Concerning the supply of informal care, it was concluded that 11 per cent of the adult population provides informal care – 15 per cent of women and 7 per cent of men – and most of them have a low level of education. Although age, sex and having a job does not seem to influence the provision of informal care, it does through the intermediation of other activities. People who spend more than 55 hours a week in work, household activities and educational activities, do not take up much informal care. And this is where the gender division in care starts. Because most women in the Netherlands work part-time, they are the actual providers of informal care. The increasing labour participation of women until now did not influence women's involvement with informal care; Dutch women work part-time and if occasionally necessary they combine this work with informal care. The report ends with the final conclusion: '. . . the actual supply of informal care is unpredictable. It depends on the demand for help within social networks and the response of the members of those networks, which means that their ideas, values and norms are important. These do not arise spontaneously in the individual or within the social network, but are informed by the attitudes of society as a whole. Feelings of solidarity with relatives and friends appear to be very strong in the Netherlands, probably because solidarity is not forced upon us as it is in some other countries.' (De Boer, *et al.* 1994)

In this conclusion about the feelings of solidarity within social networks in the Netherlands, and the willingness of citizens to provide informal care, much is hidden. This conclusion does not tell us that it is especially the lower educated women with the lower incomes who provide care, it does not tell us that during the last years the demand for informal care increased because of the reduction of professional care, it hides the declining quality of professional care and it does not say a word about the influence of network solidarity on the 'choice' of women to work part-time.

What it does say is that the willingness of Dutch women to give priority to informal care – for children, elderly parents, other relatives or neighbours – above financial and economic independence, is enormous, especially among the lower educated women. Dutch women appear to be carers in the first place, and that is why they accept the consequences of the 'caring society', and that is also why a political debate about care did not become highly contested despite the situation with respect to care.

The debate about care in the Netherlands can be summarized as follows: care is the duty of the citizen, every citizen has to provide informal care to 'significant others'. This care should be provided in particular by the citizens who have time to do so, which means housewives. Informal care supplied by housewives (whether wives, daughters, nieces or grandmothers) is so much part of the Dutch culture, that a reduction of state supplied care hardly leads to a debate about the withdrawal of the welfare state, the state's responsibility for care or the way taxes are needed for maintaining professional care. Only professional carers and their organizations challenge the state's care policy, because they experience an increasing stress, burn-out among the carers and an intolerable neglect of the care dependants. The main focus of the debate is, however, on how to provide the necessary informal care, whether women should reject paid jobs because of the necessity of providing informal care and whether to give flowers or support to informal carers.

DAILY CARE AND THE WELFARE STATE

Underlying the paradox of care are two central tendencies: the first is that care retains its gendered character, while worldwide women are increasingly participating in the labour market. The entrance of men into the domain of care, the status of men as carers, or the employee with caring responsibilities – none of these found their way into public awareness or public policies in the same degree as the female worker did. Instead of that a reduction and devaluation of daily care seemed to be the only option for employed women who did not want to become overloaded or stressed. Alternatives like private nannies and cleaners, home helps, institutionalized child care, homes for the elderly and so on to a certain degree solved this reduction of personal daily care, but only in a limited way and nowhere did they offer a good enough alternative for the withdrawal of women from care. The second general tendency underlying the paradox of care is that although in current public policies a strong 'care-debate' is going on, this debate focuses especially on the citizen's personal duty to care. The quality of care, the state's responsibility to care and the human rights of care dependants are all getting less attention in the public debate of the welfare states than the citizen's own responsibility to claim care as little as possible and the citizen's responsibility to give care as much as possible. So while care has never been discussed as much as today, it results in the stigmatization and devaluation of care givers and receivers. It is as if a new definition of citizenship has become dominant; someone without persons to care for and someone without a need to be cared for. The strong, sane, healthy, capable and productive human being becomes the standard citizen.

Let us see, from this perspective, what we can say about the development of modern welfare states.

CARE AND THE EVALUATION OF THE WELFARE STATE

About a decade ago a feminist debate began about whether the welfare state was either patriarchal or women friendly. (Hernes 1987, Siim 1990) In this debate the welfare state was evaluated by such criteria as its policy towards women's autonomy, women's labour participation and sex-segregation in the labour market, the quality and quantity of its caring provisions, women's political participation, and reproductive right.

In this debate empirical and theoretical research underlined some general conclusions. There is not one paradigmatic women friendly welfare state; specific countries have their specific kind of welfare state and it depends on the criteria whether a welfare state can be characterized as women friendly or not. Liberal welfare states show less sex segregation than social democratic and corporatist welfare states, but there exists more inequality among women. Social democratic welfare states have more care provisions of good quality than in liberal and corporatist welfare states, but also have a strong gender gap between the private and the public sector. Corporatist welfare states seem to have better benefits for mothers but the labour participation of mothers is low and thereby their autonomy too. (Esping-Andersen 1990, Langan and Ostner 199, Orloff 1993).

The criteria for the evaluation of welfare states from a gender perspective are ambiguous. Nevertheless we can conclude that 'male-criteria' like decommodification and equal rights in social security are not sufficient to take account of women's interests. Decommodification denies women's interest in and actual need to employment (because of the goal of financial independence). Equal rights in social security neglect women's double interest in social welfare (related to family life) and social security (related to employment) and their aim to get men involved in care.

Without denying the importance of these dimensions, I think history forces us to rethink the current developments in welfare states and the criteria we use to evaluate them. In doing so two themes need attention. First, current welfare states are increasingly converging in the direction of the liberal-type of welfare state, which means that instead of being 'patriarchal' or 'women friendly' they are developing an *indifferent* attitude toward women's interests.

Second, the welfare states' policies towards daily life, and in particular towards care need to be added as a criteria to judge the character of the welfare state. It is by using this criterion that the growing indifference of welfare states towards women's interests can be illustrated. In analyzing the consequences of the developments in welfare states with regard to personal life and well being it is of great importance to take account of the different social and cultural values with regard to care. The meaning of informal or professional care also depends on the quality of the supplied professional or informal care as well as on the meaning of care to the providers and recipients of each kind of care. The association of women, female gender-identity and the expectations or claims on women as carers form an essential part of this judgement. That is why we are, in my opinion, moving into a new stage of rethinking female indentity and care, a stage which is much more complicated than it was some years ago, a stage also where women are much more vulnerable to claims on the relational parts of their identity; current developments in welfare states not only challenge the identification of women with care, they challenge care itself.

What can be said from this point of view about the acknowledged ideal types of welfare states as they are described by Esping-Andersen and Langan and Ostner? Looking at the social democratic welfare states, the commodification of women has increased and since World War II women have depended more on a waged income than before the expansion of the welfare state. Most women began working in the public sector of the labour market. This increasing labour participation of women was guided by the introduction of state supplied care provisions. These provisions partly replaced informal personal care and partly made informal personal care possible for workers. However, since the introduction of state care provision the quality as well as its effects on daily life have been topics of concern in the public and political debates, and among carers and receivers of care. Not to be ignored in these debates is the fact that women still have many problems with combining work and care, and therefore reveal a certain ambivalence towards the notion of the 'worker citizen' and the reduction of personal care implicated in it.

In liberal welfare states the commodification of women is based on the free market ideology and therefore concerns lower educated women in particular, in contrast to the social democratic welfare states, a human needs approach to the needs of the care dependents, nor of those of the carers. In the same way as the market has to regulate jobs and incomes, it was supposed to regulate care. The consequence is, as many Anglo-North American surveys show, a downgrading of care: low paid women have hardly any opportunity to find acceptable care for their children, elderly parents and other family members needing care. The caring provisions available to them are of poor quality, only the upper classes have access to personal care – they can buy the personnel who provide it – and 'payment for care' alternatives for the reduction of institutionalized care give the impression that the state or the local government is at least concerned with carers.

Corporatist welfare states 'protected', at the expense of women's autonomy, personal care. Women were indirectly, via breadwinner wages and secondary benefits for women without a breadwinner, the suppliers of personal care, at least until the 1980s. Nowadays these carers' provisions are under attack in most corporatist welfare states. Now that women enter the labour market at the moment of the withdrawal of the welfare state, marketized care seems to be becoming the alternative to the care provided formerly by housewives. Corporatist welfare states do not have the public care-oriented tradition of social democratic welfare states; care belongs to the private domain and there it remains, even if the carers are going public.

From this description of the current typology of the three welfare states we have to conclude that the commodification of women's labour, which took place at different moments and for different reasons in the different welfare states, leads to three alternatives towards the care women in the labour market left behind: state supplied care, marketized care and reduction of care. There is a 'rationalized marginalization' of care at present in all three options; the government, as well as the market and employers, calculate the most minimal care that is necessary to maintain economic production. That is the rationality of reducing parental leaves, reducing the available home help, reducing the number of homes for the elderly, diminishing the number of employees in home help services, stigmatizing care dependents and giving small amounts of payment. On the other hand, there is evidence that the meaning, forms and quality of daily care and its level of institutionalization and professionalization varies too much within each of the three ideal-types of welfare states to conclude that a certain level of decommodification implies automatically a certain level of rationalization of daily care. For instance Leira (1990) showed us that the professionalization of care in Norway differs a lot from that in Denmark or Sweden, although all three are characterized as social democratic welfare states. The consequences of these differences for the rationalized marginalization of care are not clear yet. The same is true for the differences between Belgium and the Netherlands; although both countries have characteristics of the mixture of corporatist and social democratic welfare states, they differ very much in the degree of professionalizing of child care. Therefore we need to rethink the dominant typology from the perspective of the relationship between formal and informal care, the rationalization and marginalization of care and its consequences for daily life, the vulnerability of care dependents and carers and the position of women. In relation to that we especially need more comparative research on these topics.

CONCLUSION

The increasing labour force participation of Dutch women is occuring at the very same time as the retrenchment and withdrawal of the welfare state. Clearly this trend pose dilemmas for those who need care and for care givers, particularly in the Netherlands, since the search for solutions is fraught with complexity that can be traced to conflicts within second wave feminism. On the one side are those who argue for the right to care: on the other side are those who claim the right not to care. The Dutch feminist movement appears to have become polarized around those two positions: one speaks of 'the colonization of the private world because of the powerful economic forces which push women to leave their intimate relationships', and the other pleads for autonomy and challenges the benefits women as carers received until now.

Yet both these positions lead into a false dichotomy of work versus care. Recent conceptions of care have sought to break away from this dichotomy by viewing care as an undeniable aspect of human life, which is to say that everyone, at least during some periods in his or her life, will be confronted with the necessity to give or receive personal care. From this perspective, care is not a gendered activity but a human activity and is connected to being a citizen in a welfare state. Thinking about the rationality of care from this perspective calls for different frameworks and criteria for evaluating care in welfare states. Such frameworks and criteria at least have to include the balancing of the rights and duties of care givers and care recipients, the harmonization of work and care and finally the degendering of care. In particular, feminist scholars can contribute to such a 'care policy' by putting care as an inclusive aspect of citizenship on the political and scientific agenda.

REFERENCES

Achterhuis, H. (1980) *De markt van welzijn en geluk*. Baarn: Ambo.

Adriaansens, H. and A.C. Zijderveld (1983) *Vrijwillig initiatief in de verzorgingsstaat*. Deventer: Van Loghum Slaterus.

Leira, Arnlaug (1990) 'Coping with care: Mothers in a welfare state', in C. Ungerson (ed.) *Gender and Caring. Work and welfare in Britain and Scandinavia*, Hemel Hempstead: Harvester Wheatsheaf. pp. 133–159.

Balbo (1987) 'Crazy Quilts: Rethinking the welfare state debate from a woman's point of view' in A. Showstack Sasson, (ed.) *Women and the State. The Shifting Boundaries of Public and Private*, London: Hutchinson. pp. 45–71.

Beukema, L. (1990) 'Kwalificatieontwikkelingen in de eerstelijns gezondheidszorg', *Tijdschrift voor Arbeid en Bewustzijn*. 4: 229–238.

Boer, A.H. de, J.C. Hessing-Wagner, M. Mootz and I.S. Schoemakers-Salkinoja (1994) *Informele zorg. Een verkenning van huidige en toekomstige ontwikkelingen*, Rijswijk: Sociaal en Cultureel Planbureau.

Brannen J. and P. Moss (1991) *Managing Mothers. Dual Earner Households after Maternity*, London: Unwin Hyman.

Ebbers, l. and S. Kaldenhoven (1993), *Wie zorgt er voor de zorgverleners*. Utrecht: Wetenschapswinkel Sociale Wetenschappen.

Emancipatieraad (1993), *Advies vrouwenmantel èn mannetrouw in de thuiszorg*. Den Haag.

Esping-Andersen, G. (1990) *The Three Worlds of Welfare Capitalism*, Cambridge: Polity Press.

Fisher, B. and J. Tronto (1990) 'Towards a feminist theory of caring', in E. Abel and M. Nelson (eds) *Circles of Care. Work and Identity in Women's Lives*. New York: State University of New York Press.

Friedan, B. (1981), *The Second Stage*, New York: Summit Books.

Gordon, L. and N. Fraser (1994) '"Dependency" demystified: inscriptions of power in a keyword of the welfare state', *Social Politics* Vol. 1, no. 1, pp. 4–31.

Hattinga Verschure, J.C.M. (1981) *Het verschijnsel zorg*. Lochem: DeTijdstroom.

Hernes, Helga Maria (1987) 'Women and the welfare state: the transition from private to public dependence', in Ann Showstack Sassoon (ed.) *Women and the State*, London: Routledge.

Hochschild, A. (1989) *The Second Shift, Working Parents and the Revolution at Home*. New York: Viking.

Knijn, Trudie (1994) Social dilemmas in the image of motherhood in the Netherlands *The European Journal of Women's Studies*, Vol. 1, no. 2, pp. 183–206.

Knijn, Trudie and Monique Kremer (1997) 'Gender and the caring dimension of welfare states: toward inclusive citizenship.' *Social Politics. International Studies in Gender, State and Society*. Vol. 4, no. 3, pp. 328–61.

Kwekkeboom, M.H. (1990) *Het licht onder de korenmaat: informele zorgverlening in Nederland*. Den Haag: VUGA.

Langan, M. and Ilona O. Stner (1991) 'Gender and welfare: towards a comparative perspective', in G. Room (ed.) *European Developments in Social Policy*. Bristol: J.W. Arrowsmith.

Lasch, C. (1977) *Haven in a heartless world*, New York: Basic Books.

Nationale Raad voor de Volksgezondheid (1991) *Advies ondersteuning mantelzorg*. Zoetermeer: NVR.

Orloff, Ann Shola (1993) 'Gender and the social rights of citizenship: the comparative analysis of gender relations and welfare states', *American Sociological Review*, Vol. 58, no. 3, pp. 303–28.

Popenoe, D. (1988) *Disturbing the nest*, New York: Aldine de Gruyter.

Qureshi, H. (1990)'Boundaries between formal and informal care-giving work'. in C. Ungerson (ed.), *Gender and Caring. Work and Welfare in Britain and Scandinavia*. Hemel Hempstead: Harvester Wheatsheaf.

Sevenhuijsen, Selma (1993) 'Paradoxes of gender, ethical and epistomological perspectives on care in feminist political theory', *Acta Politica* 28, No. 2, 131–149.

Siim, Birte (1990) 'Women and the welfare state. Between public and private dependence. A comparative approach to care work in Denmark and Britain', in C. Ungerson (ed.) *Gender and Caring. Work and Welfare in Britain and Scandinavia*, Hempel Hempstead: Harvester Wheatsheaf.

Singer, E. (1989) *Kinderopvang en de moeder-kind relatie*, Deventer: Van Loghum Slaterus.

Staccy, J. (1991) *Brave new Families. Stories of Domestic Upheaval in Late Twentieth Century America*, New York: Basic Books.

Stuurgroep Toekomstscenario's Gezondheidszorg (1992), *Ouderen in het jaar 2005, gezondheid en zorg*. Rijswijk Den Haag: VUGA.

Swaan, A. de (1989), *Zorg en de staat*. Amsterdam: Bert Bakker.

Tjadens, F.L.J. and C. Woldring (1989), *Informele zorg in Nederland. Zelfzorgproblemen, behoefte aan zorg en praktisch-instrumentele onderlinge hulp*. Nijmegen: ITS.

Tronto, J. and B. Fisher, (1990) 'Toward a feminist theory of Care', in E. Abel and M. Nelson (eds) *Circles of care: work and identity in Women's Lives*, Albany, NY: Suny Press.

Ungerson, C. (1983), 'Why do women care?' in Jane J. Finch and Dulcie Groves *A labour of love: Women, work and caring*. London: Routledge and Kegan Paul.

Ungerson, C. (1990) 'The Language of Care: Crossing The Boundaries' in *Gender and Care: Work and Welfare in Britain and Scandinavia*. C. Ungerson (ed.). Hemel Hempstead: Harvester Wheatsheaf.

Veerman, T.J. (1989), *Ziekteverzuim in de gezinsverzorging*. Amsterdam/Leiden: NIA.

Waerness, K., (1984) 'The rationality of caring', *Economic and Industrial Democracy*, Vol. 5, p. 185-211.

Waerness, K. (1990) 'Informal and and formal care in old age: What is wrong with the new ideology in Scandinavia today' in (ed.) C. Ungerson, *Gender and Caring: Work and Welfare in Britain and Scandinavia*. Hemel Hempstead: Harvester Wheatsheaf.

WWR (Wetenschappelijke Raad voor het Regeringsbeleid) (1990) *Een werkend perspectief*. Den Haag: SDU uitgeverij.

Wheelock, J., (1990) *Husbands at Home. The Domestic Economy in a Post-Industrial Society*, London: Routledge.

9 Citizenship, Caring and Commodification

Lois Bryson

The nature of the domestic relationship between partners within families has received relatively little research attention. Though a recent phenomenon itself, much more attention is being paid to caring, particularly to mothering, despite a quite clear underlying theme in feminist theory that women's domestic labour is exploited by men. Heidi Hartmann's (1981) classic discussion of patriarchy is just one much quoted feminist tract that, as a consequence of heterosexual marriage, clearly sees women's position within capitalist societies as involving domestic exploitation. She also sees this exploitation as typically impinging on the commodification of women's labour. This important element of socialist feminist theorizing was largely discarded at the same time as the justifiable rejection of the explanation of patriarchy in terms of a dual system of oppression, based on sex and capitalism (Young 1981). This thesis has been revisited lately in a number of works, as the importance of the family site has been rediscovered and as the promise of second wave feminist pressure to deliver an egalitarian family and male reform has not materialized (Delphy and Leonard 1992; Dempsey 1992; McMahon 1994).

The unfairness of the domestic division of labour as a social issue is one which is not far beneath the surface in many societies. In Australia, for example, when the research material on which this chapter is based is presented to students, or in public lectures, women readily respond to the picture of a gendered and unfair internal family division of labour, while men are often discomforted or vehemently reject the idea that they do not make an equal domestic contribution. Women in Australia often talk of taking on a partner as gaining another child, while at the same time, media coverage, usually, though not always, written by men, extols the virtues of the new age male's vastly increased contribution to family activities (McMahon 1994).

Despite very general popular concern about the issue, at least among women, social scientists have produced relatively little detailed empirical information on how much difference having a male partner makes to the domestic work of women. This lack of empirical information hampers the assessment of the validity of what came, prematurely, to be a discarded theory about the exploitation or expropriation of women's domestic labour by men. The analysis of time use provides a basis for reassessment of the value of approaching the issue of gendered citizenship from this perspective.

THE RESEARCH

In this chapter the amount of time men and women spend in both paid and unpaid work is compared where women have and do not have partners, and when they have and do not have children. The influence of other factors such as age of children and employment status have also been examined.[1]

The analysis reported on in this chapter is based on data from time use surveys. Such surveys have a long history and became internationally standardized as a research tool during the 1960s. Information is typically collected on the basis of a 24-hour diary and because the diary covers all activities undertaken during the survey period, the data simultaneously provide a picture not only of respondents' involvement in paid and unpaid work but also in personal maintenance activities and leisure as well. Much research has (Robinson 1980) shown that the activities that people report via a diary do provide a reliable account of the way their time is apportioned. It has also been found that data gathered through the diary method generally are strongly supported by findings from related forms of surveys (Baxter 1993; Berk and Berk 1979; Bittman and Lovejoy 1993), and other research which has used observational and other, less readily quantifiable, methods of collecting information about daily behaviour (Dempsey 1988; McMahon 1994).

While it is the intention of this study to ultimately include a number of countries in the study, to date only Australia and Finland have been compared, using national data collected in 1987.[2] There are clearly limitations in comparing only two countries, but the two compared to date do have a number of similarities and differences that prove valuable for the task of raising key questions about gender relations. Of particular interest is the fact that Finland has the highest proportion of women in full-time employment of any OECD country (at the time of the survey, about 80 per cent in paid employment and only 10 per cent in part-time work), while Australia falls in the middle group of countries (with about 50 per cent in paid employment and 40 per cent working part-time). In terms of the commodification of women's to men's labour, the gender gap was 5 per cent for Finland, that is 5 per cent more men than women were in the labour force, whereas for Australia the figure was 22 per cent in 1992, though it continues to fall steadily (Perry 1993: 42). The two countries have similar rates of sole female parents, 13 per cent of all families with children (Perry 1993: 39–40).

The countries not only vary with respect to women's employment, they also have contrasting welfare state regimes. Welfare states are routinely classified by researchers and commentators in terms of their package of social policies and the ideology which underlies these. When approached in this way, Finland is generally classified with other Scandinavian nations as having a 'social democratic' welfare state regime (Esping-Andersen 1990; Kangas 1992). Social democratic regimes are recognized for their extensive and universally based citizenship rights, generous levels of provision and well developed services and entitlements. Australia, on the other hand, is usually classified as a liberal welfare state regime along with other English-speaking nations, notably Canada, New Zealand, UK and US. Liberal regimes are less generous, provide support which is often targeted and means tested, lack universal provisions and focus less on comprehensive and equal citizenship.

There is some debate about the accuracy of the conventional classifications of the Australian welfare state because it does deliver some more egalitarian social patterns than a number of the other liberal welfare state regimes. This has been explained in terms of Australia's historically strong and politically effective labour movement. Nonetheless, even its critics mostly accept the broad classification. Frank Castles and Deborah Mitchell (1991), would however modify it somewhat by using the qualifier that Australia and New Zealand are more correctly seen as 'radical' liberal welfare states. Because of the strength of its labour movement, Castles (1985) has specifically described the Australian welfare state as a 'wage earners' welfare state', a description which historically, however, is more accurately read as a white, male, wage earners' welfare state (Bryson 1992).

On the basis of their respective welfare state regimes it would be expected that citizenship would be more egalitarian and less gendered in Finland than in Australia. A research objective here is to examine whether this is so, through a consideration of patterns of caring labour and commodified labour for women and men. Caring labour is approached through the amount of time spent in unpaid family labour (domestic and child care) and commodified labour through time spent in paid labour. How women and men spend their time in these activities, particularly because of their unequal reward systems, can be taken as a reflection of broader gender power relations. The analysis attempts to set the findings against notions of equal citizenship and the nature of the welfare state regimes of the two countries.

THE RELATIONSHIP OF CARING AND COMMODIFIED LABOUR

The relationship of time spent in paid and unpaid work by men and women according to their family status is set out in Table 9.1. It needs to be noted at the outset that work is generally underestimated by these overall figures and to a much greater extent in the case of unpaid work, because only one activity at a time is recorded. In the 1987 Australian survey, respondents were invited to add other secondary activities, but this was not done systematically and so these entries have not been analyzed here. It is very clear from the data where people did opt to mention additional activities, that much information about the extent of domestic labour is lost when multiple patterns are not systematically investigated.

Child care times, for example, nowhere near cover the times for which young children must be supervized. It is clear that many other activities are also likely to represent a doubling (or trebling or more) of tasks. Laundry, for example may be in the machine, a meal cooking and the baby being fed, or played with all at the same time. Hence counting only a primary activity seriously underestimates the intensity of the work actually done. In particular, this underestimates women's activities as they do more domestic labour and it is domestic work which, it has been found, is more often carried out on a multiple task basis.

As Table 9.1 clearly indicates, whatever their marital status, women do more domestic labour than men of similar family status. Married mothers do the most unpaid work, followed by lone mothers. The difference between them can be seen as one explicit cost, in unpaid work time, for women of supporting their partners. Inspection of the figures for lone male parents suggests that there is also a time cost in respect of a female partner for Finnish fathers, whose unpaid work times are somewhat higher than those for lone fathers. However, partnered Finnish fathers still do just half the amount of unpaid work of Finnish partnered mothers. This is not the case in Australia, the few male lone parents in the sample have higher unpaid work times than their married counterparts. However because

Table 9.1   Paid Work, Unpaid Work and Family Status

Time Spent	Australian			Finnish		
Grand mean (*mins per day*)	*Paid Work*	*Unpaid Work*	*Total*	*Paid Work*	*Unpaid Work*	*Total*
Married* women with children	102	393	(495)	202	310	(512)
Married women without children	91	283	(374)	183	214	(397)
Lone mothers**	90	321	(411)	230	237	(467)
Single women	143	206	(349)	139	166	(305)
Married men with children	327	142	(469)	318	160	(478)
Married men without children	169	171	(340)	221	133	(354)
Single men	235	122	(357)	196	113	(309)

* married includes legally married and partnered.
** there were very few sole fathers in each country so they have not been included.

of the small numbers of lone fathers in the samples, further investigation would be necessary to confirm such preliminary observations. Nonetheless these preliminary observations support a general trend which finds in Finland a greater degree of gender parity, both within families and within the workforce.

When we combine times for both unpaid and paid labour we find that there is far greater gender balance than is the case when they are treated separately (see Table 9.1). Nonetheless, the aggregate time spent by women with partners and children remains greater than for all men in both countries. Single men and women have the closest aggregated time commitments, though this still has the strongly gendered element that women's unpaid work time is greater than their paid, while the reverse is so for single men. The strength of the ascriptive nature of unpaid tasks is certainly underscored by the finding that, in each society, women of each family status do on average more unpaid domestic work than the equivalent category of men (and this would still hold if lone fathers were included). In fact only in one case does any male category (Australian married men without children) do more than a category of women (single Finnish women). As will be discussed later in the paper, unpaid work times for Australian married men without children are bolstered by labour which has a discretionary, 'hobby' element to it.

The pattern for unpaid work must also be understood in terms of the pattern of paid labour. It is not that men, when they are not doing household labour, are doing nothing. They do the main share of the paid work of the society. This is significant, however, because of the different reward patterns associated with each type of work. As well as financial gains, the domain of paid work offers tangible rewards by way of power and status. It also seems that there are more psychic rewards from paid work than from most unpaid work. One of the classic studies of time use carried out in the US in the 1970s, considered how women and men felt about the tasks in which they were engaged. They were asked about the 'psychic' rewards that they derived from household tasks, leisure and paid work. What was discovered, not surprisingly, was that those activities designated as leisure were seen as the most pleasant. A wide range of household tasks were the least pleasant, though meal preparation and child care were classified as mixes of work and leisure. Market employment was viewed as more similar to leisure that other household tasks. As Berk and Berk expressed their findings, 'psychic rewards from employment may well exceed the psychic rewards from much of household work' (Berk and Berk 1979: 230). Further research is called for into this issue, but we need to remain aware that paid work does have a range of key benefits over unpaid work when we are assessing the issue of gender equity and domestic labour. It is not just a matter of an equitable distribution of time expended but also of rewards and satisfaction gained, against a background of what one is prevented from doing.

Table 9.2 shows the ratio of women's to men's time expenditure in three family status categories. Equal patterns would be expressed in men and women each doing 50 per cent of the paid and 50 per cent of the unpaid labour. For no category is this the case. Partnered parents in Australia have the most skewed pattern. In this category, for every 100 minutes of unpaid work that is done, women average 73 or about three times the 27 minutes that men average. On the other hand, women are involved in only 23 minutes of paid work for every 77 by men, or less than one third of the male rate (see Table 9.2).

The unpaid work ratio of women to men where there are no dependent children, is relatively similar across the two countries, ranging from 60 to 63 per cent (though the actual amount of unpaid work time is less in Finland). This suggests that the greater equality in Finland must be seen as achieved more through the commodification of women's labour that the sharing of caring labour. This is also demonstrated by the fact that of all categories of women, sole female parents in Finland who do not have a partner with whom to share unpaid labour, have the highest levels of paid employment (see Table 9.1) and in fact come second to partnered fathers, of the seven Finnish categories.

Figure 9.1 sets out in graphic form the patterns of domestic activities of Australian women and men at various stages of the life course, drawing on the same 1987 survey data. The figure clearly indicates that Australian men transfer much of their domestic responsibility to their partner on marriage, and perhaps more surprisingly, that this on average amounts to a greater increase in partnered women's workload than accrues from having a child under five years of age (Bittman 1991: 54). It is

Table 9.2 Women's Paid Work, Unpaid Work and Family Status

Average Time Spent by Women as % of Total of Women's and Men's Time in Each Category	*Australian Women*		*Finnish Women*	
	Paid Work	*Unpaid Work*	*Paid Work*	*Unpaid work*
Partnered with children	23	73	39	66
Partnered without children	35	62	45	61
Single	37	63	41	60

also interesting that for retired women and men who live alone, the amount of time spent in domestic labour is almost identical. This is at a stage of the life cycle when the rewards from paid labour no longer compete. A similar analysis for Finland does not show a similar transfer of domestic responsibility to women on partnering but also demonstrates that older retired men take less domestic responsibility.

The gap between Australian women's and men's paid work times widens if breaks at work, travel and job search are also taken into account. This extra time is mainly made up of travelling time and it increases the difference between women and men in Australia and between the nations. These additional activities add on average 70 minutes to the daily paid work time of Australian partnered fathers and 52 minutes per day to that of single men (see Table 9.3). The average for married men without a child at home is lower, at 34 minutes, partly because of the diluting effect of a high proportion in the category of older men not in employment. The category of Australian women with the highest additional work times is single women at 31 minutes per day. For the other three categories, their patterns are much closer to Finnish women's patterns ranging between 15 and 21 minutes. The relatively short travel times of Australian women confirm a characteristic of women's employ-

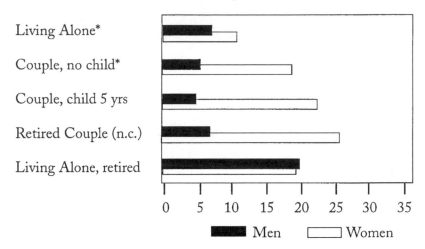

Figure 9.1   Australian Women's and Men's Unpaid Work Times by Life Course Stages (hours per week)

* below retirement age
Source: Bittman, (1991): 54.

ment which has been recorded in the research over a number of decades (for example Bryson and Thompson 1972: chap 4). This is that women tend to choose jobs closer to home than men. This is particularly so for those with family responsibilities, as this interferes less with their domestic responsibilities and allows a maximization of financial benefit from the hours that are devoted overall to paid employment. This in turn however, reduces their capacity to choose the most advantageous job and can be readily seen as one of the negative influences of domestic responsibility on career prospects, and thus an aspect of exploitation.

It has been traditional to use working hours as an index of the degree of development of a country's welfare state. The shorter male working hours in Finland, then, can be taken as a reflection of a more developed pattern of decommodification of labour. The shorter additional work time spent by men in travelling, breaks and job search can be seen to strengthen the conclusion that Finnish men have superior working life conditions to Australian men. However, I am not concerned to pursue here

Table 9.3   Total Extra Paid Work Time* and Family Status

| Total Extra Paid Work Time | | | | | | | |
Grand Mean (mins/day)	Lone Mothers	Married Mothers	Married Fathers	Single Women	Single Men	Married Women No Children	Married Men No Children
Australian	21	21	70	31	52	17	34
Finnish	25	19	28	15	19	21	21

* Figures include working time and travel, breaks and job search.

the analysis of the relative position of men as workers. This would point us toward issues of the decommodification of labour and the history of class politics (for example Castles 1978; Korpi 1989; Kangas and Palme 1992). We would then quickly be led back to 'mainstream' approaches to understanding the welfare state, of the Esping-Andersen (1990) variety and such approaches do not adequately encompass women's working patterns and interests (Sainsbury 1994; Bittman, *et al.* 1994). Cross-national differences in the average hours spent in paid employment among women, are rarely confronted directly in these conventional analyses. Yet the gap between Australian and Finnish women is three times that of the gap for men and it is in the opposite direction to that which would be predicted on the basis of the level of development of the respective welfare states. Unlike their male counterparts, Finnish women do more, and much more, paid work than Australian women.

MEN'S EXPLOITATION OF WOMEN'S UNPAID DOMESTIC LABOUR

As well as encompassing the capacity of unpaid work to interfere with the commodification of women's labour, the thesis of the exploitation of women's domestic labour by men is also illuminated by an analysis of the detailed distribution of family responsibility for domestic activities, that is through a consideration of precisely which tasks are done by women and men. Ken Dempsey (1992) is one researcher who has undertaken such a detailed investigation as part of a 17 years community study of a rural town in Victoria, Australia, which he calls 'Smalltown'. He highlights the capacity of domestic labour to 'interfere seriously with leisure, paid work and career advancement' (Dempsey 1988: 421) and identifies aspects of domestic work which are likely to affect the extent of exploitation. He thus distinguishes tasks according to their '(i) frequency and regularity of performance; (ii) the extent to which they impede leisure and paid work; and (iii) their propensity for placing the performer in a subordinate relation to other actors in the situation.' He divided work according to its routine nature, that is tasks that need to be done daily or no less than weekly, for example cooking, child care and laundry. Among non-routine tasks he includes gardening, painting and cleaning windows. It is the routine, persistent tasks which he sees as primarily constitutive of exploitation, because they tend to have no definite time boundaries and they are difficult to postpone. Therefore they are much more likely to interfere significantly with other activities. Importantly they are 'more likely to entail the provision of personal services', thus having a 'propensity for placing the performer in a subordinated position' (Dempsey 1988: 421).

Most major unpaid domestic tasks fit within Dempsey's definition of those routine persistent tasks which involve exploitation. When we examine the distribution of cooking, laundry, shopping, child care and other domestic tasks, we find that the patterns are highly predictable with women in both countries doing much more than men in all tasks except those traditional masculine tasks of household maintenance which here are referred to as 'other domestic' activities. For almost every task for each family status for both women and men, full-time employment reduces the amount of time devoted to them, especially for Australian women. It is striking that part-time employment, which is common among Australian women, has relatively little effect.

As is the case overall, Australian women do most in terms of most of the individual domestic tasks, followed by Finnish women, while men from the two countries do far less and their patterns exhibit the greatest similarity. Despite the predicability of the general trends it is instructive to consider the major tasks separately, because the more detailed picture offers an opportunity to assess the constraints that operate and the effects associated with family status, across the life course. This sheds detailed light on the applicability of the hypothesis of men's exploitation of women's labour.

Cooking

The pattern of time spent in cooking (defined as covering food and drink preparation and cleaning up) is consistent with the aggregate figures for unpaid work, and the picture that has already emerged in the national trends (see Table 9.1). The amount of cooking time spent by the most committed category of women, Australian married women with children, is 107 minutes per day. This is just on five times that of Finnish married fathers who do least, on average, 22 minutes per day. Virtually the same amount is done by their Australian counterparts (23 minutes). Finnish married mothers do considerably less than do their Australian counterparts at 83 minutes per day, or just under four times the amount of the lowest ranking Finnish husbands with children (Table 9.4). The greater development of the Finnish welfare state is relevant here, as children are provided with a cooked meal at school, whereas in Australia, individual families are responsible for a child's food at school as well as at home. It is noteworthy, however, that having a child leads to an average difference of only four minutes per day for Australian mothers over married women without children and a difference of two minutes a day for Finnish women.

Table 9.4 Cooking and Family Status

Cooking Grand Mean (mins/day)	Lone Mothers	Married Mothers	Married Fathers	Single Women	Single Men	Married Women No Children	Married Men No Children
Australian	84	107	23	63	34	103	32
Finnish	70	83	22	60	32	81	24

The rankings are identical for each country with married women in both countries responsible for carrying out the bulk of these tasks. For each category, Australians spend more time in cooking than do Finns, though apart from the two top-ranking categories of married women, the differences are slight. Lone mothers rank third as a family type, and this supports the exploitation thesis, since contrary to what seems to be an intuitive logic, sole parenthood does not involve increased domestic burdens. The fourth female category, in terms of time spent in cooking, consists of single women, confirming the ubiquity of the gender dimension. Dempsey, in observing and surveying all family members in the rural community he studied, highlights the mechanisms through which the domestic situation remains exploitative of women. He found in the situation of young girls, processes through which exploitation is perpetuated. Adolescent girls in 'Smalltown' already provided domestic labour for their brothers and their unpaid labour time was higher. Their brothers then, he suggests, 'enter their own marriages committed to the view that women exist primarily to serve as carers and nurturers of men and their off-spring', rather than independent breadwinners (Dempsey 1988: 420).

The traditional gender order is reflected in all the rankings. The times for single women are virtually the same for the two countries and are double single men's, who, lacking the services of a partner, fall at the fifth rank position, but at the top of the male rankings. They are followed by married men without children and last are married men with children. For the two categories of Finnish married men the times are very similar, confirming, as for women, that dependent children are not a great additional burden as far as time spent on cooking is concerned.

Having a child is not significantly related to cooking time for either men or women. However, except for single Australian men and women, employment status is significantly linked. The higher the number of hours of paid work, the less the time spent in cooking. The extra average time spent by married Australian women over Finnish women is largely accounted for by the fact that they are less likely to be in full-time employment. When this is taken into account their cooking times are much more similar. Part-time work does not have the effect of reducing cooking time. Even so full-time employment does not reduce women's times to levels equivalent to those of men and this supports the exploitation thesis. An inspection of the small numbers of lone fathers suggests their average time would fall below all categories of women, but they would be at the top of the male categories. This merely reinforces the key role of gender, rather than solely practical demands, in the expenditure of time on cooking.

Employment status also makes some differences for men. We find that for most family categories, those who are not in paid employment, men as well as women, have higher cooking times. However, except for two smaller sub-categories injured/disabled Australian men and Finnish single men whose employment is recorded as home duties, the recorded average times for these men still fall well below those of women.

The association of cooking times with age is striking for virtually all sub-categories: time devoted to cooking generally increases with age. This, it can be suggested, may represent in part the leisure element that Berk and Berk (1979) noted for cooking in their US study. When the national times are plotted by age and sex we find that the graph line for Finnish women crosses that of Australian women around the age of 70 years, when few are in employment. The absolute time they spend in the preparation of food and drink and cleaning up after these activities in both countries, is well below the average time that they spend consuming the food and drink that is produced.

Laundry

Laundry, which consists of washing, ironing, the collecting of clothes and the putting away that is involved, represents the extreme of segregation of domestic labour, and it could be said, the utmost in men's exploitation of women's labour. On average, the time women in both countries spend on this task is nine times that of men. Women's laundry time in Australia ranges from a high of 50 minutes per day for married women with children to a low of 23 minutes per day for single women (see Table 9.5). For Australian men the number of minutes ranges from a high of 9 for single men to a low of 3 for those who are married with children, or one-17th of the daily average of women of the same family status. Among Finnish married parents, women's contribution is proportionally even greater, being 26 times that of men.

Table 9.5   Laundry by Family Status

Laundry Grand Mean (mins/day)	Lone Mothers	Married Mothers	Married Fathers	Single Women	Single Men	Married Women No Children	Married Men No Children
Australian	46	50	3	23	9	43	4
Finnish	20	26	1	16	5	22	2

As with other unpaid labour, Australian women do more, but in this case much more, while Finnish men do considerably less. Some of the variation, again, is accounted for by the fact that Australian women are less likely to be in full-time employment, and this does reduce women's, but not men's laundry time. However, a genuine national difference remains across all categories. This seems likely to represent a cultural difference, partly based on climatic conditions and varying approaches to dealing with laundry.

The rank order of the categories by family status and gender is similar to cooking, with one modification. Children are more demanding with regard to laundry and Australian lone mothers move from third to second position in the rank order. Finnish lone mothers maintain their third rank on the national scale, but their time expenditure is much closer to that of married women without children, than it is for cooking.

Other Housework

When we come to the composite category 'other housework', which includes such activities as general cleaning, floor care, dusting and tidying, we find that the gender differences are not as great as for laundry but they do conform to the general pattern. Married mothers again have the greatest time commitment, followed, for Australia, by married women without children and then sole parents. For Finnish women, the order of sole parents and married women without children is reversed, but there is only one minute's difference in their times in any case. This is the only activity in which Finnish times are gener-

Table 9.6 Other Housework and Family Status

Other Housework Grand Mean (mins/day)	Lone Mothers	Married Mothers	Married Fathers	Single Women	Single Men	Married Women No Children	Married Men No Children
Australian	36	55	11	33	10	47	11
Finnish	46	49	23	34	20	45	25

ally higher than for Australia, indicating the inclusion of a rather wider range of activities in the category.

For Finnish women the times are not greater than for Australian women in absolute terms except for lone mothers, but they are relative to cooking and laundry, where Finnish women have a considerable advantage. Though still lower than Finnish women's times, Finnish men's times are considerably higher than Australian men's. Age of youngest child makes no significant difference for any category, but employment, particularly for women has once again a significant reducing effect.

Other Domestic Activities

Other domestic activities covers broadly those household activities that have traditionally been seen as men's work. This includes garden and pool maintenance, car repairs, house improvements and providing transport where this is not elsewhere classified as it is in relation to employment, child care and leisure.

Here we find a reversal of the pattern for cooking, laundry and other household work, with men being most active. Australian men are more involved than Finns, something which can be taken as part of the more gendered pattern already established for Australia. The activities included in the category are those that have traditionally been seen as male activities.

These activities are largely those which Dempsey excludes from his definition of exploitation. These are not tasks of a routine nature, that is, tasks that need to be done daily or no less than weekly for example. These fit his definition of non-

Table 9.7　Other Domestic Activities by Family Status

Other Domestic Activities Grand Mean (mins/day)	Lone Mothers	Married Mothers	Married Fathers	Single Women	Single Men	Married Women No Children	Married Men No Children
Australian	24	27	49	26	31	27	73
Finnish	11	14	41	11	18	18	42

routine tasks, as already outlined (Dempsey 1988: 421). The only category of activity in which men do play a greater role than women we find involves the very tasks which are not likely to be exploitative.

Age of youngest child is significantly associated with time spent on these activities for Finnish married mothers and fathers and for Australian married fathers. Having a young child decreases the time spent and not having a child under 15 years of age significantly increases the time spent on these activities. These findings certainly support Dempsey's views of these tasks as more freely chosen and not merely subject to the inexorable demands of familial duty.

Married men with no children at home expend the most time on these traditionally male activities in both societies. In Australia the high amount of time expended among this category is explained by men not in employment and this suggests they are pursuing these activities as something of a hobby. In Australia single men come next, while in Finland they have the same times as married women with no children. The four categories of women in Australia have very similar weekly times, with sole mothers actually expending least time of any Australian category, reinforcing the interpretation that such activities are not obligatory for parents. In Finland lone mothers also have the lowest rates, along with single women. The generally higher time expenditure in Australia seems to be partly associated with lifestyles. Outdoor activities are possible throughout the year in Australia where they are not in Finland and separate dwellings, with gardens, are more common in Australia and these present more scope for home maintenance activities.

Child Care

The coding of child care in the time use surveys includes time spent on caring by parents for their own children and also time devoted to caring for the child of others. This means that it is meaningful to assess child care times across the board, even for those who do not have a child. When we consider the time spent by those without a child in the household we find the average times devoted to this task much higher in Australia than Finland. Single Australian women put most time into this form of child care, at 17 minutes per day on average. This does not seem to be specifically associated with older age groups, that is grandmothers caring for grandchildren, but a general pattern across the age range, though it decreases after 55 years. It is, however, significantly associated with not being in employment (part-time or full-time) or being a student. The pattern of much higher rates of informal child care being provided by other than parents holds across all groups in Australia and is explicable by the much poorer public provision of child care. Once again we find a reflection of the more developed Finnish welfare state.

The figures for child care in Table 9.8 are deceptively low, an artefact of working with averages. When only parents with children of the relevant age are considered in isolation the figures are 2 to 3 times higher. It must also be borne in mind that the data omit care as a parallel activity accompanying other activities. While recognizing this under statement of actual time involved, the pattern nonetheless confirms the broad picture for other unpaid work, with Australian women expending most

Table 9.8   Child Care and Family Status

Child Care Grand Mean (mins/day)	Lone Mothers	Married Mothers	Married Fathers	Single Women	Single Men	Married Women No Children	Married Men No Children
Australian	72	99	27	17	5	10	6
Finnish	46	94	37	3	2	5	2

time, followed by Finnish women. Having a child below 5 years of age, not surprisingly, has a strong effect on increasing the time spent in child care, especially by Finnish mothers. This pattern is linked to the well developed maternity and child care provisions associated with employment, which tends to ensure that almost all mothers with young children do care for their own children for a period, supported financially by a range of decommodified rights.

When it comes to child care married mothers are far ahead and there is little difference between the two societies. Sole parents come next with Australian lone mothers doing more unpaid child care than their Finnish counterparts. This again is something that must be understood in the light of the public provision of child care as well as the employment patterns in the two societies.

Married fathers are the only other category with their own children in the household and Finnish fathers spend 37 minutes in child care per day compared with Finnish married mothers, who spend 94 minutes. Finnish fathers do just on 25 per cent more child care than Australian married fathers, who are involved least on average of any category. Australian married mothers average 99 minutes of child care, compared with 27 minutes for Australian married fathers. In the wider gap between male and female parents in Australia than in Finland, we have another illustration of greater gender inequality than in Finland.

When it comes to caring for other children, single Australian women do most, followed by married Australian women without children and then married men without children. The Finns, both women and men, are far less likely to provide care for other than their own children, something which can be explained by the far superior arrangements for child care that are provided by the state. The superior welfare state provisions actually underscore the contribution of Finnish, *vis-à-vis* Australian, men to the care of their own children, as their higher contribution is on top of these better provisions within the public arena. Finnish fathers' child care then, is clearly a contribution to family work which can be interpreted as an aspect of greater gender equality.

As with so many unpaid tasks, full-time employment strongly reduces the amount of time spent in child care by Australian women and non-employment, such as being a pensioner or being disabled, strongly increase it for Finnish women and indeed single Australian women.

A clear pattern of weekend influence occurs for child care for parents of both sexes in Australia. Mothers, both lone and married, do significantly less child care at weekends. The trend for Finnish mothers, solo and in dual parent families, is in the same direction, though this is not as strong and does not reach statistical significance. This suggests the conclusion that weekday child care is made less onerous in Finland by good collective provisions and therefore there is not so much incentive for mothers to seek a break from child care at weekends. Married fathers in both countries do significantly more child care at the weekends.

Shopping

Shopping is an activity in which the rates for women and men are quite close together. This is the only activity in which lone Australian mothers spend more time than married women. Other research suggests that this might be due to the potential of shopping to offer a leisure element as well as having a utilitarian value (Cant 1991). Alternatively it could be that because Australian lone mothers are likely to be quite poor they must shop particularly carefully. Robin Douthitt (1993) suggests that Canadian welfare recipients expend extra effort on unpaid work as a way of conserving their meagre resources and that this needs to be recognized as needed time when social security policies are developed.

Table 9.9   Shopping and Family Status

Shopping Grand Mean (mins/day)	*Lone Mothers*	*Married Mothers*	*Married Fathers*	*Single Women*	*Single Men*	*Married Women No Children*	*Married Men No Children*
Australian	59	55	30	44	33	53	45
Finnish	44	44	36	42	36	43	38

The next category of Australian women with high shopping times, is married mothers, but women without children are not far behind. Married men with no children come next, something again which can be explained by the high number who are not employed, in conjunction with the element of recreation which attaches to shopping time. Single women come next and a fair way behind are single men and last married fathers.

The Finnish pattern for women across categories is much more even, with only two minutes between the daily times of each group. For men, the levels are slightly lower, but again there are only two minutes between the high (38 minutes) of married men with no children and the low (36 minutes) of married fathers and single men. These patterns of shopping times in Finland and Australia are gendered, though only slightly so and they are less affected by marriage than most other activities. For Finnish parents with children and Australian fathers, full-time paid employment reduces shopping time. For married Australian mothers the trend is in the same direction though it does not reach statistical significance. Day of the week, as would be expected, has a significant effect for all groups except Australian single persons.

CONCLUSION

At first glance the picture that emerges from this consideration of women's and men's time use induces no substantial surprise. It certainly is well known that women do most of a society's caring labour and that women's labour is less commodified than the labour of men. It is well known too, though outside the scope of this study, that men enjoy a vast advantage in terms of the economic, power and social status rewards within the labour market. The data also confirm that Finland, with its social democratic welfare state more explicitly focused on equal citizenship, has achieved greater gender equality than Australia, with its less developed liberal welfare state. Nonetheless Finnish women's time use patterns are not as different from Australian women's as might be expected and Finnish and Australian men's are much closer than might be expected.

What is perhaps most surprising is that there are such significant differences between women and men. If equal citizenship is being approached, at least in Finland, this would hardly be expected. With such differences remaining in both countries we need to seek an explanation. In the absence of a social revaluation of the social importance of traditional caring labour, paid labour provides the main economic and social rewards. Yet the evidence presented here suggested that in both social democratic and liberal welfare states, access to paid labour remains dependent on sex. The only sociological explanation which seems to address this continuing imbalance is the notion of exploitation and the usurpation of advantage by men of the benefits of women's contribution to the socially necessary caring project on which societies basically depend. Women's caring labour effectively underpins men's advantage in the market and in the public world more generally.

The proportion of the household's unpaid work which is undertaken by women and men remains similarly unequal in Australia and Finland except for those with children at home. Finnish men in these latter households do make greater contributions to child care than Australian men but still the gender gap remains greatest in these families. Finnish women nonetheless spend considerably less time on domestic labour than Australian women and this is consistent with the greater commodification of their labour. At the time of the surveys, the gap between the proportion of women and men in the labour force in Finland was only five per cent, whereas for Australia it was 22 per cent, though gradually reducing over time. Finnish women are, however, mostly employed full-time. Their reduced domestic load is due far less to changes in men's behaviour than to the effects of this greater labour force participation. Australian women working full-time, like Finnish women, significantly reduce their domestic labour, but men hardly increase theirs. Given that Australian women are increasingly entering the workforce, it can be predicted that their very high rates of domestic work will decrease. However, they are entering a labour market which is calling for flexibility. This means that increasingly employment opportunities are for part-time work and this does not have the same reducing effect on unpaid work.

A detailed consideration of the household contribution of women and men clearly shows that it remains women who are more likely to undertake those routine tasks which have the greatest propensity to be exploitative, that is, they still do the tasks that are much more likely to interfere with leisure, paid work and career advancement. It becomes clear that changes that are leading to a greater convergence of the activity patterns of women and men are being driven almost exclusively by the factors that draw women into the labour market. This increasing commodification in both countries is underpinned by a range of state policies and programmes which support it, such as parental leave and child care, and these are better developed in Finland than Australia. Men's patterns have not changed significantly and they are still effectively exploiting women's domestic labour, not a sound basis on which to build equal citizenship. The exploitation thesis also helps to explain why women's position in the labour market remains subordinated and emphasizes the importance of the feminist view that the key to achieving gender equality without obliterating difference is through the revaluing of caring labour. However, the analysis only reinforces the difficulty of achieving this project because of the force of history and entrenched interests that are involved.

NOTES

1. A major statistical technique that has been used throughout the analysis is Multiple Classification Analysis (MCA). This technique is derived from multiple regression analysis and is used throughout the world by national statistical agencies for the multivariate analysis of time use data. A series of means (grand means) are computed for each dependent variable (in this case the amount of time spent on various activities). A table is compiled giving grand means for the designated categories, married mothers, lone mothers, married women without children, single women, married fathers, married men without children and single men. The deviation of the mean for each sub-category is then computed from the grand mean for selected factors (for example employment, education, age). The MCA data is interpreted in terms of deviations from the grand mean. These deviations convey the magnitude of the effect of a particular category (for example the effect of having a child between 0–4 years, being unemployed, having a tertiary education) and can be positive (more than the mean) or negative (less than the mean) (SPSS Inc. 1988: 375–6). The MCA tables have not been included in this chapter, though comments are made on the findings from this analysis at various points in the chapter.

2. The project is a joint one with Michael Bittman, the study being origi-
    nally made possible by a grant from the Australian Research Council in
    1992, and an additional grant for the 1994–5 period. The analysis on
    which this chapter is based also forms part of my research programme
    for the Institute of Advanced Studies of the Australian National
    University's 'Reshaping Australian Institutions' Project.

REFERENCES

Baxter, Janeen (1993) *Work at Home: The Domestic Division of Labour* Brisbane:
    University of Queensland Press.
Berk, S. F. and Richard A. Berk (1979) *Labour and Leisure at Home* Beverley
    Hills: Sage Publications.
Bittman, Michael (1991) *Juggling Time* Canberra: Office of the Status of
    Women, Department of the Prime Minister and Cabinet.
Bittman, Michael and Frances Lovejoy (1993) 'Domestic Power: Negotiating
    an Unequal Division of Labour within a Framework of Equality' *Australian
    and New Zealand Journal of Sociology* 29 (3): 302–21.
Bittman, Michael, Lois Bryson and Sue Donath (1994) 'Men's and Women's
    Welfare State: Tendencies to convergence in Theory and Practice?' in
    Diane Sainsbury (ed.) *Gendering Welfare States*, London: Sage.
Bryson, Lois (1992) *Welfare and the State: Who Benefits?* London: Macmillan.
Bryson, Lois and Faith Thompson (1972) *An Australian Newtown*, Ringwood:
    Penguin.
Cant, Rosemary (1991) 'Tending Work: Caring for Children Who are
    Disabled' PhD thesis, University of Newcastle.
Castles, Francis G. (1978) *The Social Democratic Image of Society*, London:
    Routledge.
Castles, Francis G. (1985) *The Working Class and Welfare*, Sydney: Allen and
    Unwin.
Castles, Francis G. and Deborah Mitchell (1992) 'Three Worlds of Welfare
    Capitalism or Four? *Governance* (5) 1.
Delphy, Christine and Diana Leonard (1992), *Familiar Exploitation: A New
    Analysis of Marriage in Contemporary Western Societies*, Cambridge: Polity Press.
Dempsey, Ken (1988) 'Exploitation in the Domestic Division of Labour: An
    Australian Case Study' *The Australian and New Zealand Journal of Sociology* 24
    (3): 420–37.
Dempsey, Ken (1992), *A Man's Town: Inequality Between Women and Men in Rural
    Australia*, Melbourne: Oxford University Press.
Douthitt, Robin (1993), 'The Inclusion of Time Availability in Canadian
    Poverty Measures' in Time Use Methodology: Towards Consensus Rome:
    ISTAT.
Esping-Andersen, Gøsta (1990) *The Three Worlds of Welfare Capitalism*,
    Cambridge: Polity Press.

Hartmann, Heidi (1981) '*The Unhappy Marriage of Marxism and Feminism*: Towards a More Progressive Union' in Lydia Sargent (ed.) *Women and Revolution* (London: Pluto Press): 1–41.

Kangas, Olli (1992), 'Macrosociological Comparative Methodology. On Regression, Qualitative Comparisons and cluster Analysis in the Politics of Social Security' Stockholm: Swedish Institute for Social Research, Stockholm University.

Kangas Olli and Joakim Palme (1992), 'Class-Politics and Institutional Feedbacks: Developments of Occupational Pensions in Finland and Sweden' Stockholm: Swedish Institute for Social Research, Stockholm University.

Korpi, Walter (1989), 'Power, Politics and State Autonomy in Development of Social Citizenship: Social Rights During Sickness in 18 OECD-countries since 1930' *American Sociological Review* 54: 309–28.

McMahon, Anthony Graham (1994) 'Taking Care of Men: Discourse and Practices of Domestic Life', PhD thesis Victoria, Australia: La Trobe University.

Perry, Julia (1993), 'Breadwinners or Childrearers? Barriers to Labour Force Participation of Sole Mothers' in Sheila Shaver (ed.) *Comparative Perspective on Sole Parents Policy: Work and Welfare*, Sydney: Reports and Proceedings No. 106, Social Policy Research Centre.

Robinson, John (1980), 'Household Technology and Household Work' in Sarah Berk (ed.) *Women and Household Labour*, Beverly Hills: Sage.

Sainsbury Diane (ed.) (1994), *Gendering Welfare States*, London: Sage.

SPSS Inc (1988), *SPSS-X User's Guide*, 3rd edn. Chicago: SPSS Inc.

Young, Iris (1981), 'Beyond the Unhappy Marriage: A Critique of the Dual Systems Theory' in Lydia Sargent (ed.) *Women and Revolution*, London: Pluto Press, pp. 43–70.

10 Women's Paradise Lost? Social Services and Care in the Quasi-Markets in Sweden

Stina Johansson[1]

The Scandinavian welfare state model with its emphasis on income redistribution and public responsibility for the production of services is in many ways facing a crisis. In Finland, and to some extent Sweden, the reassessment of the model has been initiated by the crisis in public financing and the changes taking place in the prevailing ideology on welfare norms,[2] as reflected in the rise of neo-liberalism and current economic crises.

The welfare state can be examined in two capacities: as a *re distributive state* and as a *service state*. The on-going debate on the redistributive state tends to focus on questions of basic security versus earnings-related security. With regard to the Scandinavian model of a service state, which has been less firmly institutionalized than the redistributive state of a longer tradition (for example, Leira 1994), the critique concerns the public monopoly on the production of services. Recent debates in the Scandinavian welfare states concern the division of labour between private and public service production and the applicability of new welfare-mix models. A vocal group of policymakers and academics argue that the state (in the broad sense of the word) should continue to occupy a central role in income security and in the redistribution of incomes. The trend, however, towards a mixed economy is inevitable in the production of services (Rothstein 1988; von Otter and Saltman, 1990; Langby 1993).

These tendencies are represented on the ideological level in new discourses on competition, efficiency, free choice and personal responsibility. In policy discussions, they are found in new models for organization, production, supervision and financing of public services that promise a more streamlined administration, which will become less cumbersome and more economical, and will provide services that will correspond more closely to the needs of the client. These are the hallmarks of what has been described as 'restructuring' in the academic and policy literature on welfare states (for example Julkunen 1992). Among some of the neo-liberal and monetary economic theories, restructuring does not necessarily imply a total dismantling of the old system of the welfare state, but rather its renewal on the basis of a multiple producer model and a mix of public, private and voluntary sectors anew.

In this chapter I will explore the ideological debates, policy-making and possible consequences around the restructuring of care work in welfare states. I want to argue that the transformation in the system of health and welfare service production has consequences for women's work and employment. In effect, it signals a new gendered social contract (Rantalaiho 1993) between women's articulated interests as care givers and care recipients in the service state. On a more general level, it will possibly imply a renegotiation of the contract between men and women with several actors, not only the state.

The chapter is divided into two sections. First, I describe the rise of the social service state and why it has played a crucial role in promoting gender equality within Nordic societies, what has been referred to by Helga Hernes (1987) as women friendly policies. Second, I present the models and practices of restructuring carework that are embedded in the concept of quasi-markets, a keyword in the discourse of restructuring. The article addresses areas of care work in Sweden in which quasi-market principles are now being employed or have been discussed as potential solutions to the economic pressures on public sector services and ideological pressures for more choice and flexibility in care giving. I focus on elderly care, but many of the same practices are occurring in other areas, such as day care and medical care. Throughout this discussion I allude to the gendered consequences for women as either care givers, employed in the care sector, or as care recipients.

THE RISE OF THE SOCIAL SERVICE STATE: WOMEN FRIENDLY POLICIES

It can be argued that it is important to recognize the historical background of the establishment of the service state when interpreting present trends in the development of the care market.

Being a housewife was the ideal set for Swedish women in the 1940s by government experts and policymakers. Some scholars have interpreted this as a strategy to keep women away from the male dominated labour market in the 1930s (Johansson and Evertsson 1994), while others have argued that valorising women's domesticity was a way of promoting the traditional family ideal and increasing the birthrate (Lövgren 1998). However, a new ideal began to emerge in the post-war period with the rising interest among policymakers and employer federations to recruit more women into paid work. Alva Myrdal and Viola Klein advocated 'Two Roles for Women' (1957) as housewives and wage-earners, in their book of that name. (Johansson, 1994b). But the question remained as to how they were to be 'drawn out' into the labour market (Hatje 1994). The long term strategy which would allow women flexibility in everyday life to combine family duties was part-time work and publicly financed child care and elderly care.

Throughout the 1970s, as more and more women entered the labour market, they sought to capture other social security benefits, such as parental leave, parental insurance, job security and occupational protection. These entitlements and social security benefits were coupled to women's social rights to paid employment. What has been referred to as the gendered social contract in Sweden (Hirdman 1990) was a set of social policies that reduced women's dependence on husbands. Underlying this contract between women and the welfare state were positive incentives for women to enter the labour market to solve the shortage of labour. But the contract also reflected women's search for emancipation.

In the 1970s the service state came into its own, with the expansion of the public sector in which women's care work became paid care work. Waged working women in Sweden are overwhelmingly in public sector employment (Axelsson 1992). Specific links between the welfare state and the labour market exist; the public sector has acted as the major employer of women, as well as providing services to enable women to combine family commitments with paid work. These links have produced women friendly policies. Public services are widely supported. A national survey finds that 86 per cent of the population want the public sector to meet the increased need of services for the elderly, and 71 per cent prefer to receive help from public employees (Andersson 1993; see also Svallfors 1992). The popularity of public services has even increased (Svallfors 1995).

The struggle for visibility and the socio-economic status of women's care work has been the core of the Nordic equality project (Varsa 1993). Is freedom of choice overtaking equality as the value guiding social policy? If so, what consequences will it have for different groups of people as clients, as receivers of services, and for women as producers of services?

At this point it is instructive to turn to a new discourse on quasi-markets, a concept employed in the analysis of the shift from publicly funded services to various forms of public/private mixes of care servicing in welfare states.

THE QUASI-MARKETS AND WELFARE SERVICE PRODUCTION

Embedded in the definition of quasi-markets are normative assumptions about efficiency, flexibility and free choice. The aim behind the concept of quasi-markets (Williamson 1975) is to intensify the allocation of resources for welfare services.

On the supply side, it is important to distinguish between the financier (purchaser) and the producer of a service. Monopoly producers, in the ideal case, are replaced by competing, independent service producers. The public sector, the private entrepreneurs, and organizations producing non-profit services, as well as the household sector can act as producers in the quasi-markets. Nevertheless, in the quasi-markets, the public sector is supposed to continue to organize and finance the services. Only the producers would compete with each other (Le Grand 1991). The market mechanism has been considered an instrument encouraging efficiency and flexibility by increasing competition in the production of welfare services.

Correspondingly, on the demand side of the quasi-markets, an attempt is made to decentralize the decision-making power of the public sector authorities by supporting reforms which will increase the opportunity for consumer choice. This is done by allocating the decision making on public financing and the use of public resources. In the quasi-markets, the production of welfare services is financed by taxation, producer subsidies and public money. Public sector financing means that the purchaser may be the municipality as a local authority, an agent acting on behalf of the consumer, or the consumers themselves. These purchasers then make their choice from the service producers available. Thus, the reallocation of resources transfers the decision-making authority (choice) from the public sector to the individual consumer, through taxation or in the form of a voucher, for example (Le Grand 1991).

When discussing quasi-market alternatives one has to distinguish between customer-run organizations (like Stockholm Independent Living) favouring the power to choose and, through municipal subsidies, pay an informal carer to look after someone in need of care (compare the British case in Ungerson chap. 7 this volume), private enterprises run by special service producers (like private medical centres), cooperatives run by professionals (children's day care centres), and forms of self-employment or firms run by one or a few persons (like examples of home care firms studied in Finland,[3] (see Andersson and Parviainen 1994). In Sweden, the first three types are in existence, whereas firms run by one or a few persons are rather uncommon, (Evertsson and Johansson 1996) or not studied empirically.

Whether quasi-markets are more efficient is an open question and needs to be empirically tested. But what I would like to focus on are the tensions and conflicts within these market strategies and the ways in which they undermine some of the key assumptions in the social service state and the women friendly policies that flowed from it. Here I want to reveal how the development of quasi-markets in the care sector has both a gendered dimension for the care giver (women as employees) and for the care receiver (women as elderly clients and women as mothers who must organize day care for children).

In the following section, I analyze tensions between theory and practice considering the rationales for quasi-market strategies, efficiency and free choice, and highlight the hidden gen-dered assumptions and likely gendered consequences using the example of elderly care.

MIXED MODELS OF WELFARE SERVICES PRODUCTION

In Sweden, a broader debate on the role of the public sector has been initiated since the 1970s by economists within and outside the Social Democratic Party (see for example Lindbeck 1972; Eklund 1981). Public criticism revolved around the expansion of public welfare provision. Demands for expansion gradually gave way to demands for change in quality of care (Stryjan 1994). Those demands represented a reaction against the strong engineering bias that had marked the expansion of social ser-vices in the Swedish welfare state (Hirdman 1989). In the most general terms, the critique underscored the contradiction between the ethics of care interaction, and the rigidity of the bureaucratized system (Beckman 1981). Many experts consid-ered the problem of how to provide greater accessibility and quality (Stryjan 1994). Murray (1987) for example, proposed a distinction between purchaser and producer of welfare services, and the idea of mixed models emerged. Casten Von Otter and Richard Saltman (1990), two sociologists and a political scien-tist Bo Rothstein (1988), followed and expanded upon mixed model design.[4]

In the new discourse that arose from the discussions of quality care and accessibility, there is emphasis on the opening of channels to the consumer. We all know that a hierarchical service organization contains conflicting interests. Potential conflicts between the providers and the consumers are obvious. A strategy for overcoming these conflicts is to place professional services under the control of the community, which is not the same as a deprofessionalization of services and care (Anttonen 1989). The aim therefore is to enhance the status of informal community actors by permitting various working and operating procedures. Within this framework, questions arise: should professional or bureaucratic standards decide, or should the organization be open for clients'/customers' preferences?

The Swedish Social Services Act of 1982 is a framework legis-lation, which mirrors these debates. It was constructed as to provide a space for innovation in organizing services at the local level. Nevertheless, the municipalities still have the ultimate financial responsibility for the welfare of their residents. In fact, however, the managing professionals function as gatekeepers and thus control access to services. This makes the ideology of actual free choice very complicated.[5]

Two Cases: Child Care and Elderly Care

Care policy in transition
During this period of care reform, there have been many initiatives and approaches to demonopolizing care. For example, in the case of child care, attempts to break the public monopoly were made as early as 1975, with five parent cooperatives, but in the 1990s this figure jumped to 933 parent cooperatives in 1992. The private alternatives have attracted mostly middle-class families, and we may be seeing a new stratification between public and private child care systems. Currently, this is not the case, but there appears to be greater ideological cleavages among different types of families and their expectations of the public child care system (Stryjan 1996).[6] It is nevertheless shown that the break more reflects a shift in ideology than a structural change.

Another gesture toward demonopolization can be seen in the creation of free schools, made possible through a voucher system in which the funds for a pupil follow him or her to his choice of schools. Free choice in care was the main rationale behind the home-care allowance of 2000 SEK (US$265) per month and per child, passed by Parliament in the summer of 1994. It enabled parents to reduce their use and costs of public child care. However, this reform was interpreted as a threat to the public care system and was immediately withdrawn when the Social Democratic Party took power again in December 1994.

Elderly care
It is important to separate changes in welfare production due to general cost cuts and changes due to the restructuring of welfare services. During the 1980s and specially the 1990s, there has been an ongoing process of cutting back services for the elderly.

In a report to the Swedish National Board of Health and
Social Welfare, Marta Szebehely (1993) states that the number
of elderly assisted by home helps or living in institutions has
decreased. According to Szebehely, the introduction of com-
petition-based reforms has proved expensive; these additional
expenditures reflect new transaction costs associated with
market-based reforms (contract negotiation and litigation, ad-
vertising, higher personnel salaries). For the most part, reduction in public care is being replaced by informal care from
family members. The difficulties in measuring the dimensions
of informal care are well known, but I can report some results
and disturbing findings. One finding is a decrease in home help
given to elderly women. Home help has been cut back for both
cohabiting women and women living alone, while men in the
same situations have not experienced similar cut-backs. The –
assumption based on gendered expectations – is that women
can care for themselves. The welfare system relies on their
competence and their silence. Another finding is that those ad-
ministering social services now assume that a greater share of
assistance will be given by grown-up children, especially daughters, to the care recipients in the event of cut-backs in public
care.

In Sweden, elderly care and care for the handicapped have
been revamped, and a range of different alternatives to the traditional public service have been developed (Socialstyrelsen,
National Board of Health and Social Welfare 1994). Thirteen
per cent of the Swedish municipalities (286 altogether) in 1994
made distinctions between purchasers and service producers.
This type of separation was most common in the big cities, and
also in cities with a right-wing majority. In 53 per cent of the
municipalities, mainly in large or middle-sized cities, special
units with their own responsibility toward staff, finances and
results have been developed. From 1994 and onwards, another
14 per cent of the municipalities will continue to develop such
units. It is important to keep in mind that only a minority
(11 per cent) of the municipalities with such units had established a link between the economic rewards and the results produced. For the most part, this efficiency model is organizational
rhetoric rather than reality.

Purchased services have been on the public service agenda in
Sweden since 1987 (Antman 1994, 40–2). In less than half of

the municipalities (44 per cent) in Sweden, private entrepreneurs are used for certain services. In home care for the elderly, private firms offer cleaning services and other services related to the household. 'Meals-on-wheels' have become a target of privatization in this modified form. Several types of organizations have been established. They can be run as a private enterprise or as a non-private associations. Like other alternative forms of management, private entrepreneurs are most frequently found in big cities or municipalities with a conservative majority. In 1993, the municipalities spent on average 3–4 per cent of their total costs for elderly care on buying privately produced services. The variation between municipalities is considerable, between 1 per cent and 42 per cent. In 7 per cent of all municipalities, and in all big cities, services from different types of cooperatives are purchased.

Vouchers, a benefit paid to the disabled or elderly person with which they are expected to purchase personal care (compare the British case in Ungerson chap. 7, this volume), were still in marginal use in Swedish elderly care (Socialstyrelsen, National Board of Health and Social Welfare 1994). In 1993 they were only in use in four municipalities, but another eight municipalities planned to introduce this system during 1994. Normally the voucher system includes only certain services in open home care (cleaning, shopping, laundry, meals-on-wheels, personal care and escort service). Only one municipality, Vaxholm, had a voucher system in elderly care also offering a free choice of nursing-homes.

Nacka in Sweden is one of the municipalities moving and having moved fast towards privatization of public home help services. Since 1982, the municipality has been run politically by a coalition of Moderates and Liberals. Changes in the provision of home help as well as in other welfare services, have been based on the introduction of vouchers, issued by the local authority. It makes pensioners eligible to obtain home help from either the public or private provider – according to their own choice. The pensioners pay a monthly fee for home help in the traditional way, but elderly clients are each issued a voucher, which represents the value of the total number of home help hours that the municipality has decided they are entitled to. Pensioners give this voucher to the service provider of their choice in exchange for care. One year after the Nacka project started, in May 1993, 12 companies had been approved by the municipality to receive vouchers in exchange for services, but the demand by clients for vouchers was low. The explanation for the low demand for vouchers from pensioners appeared to be that they were satisfied with the municipal system of publicly financed home help (Sparks and Olsson-Hort 1993).

In another Swedish municipality, Lidingö, a different approach to reforming the home help system was adopted. Rather than encouraging private providers to enter into all areas of home help, the local municipality decided to stop providing auxiliary services entirely, thus forcing people who need these services to assume their full cost. The total cut-back policy applied to cleaning, to 'meals-on-wheels' and to grocery deliveries. For those primary care services still provided by the municipal home helpers, the range of income-based fees was raised at the beginning of 1993.

Problems of Internal Integration

The present criticism (1994) of the public services in Sweden is formulated from the top-down perspective, from ruling political parties and from some ideological think-tanks like the neoliberal Timbro group. Little systematic knowledge is collected about the private enterprises and the third sector. Peter Ström (1994) concludes that the privatizing of elderly care has been undertaken in a climate remarkably absent of critical evaluation (see also Gustafsson 1994). Saltman (1994) finds that the reforms in health care have been harder to implement than expected. 'While rapid policy mutations may prevent major mistakes, they often leave little time to think through likely problems and to develop barriers to perverse consequences. Progress has also been slowed by worried personnel and reluctant unions, particularly in the current recessionary economic environment.' (p. 291)

In cases where evaluations were made there was no clear cut evidence that cost-savings were achieved through mixed models.[7] In some municipalities the elderly care has become less costly, while in other municipalities the cost has risen (Ström 1994). Saltman (1994) finds in his comparative investigation of the transformation of health care systems in different countries, among others Finland and Sweden, that the costs of

transition have been substantially higher than national moni-
toring and evaluation activities indicate and that these higher
costs will be recurring.[8] The struggle to keep the public services
intact is very visible in the recent Swedish debate, if we bring
the staff and the clients into focus.

Within this discussion, there are some who argue that to be
able to supply varied services of good quality at a low price is a
question of work organization. In this context, the task for big
enterprises is to organize work in a rational, often Taylorized
way. Whether good quality care is lost in the reorganization
process requires close empirical research. But one cannot
ignore the fact that small firms consisting of a few persons
cannot operate on this scale and in this way. Only in highly specialized care, like chiropody or hairdressing, where the individual patient buys care with vouchers or at their own expense,
will the small enterprise have a chance to compete with larger
organizations. This opens up the question of whether non-
standardized services will develop in the long term. One might
begin such an investigation by focusing on the situation of the
self-employed, their workload, quality of work conditions and
their attempts to control their work and life situation.

Problems of Legitimization

From one perspective, there appears to be a disjuncture
between the policy rhetoric and the changes that are possible in
the organization of care. This can be seen in the competing
needs and interests of the different parties involved. Potential
conflicts exist between the providers and the clients. The
former want to live an economically predictable and independent life. The latter prefer a flexible service corresponding to
their needs. The community prefers to support the least costly
services. Then there is the broad interest group of Swedish
women who make up the majority of employees in the public
sector. Most prefer to work outside the home and as full-time or
nearly full-time workers. However, in private care enterprises
in Sweden, the trend is toward reduction of working hours (one
sees an average decrease from full employment to 50–60 per
cent of working hours). Even if there has been a reduction in
working hours for those who work in public care services, the
percentage of personnel hired per hour is still substantially

higher than in private firms. Nevertheless, these employees are expected to fulfil a minimum standard of care.

Another deterioration in the shift from public to private care refers to the differences in responsibility for the up-dating of occupational knowledge and regular training of the care providers. Within the Swedish public sector, it was an obligation of the employer to improve and update the skills of employees. The private employer considers it the duty of employees to upgrade their education, but the firm is not required to give time off or pay for education during paid working hours.[9] In practice this means that in private firms, unpaid working hours are increasing, compared with public employment. What was once a benefit won through hard fought worker organization, is now felt to be symbolic and an actual loss by many care workers.

Among actual care givers themselves, (assistant nurses, home helps in public employment), and care recipients, privatization as a strategy is not popular (Ström 1994). The defence of the public sector among staff and clients, and the silence about the privatization process, must partly be understood as a defence of generous working conditions, which are not found in private enterprises.[10] The needs and interests of the individual employee or even the clients, are sacrificed in order to fit the needs of the rationalizing mechanisms of the work organization. Lack of continuity in care giving, frequent change of individual care givers are major complaints among clients as a results of the care reforms (Ström 1994). A flexible organization does not always work in accordance with the client's needs.

The Organized Pensioner

Two strong pensioner organizations, the PRO, linked to the Social-democrats, and the SPF, linked to the Moderate party, together representing more than half a million pensioners (Sweden has a total of 8 million inhabitants) cooperate rather than compete when it comes to lobbying for the social and economic welfare of their members (Sparks and Olsson-Hort 1993). The biggest one, the PRO with 375 000 members, is of the opinion that 'Care for the elderly should not become commercial – one should not make money out of it.' The other one, the SPF, takes a more positive stance towards privatization. 'We do not require privatization, but we do demand that (private companies) be subject to the same rules as the municipal services . . . in order that competition can take place, . . . competition is important.' Representatives from both groups, however, are united in their concern that privatization of home help would increase the cost of services. It has been a central challenge for both organizations to work against increased fees for social services throughout the country. (Sparks and Olsson-Hort 1993.) It seems as if both individual pensioners and their organizations are very slow to adapt to the new ideology and practice. According to one PRO representative, some pensioners are very sceptical of the changes. They believe that the old system worked well, and that public care has gradually become more effective even before the voucher system was introduced, putting it in a better position to compete with private care.

CONCLUSION

I have described a debate on restructuring of welfare services in its ideological discourse and given some examples from an ongoing transformation of social service practices in Sweden. What are the implications of these changes for the care receiver, the care giver, and the broader commitment to equality that has existed in the Swedish social services? Finally, what are the possible scenarios in the ongoing process of privatization of social services, which thus far can be defined as semi-privatization?

The implications for care receivers are dramatic. The ideology of equality has been replaced by class differentials as well as gender inequalities. Services have become more costly, and especially long-term care for the elderly has turned out to be extremely costly in some municipalities. This puts a class-dimension to the question of elderly care.

In addition the changes for care givers are severe. Due to tradition and a more limited private labour market for women, cuts in the public sector can be expected to be difficult for Swedish female wage earners. Loss of control and limited equality in the labour market will be the price many wage earning women will have to pay for more 'consumer choice', which may exist in theory but not necessarily in practice.

Privatization does not necessarily mean that public choice will increase. The gap between ideals and realities is obvious. The municipality and a private enterprise, usually a civic organization, can draw up a contract whereby services will be bought and sold. Even if criticism of the public services was justified, given the possible scenarios in privatization, there is a continuing strong line of defence of the public services. This is true of public sector employees who obviously are losing their 'woman friendly' position on the labour market, but in addition they have lost their professional control over the criteria for the quality of care. But there is also resistance from care recipients who have come to expect a well-developed, predictable, tax-financed system of public services.

Not to be ignored in this discussion are the gendered consequences of these changes. One can see these on many levels: women as care recipients can no longer count on quantity or quality of care: female relatives of the old and disabled have to pick up the care deficit, and female employees face unemployment, as indicated by the statistics on redundancy of care workers in Swedish municipalities (Szebehely 1993). Over the long run, loss of jobs and fewer paid working hours may result in a lower standard of living and poverty in old age for many women who will receive lower pensions, particularly those who were not wage earners for the minimum period of 30 years, now required for a full pension.

The state-feminist gender model woven into the Nordic welfare state has guaranteed women individualization and emancipation through education, work of their own, professionalization and of their own earned income. The service systems of the welfare state, within the division of labour prevailing within society, have become employers of women, while at the same time, care, treatment and services are supported and provided by complex professional and bureaucratic institutions (Simonen 1994). According to the Social Services Act, from 1982, social services and assistance as well as health care are to be provided to all residents of Sweden on equal terms. The social service state prevented the class differences and stratification in care and access to care that is the hallmark of liberal welfare states.

The 'Folkhem-model' was a vision motivated from human values of equality. All citizens became involved in a complex and economically productive relation together with the state, in order to expand the labour market, to bring about a balance between regions, to create a labour market for both men and women, and so on. However, this framing of equality no longer resonates with those remaking the Swedish welfare state, in the light of unemployment, the globalization of labour markets, and general anxiety around the current financial crises. At this stage of reinventing private care services and more competitive markets, there are many possible scenarios.

A possible scenario is that there will be different layers in the care system. One could imagine an elite care system where middle-class clients and middle-class professionals contracted with each other within the 'normal' labour market, not necessarily the public sector. The well educated demand high quality services for their needs: the professional elite seek to maintain their privileges and status by providing high quality care and service. Today within the public sector the best educated and most professional groups organize to maintain their privileged status, and could, in a highly competitive system, increase the social rewards for their competence. In a privatized or semi-privatized system elite clients can organize themselves in order to demand high quality services, and the public/private mix of service producers might then provide better services at lower cost. From the literature (see for instance Abbott 1988, 122ff) it is well known that professionals who serve high status clients enhance their status as professionals.

But the second layer of care would include different contractors, groups of semi-employed care givers and client groups with the least say. In these grey and black markets of care, self-employed women providing care at home in the flexible (risky) labour market would advertise their flexible services, extending the range of provision towards the less specialized and standarized tasks.

What has not been seen in this set of debates and discussions around crises in care is a new vision, one that would sustain the ideal of equality between generations, classes and genders. The ideal of decentralization and customers choice lay outside the political sphere, and thus outside the spheres of justice and solidarity that have characterized Swedish social democracy and the vision embodied in the 'Folkhem-model'. The paradise lost will affect all citizens.

NOTES

1. This chapter is based upon a co-authored paper with Leila Simenon delivered at the 'Crossing Borders' conference. This version of the paper concentrates on the Swedish case only. I want to thank Barbara Hobson for her extensive editorial work on this article and her inspiring comments on various versions of this chapter.

2. The idea of a project proposal 'Restructuring of the Welfare State, productivity and effectiveness of social services' (Heikkilä *et al.* 1994) has been developed in this article.

3. Researchers make a distinction between 'blue' and 'red–green' entrepreneurship. The blue market model relates to big firms, privatization of public services and to real competition between big service producers. Red–green entrepreneurship is a concept used in relation to small and family firms, to small entrepreneurship. (cf. Heinonen 1993, 139–141.) In Finland, the red–green model is developing in the form of self-employment and small care firms, whereas in Sweden it is developing in the form of cooperatives. Finland, however, lacks any major enterprise in the field of care and nursing, unlike Sweden. Whether there is true competition or not can be questioned, which makes the market-colour unclear.

4. Much of this discussion was applied to health care services, but was also discussed more generally in relation to social services: (For an overview of the discussion see Antman 1994); see also Blomqvist 1980; Bergman 1983; Jönsson and Rehnberg 1986; Palmlund 1984, 1986; Hugemark 1994).

5. Tensions concerning leadership can be handled differently by organizations (for an overview see Evertsson and Johansson 1996).

6. Until recently, the middle class was over represented in public child care, but now the class structure of families who have children in public day care corresponds to the class structure of the total Swedish population.

7. In Sweden the debate on social welfare costs is controversial, and the method of measurement is questioned. Several other factors complicate such estimations. One such confounder is the radical tax-reform of 1990 which influenced GNP. Another confounder is the Swedish agreement to neglect fluctuations in productivity within the public sector. The productivity is always set to zero. (Korpi 1992)

8. To become a private entrepreneur then becomes less attractive, as it is costly and time consuming to arrange all these benefits privately. The radicality of breaking away from cemented structures and strong hierarchies to become self-employed is not as recognized alternative in Sweden.

9. Some established firms, however, for example Svensk Hemservice AB, advertise their extensive staff training scheme. According to Ström (1994) public home care used five per cent of the paid working hours per employee for training, compared to the entrepreneurs who used two per cent on average.

10. Little is known about attitudes and strategies among those who have left employment in the public sector. Between 1990–4 the number of unemployed home helps, for example, increased by 14 000 (Lars Thörn, Swedish Municipal Workers Union, fax message 20 April 1994). In Sweden, there is a lack of empirical studies on self-employed people and their relation to work.

REFERENCES

Abbott A. (1988) *The System of Professions. An Essay on the Division of Labor*. Chicago and London: University of Chicago Press.

Andersson L. (1993) *De äldre och välfärden – vem ska ta hand om omsorg och vård? (The elderly and welfare – who should be the carers?)* Tidskriften Äldrecentrum 4.

Andersson, S. and T. Parviainen (1994) *Hoivayrittäjänä maaseudulla. (As a care-entrepreneur in the countryside)*. Maaseudun uusi aika. Maaseututkimuksen ja -politiikan aikakauslehti 1/1994, 13–17.

Antman, P. (1994) 'Vägen till systemskiftet. (The road to the system shift)' in Rolf Å. Gustafsson (ed.) *Köp och sälj. Var god svälj? (Buy and sell. Please accept?)* Stockholm: Arbetsmiljöfonden.

Anttonen, A. (1989) *Valtiollisesta yhteisölliseen sosiaalipolitiikkaan (From a state social policy to a community social policy)*. Helsinki: Sosiaaliturvan keskusliitto.

Axelsson, C. (1992) *Hemmafrun som försvann. (The Housewife Which Disappeared.)* Dissertation, Stockholm University.

Beckman, S. (1981) *Kärlek på tjänstetid (Love during working hours.)* Stockholm: Arbetslivscentrum.

Bergman, L. (1983) *Avgifter på offentlig service? (Payment for public services?)* Ekonomisk Debatt, 2.

Blomqvist, Å. (1980) *Konsumentönskemål eller expertvälde? (Consumer´s choice or expert rule?)* Ekonomisk Debatt, 3.

Eklund, K. (1981) *Nu krävs en historisk kompromiss. (A historical compromise demanded.)* Dagens Nyheter, 21 January.

Evertsson, L. and S. Johansson (1996) *The home help and home nursing services. A survey of research findings*. Stockholm: Arbetsmiljöfonden (Swedish Council for Work Life Research).

Gustafsson R.Å. (ed.) (1994) *Köp och sälj. Var god svälj? (Buy and sell. Please accept?)*: Arbetsmiljöfonden Stockholm.

Hatje, A-K. (1994) 'Triangeldramat mor, barn och industri'. (The triangle drama between mother, child and industry) in Baude and Runnström (eds) *Kvinnans plats i det tidiga välfärdssamhället*. (Women's role in the early welfare society.) Stockholm: Carlssons.

Heikkilä, M., T. Karjalainen, A. Kovalainen, T. Melin and L. Simonen (1994) *Restructuring of the Welfare State, productivity and effectiveness of social services*. Helsinki: Research Design. STAKES/Social Research Unit Theme 8.

Heinonen J. (1992) *Kattotarinasta monikärkiseen pohdintaan (From a grand theory into rethinking from various perspectives)* Helsinki: Gaudeamus.

Hernes, H.M. (1987) *Welfare State and Women Power.* Oslo: Universitetsforlaget.

Hirdman, Y. (1989) *Att lägga livet till rätta – studier i svensk folkhemspolitik. (To regulate life – studies in the policy of the Swedish folkhome)* Stockholm: Carlsson.

Hirdman, Y. (1990) *Genussystemet. Demokrati och makt i Sverige. (The gender system. In Democracy and Power in Sweden)* chap 3, I SOU 1990: 44.

Hugemark, A. (1994) 'Hur personalen glömdes bort – ekonomerna i sjukvårds-debatten 1979–1993. (How the staff was forgotten – economists in the debate on health care 1979–1993.)' in R.Å. Gustafsson (ed.) *Köp och sälj. Var god svälj? (Buy and sell. Please accept?)* Stockholm: Arbetsmiljöfonden.

Johansson S. (1994) 'Ommöblering i folkhemmet. Nytt vin i gamla läglar?' (Rearrangements in the folkhome. New wine in old barrels?) in L. Simonen (ed): När gränserna flyter. *En nordisk antologi om vård och omsorg. (When the boundaries shift.)* Helsinki: STAKES Rapporter 134, 31–49.

Johansson S. and L. Evertsson (1994) 'Resonemangsäktenskap i välfärdsstat. Exemplet social hemhjälp' (Marriage of convenience within welfare state.) in L. Simonen (ed): *När gränserna flyter. En nordisk antologi om vård och omsorg. (When the boundaries shift.)* Helsinki: STAKES Rapporter 134, 11–30.

Julkunen, R. (1992) *Hyvinvointivaltio käännekohdassa (Welfare state at a turning point).* Vastapaino. Tampere.

Jönsson, B. and C. Rehnberg, (1986) *Effektivare sjukvård genom bättre ekonomistyrning. (More effective health care through better financial control.)* Ekonomisk Debatt, 2.

Korpi, W. et al. (1992) *Halkar Sverige efter? (Does Sweden lag behind?),* Stockholm: Carlsson.

Langby, E. (1993) *Vinter i välfärdslandet. (Winter in the Country of Welfare).* Stockholm: Brombergs.

Le Grand, J. (1991) 'Quasi-markets and social policy' *The Economic Journal,* 101 (September), 1256–67.

Leira, A. (1994) *'Caring and the Gendering of Citizenship'* paper presented at the XIIth World Congress of Sociology, Germany: Bielefeld.

Lindbeck, A. (1972) *Centralisering contra decentralisering i svensk blandekonomi. Blandekonomi på villovägar? (Centralizing vs. decentralizing in a Swedish mixed economy.)* Stockholm: SNS.

Lövgren, B. (1998) *Hemarbete som politik. (Housework as Politics.)* Dissertation Acta Universitas Stockholmensis, 49.

Murray, R. (1987) *Den offentliga sektorn – produktivitet och effektivitet, (Public sector – productivity and effectivness.)* bilaga 21 till LU 87 SOU : 3.

Otter, C. von and R. Saltman (1990) *Valfrihet som styrmedel. Fem artiklar om den offentliga sektorns möjligheter. (Consumers choice as an instrument of control.)* Stockholm: Arbetslivscentrum.

Palmlund, I. (ed.). (1984) *Effektiv offentlig sektor? Den offentliga förvaltningens roll i samhället. (Efficient Public Sector?)* Stockholm: Liber förlag.

Palmlund, I. (ed.). (1986) *Utvärdering av offentlig verksamhet? Den offentliga förvaltningens roll i samhället. (Public sector activity evaluated?* The role of public administration in society.) Stockholm: Liber förlag:

Rantalaiho, L. (1993) 'The gender contract' in Hannele Varsa (ed.), *Shaping structural change in Finland. The role of women.* Helsinki: Ministry of Social Affairs and Health. Equality Publications. Series B: Reports 2. 1–9.

Rothstein, B. (1988) *Socialdemokratin och välfärdens institutioner. (Social-democracy and the institutions of social welfare.)* Tiden nr 8.

Saltman, R.B. (1994) 'A conceptual overview of recent health care reforms'. *European Journal of Public Health*, Vol. 4, No. 4, 287–93.

Simonen, L. (ed.). (1994) *När gränserna flyter. (When the boundaries shift).* En nordisk antologi om vård och omsorg. Helsinki: STAKES Rapporter 134.

Socialstyrelsen (1994) 'Alternativa styr- och driftformer inom äldre- och handikappomsorgen'. (Alternative forms of management in care for the elderly and handicapped.) Kartläggning: *Delrapport 1*: January.

Sparks, S. and S. Olsson-Hort, (1993) 'Changes in the public/private mix. Private provision of home help in Sweden' working paper Sweden: Lund.

Stryjan, Y. (1994) 'Cooperatives on the Welfare Market: The Swedish Case' paper presented at the XIIth World Congress of Sociology, Germany: Bielefeld.

Stryjan, Y. (1996) *Systemskiftets irrgångar (System shift on the wrong track).* Stockholm: School of Business, Stockholm University.

Ström, P. (1994) 'Hur påverkas de gamla och personalen av hemtjänstens privatisering?' (How are the elderly and the employees influenced by the privatization of home care?) in Gustafsson (ed.) *Köp och sälj, var god svälj? (Buy and sell, please accept?).* Stockholm: Arbetmiljöfonden.

Svallfors, S. (1992) 'Den stabila välfärdsopinionen. Attityder till svensk välfärd 1986–92'. (*The stable opinion about welfare. Attitudes to welfare in Sweden 1986–92*) Opinioner kring 1991 års skattereform, rapport 4. Umeå: Sociologiska institutionen.

Svallfors S. (1995) (ed.) 'In the Eye of the Beholder', *Opinions of Welfare and Justice in Comparative Perspective.* Umeå University.

Szebehely M. (1993) *Hemtjänst eller anhörigvård? Förändringar under 80-talet. (Public home care or family-based care? Transitions in the Swedish Welfare State during the 1980s).* Stockholm: Socialstyrelsen (National Board of Social Health and Welfare).

Williamson, O. (1975) *Markets and hierarchies.* Analysis and antitrust implications. London and New York: Free Press.

Varsa, H. (ed.) (1993) *Shaping structural change in Finland. The role of women.* Helsinki: Ministry of Social Affairs and Health. Equality Publications. Series B: Reports 2.

Index